# BUY THE TRUTH
# SELL IT NOT

# BUY THE TRUTH
# SELL IT NOT

# M. SHAH

# Contents

## <u>Dedication</u>

This book is dedicated to all who love
and are seeking the truth.

Whoever is careless with the truth
in small matters, cannot be trusted
with important matters.
Albert Einstein

# Introduction

Thee (alone) we worship; Thee (alone) we ask for help. Show us the straight path (Surah 1: 5-6 The Holy Quran-Pickthall Translation).

**"Ih'dina Sirathwal Musthakim" (Show us the straight path (Surah 1:6)**

This is the prayer, every Muslim prays as they recite the Holy Quran from the very first Surah (chapter) that Allah would show them the straight and true path. In other words, they pray that their god-Allah would lead them to the truth. It is really a wonderful prayer.

I firmly believe that every human being has an earnest desire of knowing the truth and to follow a straight a true path. No one wants to believe in lies and deception. But, tragically, some people are deprived of the truth. They are forcefully compelled to believe whatever is indoctrinated to them. They are forbidden to ask questions, and even discouraged to reason for something they have difficulty to believe.

*In Surah Al Ma'ida 5: 101 "O ye who believe! ask not questions about things which if made plain to you may cause you trouble. But if ye ask about things when the Qur'an is being revealed they will be made plain to you:*

*"Some people before you did ask such questions and on that account lost their faith."* (Surah 5: 102)

**Bukhari Hadith 9. 392: Narrated Sa'd bin Abi Waqqas:**
The Prophet said, "The most sinful person among the Muslims is the one who asked about something, which had not been prohibited, but was prohibited because of his asking."

Every human being is curious about things in his/her settings and surroundings. From a very early stage, a child starts to ask question like what, how, when, why and so on. Once a child is discouraged and deprived of asking questions, it surely destroys the creativity and productivity of a child. Asking questions has caused people to find solutions of the enigmas of life. It is pathetic and tragic that the sometime religious leaders of Islam discourage Muslims to ask questions as they follow the pattern of their prophet in this manner. Every question raised about Mohammad or the Quran is considered a blasphemy. Any non-Muslim especially in a dominant Muslim country once he questions the credibility of the prophethood of Muhammad or authenticity of the Qur'an faces the death penalty. That's why freedom to reason about the Islamic faith is taken away from Muslims and non-Muslims alike. The books that shed the truth about Mohammad, and the Qur'an have been banned or burnt and the sources that could bring important, imperative, and valuable information in revealing the truth about Islam are blocked very strictly, sternly, and aggressively.

One must ask this question that if Islam has the truth as many Muslims claim, then there is no need to keep it away from the scrutiny. The truth always prevails and it defends itself.

Mohammad himself was told to ask from the people of the book (Jews and Christians) concerning the doubts he had about his revelation. *"And if thou (Muhammad) art in doubt concerning that which We reveal unto thee*, then question those who read the Scripture (that was) before thee. Verily the Truth from thy Lord hath come unto thee. So be not thou of the waverers. *And be not thou of those who deny the revelations of Allah, for then wert thou of the losers.*" (Surah 10:94-95 Pickthall)

This Quranic verse is very vivid and explicit that it should serve as a beacon for Muslims to examine the authenticity of their holy book and legitimacy of the prophethood of Muhammad. Any self-centered prophet or religious teacher can make any claim in order to gain attention of self-promotion and self-exaltation.

**The Bible tells us that people living in Berea authenticated the truth about what was preached to them** by searching the Scripture daily. *"These (Bereans) were more fair-minded than those in Thessalonica, in that they received the word with all readiness, and searched the Scriptures daily to find out whether these things were so"* (Acts 17:11). No body discouraged the Berean Christians from examining the teachings that was taught about the Christian faith.

The truth defends itself. Someone asked Charles H. Spurgeon to defend the Bible. His answer was very simple but still so profound. He said, "Defend the Bible? It would as someone wants to defend a lion! Unchain it and it will defend itself.

Truth is the most powerful weapon in the world. It is also the most valuable thing in the world.

Winston Churchill said, the most valuable thing in the world is the truth and that in fact it is so valuable that it is hidden by the body guards of lies.

It is a historical fact that many people had dreadful doubts and quantifiable question marks about the dubious, suspicious, and ambiguous revelation of Muhammad and about the veracity and originality of his **CULTIC Belief System** including his own tribe from the very dawn of Islam. And, he himself was not sure about his revelations either.

### Sahih Al-Bukhari Hadith 1.92 Narrated by Abu Musa:
The Prophet was asked about things which he did not like, but when the questioners insisted, the Prophet got angry.
He then said to the people, "Ask me anything you like." A man asked, "Who is my father?"
The Prophet replied, "Your father is Hudhafa."
Then another man got up and said, "Who is my father, O Allah's Apostle?"
He replied, "Your father is Salim, Maula (the freed slave) of Shaiba."
So, when 'Umar saw that (the anger) on the face of the Prophet he said, "O Allah's Apostle! We repent to Allah (for having offended you)."

I certainly admire Muslims who take their religion so seriously. Many of them pray five times a day, observe the month of Ramadan when they fast for thirty days, if they cannot fast, they feed the poor instead for the sake of accumulating deeds (religious points). Many Muslims have the desire of going to Mecca for the Hajj (pilgrimage to Mecca) which, is one of the pillars of their faith and as they believe that it will add up to their religious/spiritual account of good deeds. Many extremists are even determined to die for the cause of Islam and kill innocent people to spread and protect Islam. For a devout Muslim, the cause of spreading and protecting Islam is more important than a human being; whereas Jesus values a human being more than a cause itself.

8

It is very sad to say that even after strict observance of all religious practices, there is no assurance of salvation and certainty about where a Muslim will spend eternity. It all depends on Allah's will and on making sure to have an accumulation of enough good deeds that would outweigh the bad deeds. There is no assurance of salvation.

In this scenario of uncertainty, with great humility, one shouldn't pray merely so earnestly "Show us the straight path", but even diligently seek the truth and should embrace the truth once it is found at every cost.

"Show us the straight path" that wouldn't be just a superficial prayer merely, but it would be a prayer from the bottom of the heart of every seeker of truth. It is very crucial to know that truth since your eternity hinges on the truth of your belief system. The truth not only affects life here on this earth but it will have an effect for eternity.

If someone want to buy a car, he wants to know the truth about the car. Anthropologists study to know the truth about the origin of man and the development of different cultures and languages. Biologists study and want to know the reality of the origin of life and everything related to it. The crime detectors spend an enormous time, different kinds of tools and equipment, and a great sum of money in order to know the truth of heinous crimes. In relationship, people want to know the truth. **Even though, we live in a world that is full of lies and deception, people still have great hunger and desire to know the truth. We hunger for honesty and truth.**

Truth is the conformity to facts or reality. It carries the concept of authenticity which is contrary to the counterfeit. It carries the concept of consistency and the idea of honesty.

There might be tolerance for treachery and deliberate denial for factual reality. But it harms more than it helps.

As John Hus (1370–1415) wrote: '
Seek the truth,
Listen to the truth,
Teach the truth,
Love the truth,
Abide by the truth,
And defend the truth unto death.'


King Solomon, the wisest man who ever lived gives us this timeless advice:

## "Buy the truth, and sell it not;

*also, wisdom, and instruction, and understanding"* (Proverbs 23:23).

# CHAPTER ONE

## THE RELIGION OF ISLAM

Every man lives in two realms: the internal and the external.
The internal is that realm of spiritual ends expressed in art,
literature, morals, and religion.
The external is that complex of devices, techniques,
mechanisms, and instrumentalities by means
of which we live.
Martin Luther King, Jr.

# CHAPTER ONE

## THE RELIGION OF ISLAM

There are numerous religions in the world. Every religion claims to be the one and only true religion and show their superiority over other faith. Some believe that different religions are different paths all leading to heaven. Even though Ramakrishna said, "Many faiths are but different paths leading to one reality, God," despite that Hindus don't go around raising their children as Christians or Buddhists. They still regard Hinduism as being superior.

The dictionary defines religion as a set of beliefs concerning the cause, nature, and purpose of the universe, especially when considered as the creation of a super human agency or agencies, usually involving devotional and ritual, observances, and often containing a moral code governing the conduct of human affairs.

In a religion, man (human beings) is trying reach to God or gods (the supreme being) through multiple efforts, struggles, and strives, with a set and system of rites and rituals; whereas in Christianity, God (the supreme being) reaches down to man (human beings) through the person of Jesus Christ. In a religion, man is trying to appease an angry God through religious practices and a sacrificial system; whereas in Christianity, God Himself did something in order to bring people into a living and dynamic relationship with Himself. That's why in Christianity, God is a God of relationship; whereas, in a religion God is far away, beyond someone's reach. The religion teaches that you do something to become something (a righteous person); whereas Christianity teaches that you become righteous first by accepting the righteousness of God in Christ and through His sacrificial death on the cross and then you will be able to do things that are pleasing to God and glorifying His name. Conclusively, a religion teaches from doing to being whereas Christianity teaches from being to doing.

Islam is a monotheistic religion in the world. Muhammad started this religion in Mecca in the Arabian Peninsula in the early seventh century. He gravitated people by claiming that he had supernatural revelations from God through the angel Gabriel but, with little success in his first thirteen years of preaching his message. Those revelations were later complied into a book called the Holy Quran. Though, Islam has some similarities with the Judeo-Christian faith, but, it has enormous differences with the foundational belief system of the same faith Islam inherited from it. Islam, presumably, endeavor to exhibit its superiority over all the religions of the world, and it claims of superseding over the monotheistic faith. With this in mind, Muslims have a delusion of world domination.

Islam means submission. It does not mean peace as sometimes people have been made to believe. Linguistically, "SALAM", means peace. It is the letter "I" that changes the meaning. Whenever and wherever the letter "I" exists emphatically and forcefully, it always changes the meaning. For example, the middle letter in SIN and PRIDE is "I". Whenever, the focus is on "I" self, it brings the absence of peace which is found very vividly in Islam.

Muslims are forced to submit to the will and ways of Allah and Muhammed even though they might have many question marks about their faith. It is also the religious duty of a good Muslim to force others to submit to Islam. That is why, terrorists condemn moderate and peaceful Muslims who do not take part in the Jihad, either financially or being active in Jihad through pen, imposing laws, or taking sword in their hand.

Some Muslim scholars refer that the "submission" would be a better translation of the word Islam. Presumably, they believe that word Islam has a twofold meaning as "peace" and "submission" and can be used interchangeably. Islam teaches that one can only find peace in one's life by submitting to Almighty God (Allah) in heart, soul, and deed. At the same time, non-Muslims can have peace and live peaceably once they exercise their total submission to Allah, and Muhammad, and by following the Sharia law imposed upon them by the Muslim community (Ummah).

The word salaam is a synonym to a Hebrew word shalom. The word "Shalom" is used as a Jewish greeting. According to the definition, Shalom (שָׁלוֹם) means *peace, completeness,* and *welfare. When it is used as greetings it* means both *hello* and *goodbye.* Shalom can refer to either peace between two entities (especially between man and God or between two countries), or to the well-being, welfare, or safety of an individual or a group of individuals.

Shalom or peace is mentioned in the Bible enormously. Jesus is called the Prince of Peace (Isaiah 9:6). God gives a perfect peace to His people (Isaiah 26:3-4; Proverbs 3:5-6).

Jesus said, *"Peace I leave with you; my peace I give you. I do not give to you as the world gives. Do not let your hearts be troubled and do not be afraid"* (John 14:27).

**The Peace that Jesus gives has a three-dimensional Aspect:**

1. **Peace with God:** "Therefore, having been justified by faith, we have peace with God through our Lord Jesus Christ, [2] through whom also we have access by faith into this grace in which we stand, and rejoice in hope of the glory of God" (Romans 5:1-2).
2. **Inner peace:** And the peace of God, which transcends all understanding, will guard your hearts and your minds in Christ Jesus (Philippians 4:7).
3. **Peace with fellow human beings:** "Make every effort to live in peace with everyone and to be holy; without holiness, no one will see the Lord" (Hebrews 12:14).

A religion requires Total Submission from its followers forcefully. Islam as a religion is not exempt from this reality either. Islam requires submission from Muslims in accordance to its name, and meaning, and from non-Muslims alike once they have an upper hand. This submission is based on fear, intimidation, and to the extent of religious slavery.

It is very incongruous that in Islam, a relationship without marriage is considered taboo, but female war prisoners are Halal (lawful). Stealing is prohibited and the thief must be punished by the decapitating of his hands, but war booty is Halal (lawful). There is full freedom to embrace Islam, but whoever reverts from Islam (apostate) must be killed by any Muslim. Muslim men can marry non-Muslim women but Muslim women are not allowed to marry non-Muslim men unless, the man first converts to Islam and then he is allowed to marry. Non-Muslims are prohibited to enter their holy places (Mecca etc.) but Muslims are allowed to go the holy places of other religions. If a non-Muslim rapes a Muslim woman he is to be killed immediately by any Muslim, but if a Muslim rapes a non-Muslim woman he is not to be killed. Infidels (non-Muslim) cannot be a witness against Muslims but Muslims can witness against non-Muslims. In Islam, Muslims can criticize other religions openly, but non-Muslims cannot criticize Islam. It is considered as blasphemy, and in the western culture, it is given a name Islamophobia or hate speech. In Islam, Muslims glean from the heretic and cultic sources that what could damage and degrade other religions. They use those sources and citations as a weapon to attack other religions; whereas, they turn either blind their eyes or trying to twist the facts documented in their own reliable, and authenticated religious sources that could be damaging and degrading to their faith.

The two main sects of Islam are: Sunni and Shiites. There is a long history of animosity between the Sunni who are in majority and Shi'ites living mainly in Iraq and Iran.

Sunni Muslims go by the name Ahl as-Sunnah which means "people of the tradition of Muhammad". They draw their religious authority from the Quran, Hadiths, and traditions (Sunna) of Muhammad. They consider the first four caliphs to be the rightful successors to Muhammad.

Shia means followers and the broader meaning is the followers of Ali. They consider Ali to be the rightful caliph after Muhammad and the first Imam and reject the legitimacy of all three caliphs who preceded Ali. Imam is the one who they believe possesses special spiritual and political authority over the community of faith. The *Twelve Imams* are the spiritual and political successors to Muhammad. The Imam is an infallible human individual who not only rules over the community with justice but also is able to keep and interpret the divine law and its esoteric meaning. Each Imam was the son of the previous Imam, with the exception of Hussein ibn Ali, who was the brother of Hasan ibn Ali. The twelfth and the final Imam is Muhammad al-Mahdi, who is considered be the universal caliph, and, who will be a champion for the Muslim world. He will deliver Muslims from the tyranny of non-Muslims, will bring peace on earth, and establish a world-wide Islamic kingdom. According to Shias, the appearing of Imam Mahdi can be hastened by creating turbulence, turmoil and, terrorism in the world.

There are millions who belong to a group called Sufism. It is a mystical-ascetic approach to Islam that seek to find direct experience of God through religious poetic chanting and dancing.

There are seventy-two sects in Islam. Some are considered cultic groups by the mainstream of sects of Islam.

Steve Keohane has stated in his book, "Mohammed" that Islam is a religion based on intimidation, and fear.[i]

There is a freedom in Christianity. A Christian has a true spiritual relationship with God and can call Him Abba Father. He communicates with God in his own language and in his own way rather than in scripted prayers of mere recitation and repetition without having any proper perception that exists in Islam.

There is no objective thinking in Islam. The objective thinkers in Islam are considered equal to an infidel. When a person challenges Islamic teachings, the life of Mohammed, or the authenticity of the Holy Qur'an, Muslims at large cannot tolerate it.

In the Islamic countries, many valuable books that reveal the truth about Islam and Mohammed have been banned. The writers have been bullied with barbarity and brutality. Any voice that seems to be a threat against Islam has been silenced forcefully.

The Bible tells us that God has created man (man & woman) with a free will. He has given every person a right to choose. God wants people to know and embrace the truth.

14

As Jesus said, *"Then you will know the truth, and the truth will set you free."* *(John 8:32.)*

## Pre-Islamic History

Islam started in the Arabian Peninsula. The inhabitants of the land are known as Semites who are the descendants of Noah's third son Shem. The people were divided into clans and tribes who were mostly nomadic (Bedou). The Bedouins selected their leader (Sheikh) among the members of the clan on the basis of wisdom and experience of the person. Each clan starts with the prefix Banu-, which means the children or descendants of, for example Banu-Hashim, Banu Lakhm, Banu Ghassan, etc. They fought each other fiercely to have supremacy over another clan or tribe in order to gain a greater hold on the resources of the land.

According to I. Q. Al-Rassooli, The Muslims state made full use of the tribal system for its military conquest and settlement purposes. The army was divided into divisions based on tribal affiliations to keep their cohesion and loyalty. The conquered territories were settled by tribes that treated the new converts from among the subjugated peoples as 'clients'.[ii] Wherever the Bedouins found oases, over there, they started some villages and towns. Their livelihood depended on tending camels, goats, and sheep. It is a male dominated society like many other ancient societies. Many tribes believed in killing girl babies, so that the first-born would be a son.

Because of its isolation, the civilization of the Arabian Peninsula spread to the area only slowly, primarily via the caravan trade. Because of the war between Byzantium and Persia, much of Yemen's spices and many goods from India moved to the Mediterranean overland.

The majority of people in Arabia belonged to animistic religions. Each city had gods and goddess. Allah was the main deity who had three daughters: Al Lat (Crescent); Al Uzzah (Venus) and Al Manah (Fate), who are also mentioned in Qur'an (Surah 53:19-20). The pagan Arabs made sacrifices-both human and animal to the goddess Al-Uzzah (Venus). Muhammad even once mentioned that he offered a sheep to Al-Uzzah when he was follower of the religion of his people. There were holy sites and shrines beside the main temple (Ka'bah) in Mecca. Once a year the tribes from different cities of Arabia would meet in the city of Mecca during an event known as the Hajj. The Ka'bah (Cube), a large cube shaped building housed 360 idols from all the tribes of Arabia. The Ka'bah was the center of Arabian religious life. Here all the warring tribes would put aside their differences as they circled the Ka'bah. From the Ka'bah they would proceed to the other shrines outside of Mecca during this five-day religious event. The Hajj was a tradition that Arabs of the peninsula remembered going back hundreds of years before Islam.[iii]

During the month of the Hajj, the people traded, arranged marriages, had a good time, and worshipped at the ka 'bah. Arab poets composed poetry to be read at the Hajj celebration. The poets acted as historians, propagandists, and spokesmen for their tribes.

The poets were very influential and well respected in the Arabian culture. When the poets challenge Muhammad about the truthfulness his prophethood, Muhammad silenced them forcefully to the point of killing them.

15

Pre-Islamic poetry has also provided a sample of the language the people spoke. An alphabet for the Arabic language was developed from the Aramaic alphabet. The Arabs were the least literate among the people of the Middle East.

Children born on the holy land around the ka 'bah were automatically considered members of the Quraysh tribe, the tribe that controlled the ka 'bah. Muhammad also belonged to this tribe.

It is ipso facto that Muhammad did not unite the Arabs of the Peninsula through dialogue, persuasion, and debate—wherein he failed miserably in his first 13 years in Mecca—but because he succeeded in 'uniting' the Arabs only through the application of force, terror, assassination, and ruthlessness as fully described in both the Qur'an and Hadith.

It is a historical fact that many of the same Arabs who had earlier falsely 'submitted' to him, apostatized the moment he died and was not there anymore to terrorize them. Once more, they had to be brought into 'Islam' by the application of the sword on a massive scale (Wars of Apostasy/ Huroub al Ridda) during the Caliphate of Abu Bakr.[iv]

Apart from the animistic religion and polytheistic faith of the Arabs, there were numerous tribes who had willingly and without coercion converted to the religion of the Jews (Mosaic faith), to Christianity or became Hanifs (believers in the God of Abraham). It was the Hebrews and the Christians in the Arabian Peninsula who introduced the concept of Monotheism long before Islam. The truth of the matter is that Islam has borrowed the concept of Monotheism from Judeo-Christian theology.

The pagan Arabs were mainly nomadic people who were always on the move in search of new resources that would provide food for them and their cattle. They had no interest in cultivating the land. The Jewish community taught the natives how to grow fruit like Apples; apricots; watermelons; pomegranates; lemons; oranges, sugarcane; bananas and almonds, etc. The greatest and most important contribution by the Jews to Arabian agriculture and subsequently their heritage was the introduction of the palm tree, which existed mostly in the fertile land of Iraq. It is called *'Tamr'* in **Arabic,** whose root resides in the Hebrew *'Tamar'* meaning *'dates'*.

The Christian faith had already spread out all over the Middle East. The Roman emperor Constantine who converted to Christianity sent the first embassy to Arabia c356 under the leadership of Theophilus Indus, who succeeded in building three churches in **Aden** and the **Himyarite** country. Both Ibn Hisham in his *(Sirah)* and Al Tabari in his *(Ta'rikh al Rasul)*, mention the conversion of Najran to **Christianity** about 500CE.

In the sixth century, there was a power struggle between the Christian Byzantine kingdom in the north of the Arabian Peninsula, successors of the Roman Empire and the Zoroastrian Persian kingdom in the northeast. Both the Byzantine and Persian kingdoms had Arab tribes allied to their cause of trade and conquest. This caused the Arabian Peninsula to become a land of refuge for those seeking escape from both of these empires. Heretic Christian sects like the Nestorians and many other cultic faiths found refuge in the deserts and cities of the Peninsula.[v]

Umar Ibn al Khattab, the second Khalifa/Caliph (successor to Muhammad), unilaterally and treacherously broke the solemn peace treaties that Muhammad himself signed with many of the indigenous Arab Christians and deported them to Iraq 635/6 CE for failing to embrace Islam. These native Arabs had as much right - if not more - to live in the Peninsula as the rising new converts to Mohammedanism.

The Christian Arab tribes, just like the Jewish Arab ones, were later forcibly dispossessed or eradicated from the Arabian Peninsula, their homeland.[vi]

# CHAPTER TWO

---

# THE TRUTH ABOUT
# THE DEITY OF ISLAM
# ALLAH

## You Become Like What You Worship

James Michener, writing in his book, The Source, tells the story of a man named Urbaal, who was a farmer living about 2200 B.C. He worshiped two gods, one a god of death, the other a goddess of fertility. One day, the temple priests tell Urbaal to bring his young son to the temple for sacrifice—if he wants good crops. Urbaal obeys, and on the appointed day drags his wife and boy to the scene of the boy's "religious execution" by fire to the god of death. After the sacrifice of Urbaal's boy the several others, the priests announce that one of the fathers will spend next week in the temple, with a new temple prostitute. Urbaal's wife is stunned as she notices a desire written more intensely across his face than she had seen before, and she is overwhelmed to see him eagerly lunge forward when his name is called. The ceremony over, she walks out of the temple with her head swimming, concluding that "if he had different gods, he would have been a different man." (Source unknown)

# CHAPTER TWO

## THE TRUTH ABOUT THE DEITY OF ISLAM

Throughout the history of humanity, man has been searching for a supreme being. There is always a longing in peoples' heart to worship someone. Some people worship a supreme being, some make creation as an object of their worship and some even worship their ancestor or things they admire and are attached to. It is because when God created man, He created man (man & woman) in His own image (Genesis 1:26). God is spirit and there is a spiritual aspect or element in every human being. That's why it is so natural for human beings to search for a supreme being who would be the object of their worship.

There are different names for God in different languages. The name itself shouldn't be a problem as long as the reality of that Supreme Being could be fully examined logically, truthfully, objectively and above all it must go through the scrutiny of the authenticated, reliable, and historical divine revelations. The deity that is an object of worship is extremely important since people become like the god they worship and serve. If they worship a god of love and compassion, they will show love and compassion. If they worship a god full of hate and judgement, it will surely reflect in their beliefs and behavior.

**Here are some of the Names for God in different languages:**

| Language | Name | Language | Name |
|---|---|---|---|
| AEolian | Ilos | Arabic | Allah |
| Armorian | Teuti | Assyrian | Eleah |
| Aramaic | Elah | Celtic | Diu |
| Cretan | Thios | Chaldaic | Eilah |
| Coromandel | Brama | Chinese | Prussa |
| Dutch | Godt | Danish | Gut |
| Egyptian (modern) | Teun | Egyptian (old) | Teut |
| Finnish | Jumala | English | God |
| French | Dieu | Flemish | Goed |
| German (old) | Diet | German | Gott |
| Gallic | Diu | Greek | Theos |
| Hindoostanee | Rain | Hebrew | Elohim, Eloha |
| Irish | Dia | Japanese | Goezur |
| Latin | Deus | Italian | Dio |
| Low Brenton | Done | Low Latin | Diex |
| Madagascar | Zannar | Lapp | Jubinal |
| Norwegian | Gud | Malay | Alla |
| Old Saxon | God | Olalu Tongue | Deu |
| Persian | Sire | Peruvian | Puchecammae |
| Polish | Bog | Pannonian | Istu |
| Portuguese | Debs | Pollacca | Bung |
| Runic | As | Provencal | Diou |
| Spanish | Dios | Russian | Bojh |
| Slav | Buch | Swedish | Gut |
| Syriac | Allah | Swiss | Gott |
| Turkish | Allah | Tartar | Magatal |
| Urdu | Khuda | Zemblain | Fetizo |

# ALLAH THE GOD OF ISLAM

*In Islamic theology, God (Arabic: ﷲ Allah) is the all-powerful and all-knowing creator, sustainer, ordained and judge of everything in existence. Islam emphasizes that God is strictly singular (tawḥīd) unique (wāḥid) and inherently One (aḥad), all-merciful and omnipotent. According to Islamic teachings, God exists without place and according to the Quran, "No vision can grasp him, but His grasp is over all vision: He is above all comprehension, yet is acquainted with all things." God, as referenced in the Quran, is the only God.* 1

*Evidently, Muslims do not worship the moon, neither revere the moon as a deity, nevertheless, Allah was worshipped in Arabia as a moon god.*

*The Christians in Arabia also use Allah, a name that refers to a divine being, but their concept about Allah is different from the Allah that Muslims worship with some similarities yet it has nothing to do with worshipping the moon as a deity. The first-known translation of the Bible into Arabic, which took place in the 9th century, uses the word Allah for God. In fact, Arab Christians were using the word Allah for God prior to the dawn of Islam. Muslims used Allah for God even in other countries apart from Arabia even when they have a particular name for God in their native language. For example, the name for God in Farsi (Persian) in Iran is "Khuda" and this is the name used for God in the Bible in Farsi language. The same can be said about Christians in Pakistan who use Khuda for God and the same word is used in the Bible in Urdu language and the word "Khudai" in Pasto and Dari languages spoken in Afghanistan, that is predominately a Muslim country where Muslim use Allah that refer to the deity they venerate.*

**Even though Christians in Arabia refer the word Allah for God but the concept of God is different from the concept of Allah that Muslims have.**

### *"Is Allah (the deity of Islam) a Moon god?"*

The deity of Islam called Allah, the native name such as in Arabic is not the matter of contention, but with what it makes its connection and all the rites and rituals that are carried out as part of the religious belief system that are linked to the pre-Islamic deity "Allah", causes something very important to be evaluated meticulously.

According to The Bible, the ancestors of modern Arabs can be traced back to Shem and are properly known as Semites. Shem's descendant Eber gave rise to two lines: Peleg's line, from which Abraham is descended, and Joktan's line, which contains the names of many Arab groups. However, many Arab tribes trace their ancestry to Ishmael, the firstborn son of Abraham. Their religion was polytheistic and was related to the paganism of the ancient Semites. The supreme beings that was adored were in origin the inhabitants and patrons of single places, living in trees, fountains, and especially in sacred stones. There were some gods in the true sense, transcending in their authority the boundaries of purely tribal cults. The three most important were Manat, 'Uzza, and Allat. These three were themselves subordinate to a higher deity; consider to be the father of Manat, Uzza, and Allat, called Allah.[vii]

The religion of Islam worship "Allah." The name Allah is not the invention of Muhammad in presenting the monotheistic concept of a deity. Abdullah, Muhammad's father,

---

1 "The God of Islam" (Wikipedia).

means the servant or worshipper of Allah. During the days of Muhammad, each Arab tribe used the word Allah to refer to its own particular high and chief god. Before Islam, Allah, the moon god, was the central focus of prayer and worship at Kaaba. Interestingly, Pagan Arabs worshipped the moon god by praying toward Mecca several times a day. **There was an annual pilgrimage to the Kaaba which was the temple of the Moon god. An animal was killed as an offering or a sacrifice to the Moon-god. The devotees run around the Kaaba seven times, and touched a black stone set in the wall of the Kaaba. They gathered on Friday instead of Saturday and Sunday for prayer and they used to give alms to the poor. There was also a tradition of throwing stones at the devil. There was fasting for the month which began and end with the crescent moon. These were all part of the pagan rites practiced by the Arabs long before Muhammad was born and they still serve as "the five pillars" of Islam practiced today.**

The Muslims claim that Allah in pre-Islamic times was the biblical God of the Patriarchs, prophets, and apostles. Was "Allah" **the biblical God** or **a pagan god** in Arabia during pre-Islamic times? The Muslim's claim of Allah as being the biblical god was essential in their attempt to convert Jews and Christians to Islam very cunningly and deceptively. They somehow succeed in doing so to those who were ignorant of the fact that Allah was a pagan god and not the deity which the people of Judeo-Christian faith have been worshiping throughout the centuries.

Remember! any religion can make endlessly admiration about its belief system, but once it goes through the historical and archeological testing, then it reveals the evidence which speaks for itself truthfully.

## WHERE DOES ALLAH COME FROM: The Origin of Allah

"Islam owes the term "Allah" to the heathen Arabs. There is evidence that it entered into numerous personal names in Northern Arabia and among the Nabatians. It occurred among the Arabs of later times, in theophorous names and on its own." Ibn Warraq, Why I Am Not A Muslim, (Prometheus, Amherst, 1995) p. 42.

- The worship of the Moon-god "Suen" (also called Nanna or Asimbabbaar) was the most wide-spread religion in the Middle East (Hall, Mark. 1985, *A Study of the Sumerian Moon-god*, Nanna/Suen; University of PA)
- The symbol of this Moon-god was the crescent moon, and was constantly found on ancient pottery or artifacts of worship. Islam adopted the crescent moon as its religious symbol.
- In Mesopotamia the word "Suen" was transformed into the word "Sin" by the Sumerians as their favorite name for the Moon-god. (Austin Potts, 1971, *The Hymns and Prayers To The Moon-god, Sin*, Dropsie College, p. 2)
- The Old Testament forbade the worship of the Moon-god (Deut. 4:19; 17:3; II Kings 21:3,5 etc.) because it often caused Israel to commit idolatry.
- While the name of the Moon-god was "Sin," his title was "al-ilah" meaning "the deity." "Ilah" is a generic Arabic word for "god" or "deity."
- "The god Il or Ilah was originally a phase of the Moon God." (Coon, Carleton S.; 1944. *Southern Arabia*, Washington D.C.: Smithsonian, p. 398)
- The pre-Islamic Arabs shortened 'al-ilah' to Allah. They used 'Allah' in the names of their children. For instance, Muhammad's father and uncle had Allah as part of their names (Abdullah-servant of Allah).

- "Similarly, under Muhammad's tutelage, the relatively anonymous Ilah became Al-Ilah, The God, or Allah, the Supreme Being." (Coon, p. 399)
- **Mohammed never defined "Allah" in the Qur'an because he assumed that the pagan Arabs already knew who Allah was.**
- Mohammed rejected all the deities of Ancient Arab such as Ilah's wives and daughters. But he kept the black stone which represented Allah.

## Arabic Pagan Worship

Islam's origins and practices have been tracked back by scholars to the ancient fertility religion of the moon god of Arabia. The Forms of Pagan Worship includes the sun, the moon, and the five planets with a living deity, and numerous god or goddess.

Moon worship was popular in various forms. The moon was a male deity in ancient India; it was also a male deity in ancient Semitic religion, and the Arabic word for the moon (qamar) is of the masculine gender. On the other hand, the Arabic word for the sun (shama) is of the feminine gender. The pagan Arabs evidently looked upon the sun as a goddess and the moon as a god. If Wadd and Suwa represented Man and Woman, they might well represent the astral worship of the moon and the sun...

The pagan deities best known in the Kaaba and around Mecca were Al-Lat, Al-Uzza and Al-Manat...They were all female goddesses." (Yusuf Ali: pgs. 1619-1623)

- In his explanation of why the Qur'an swears by the moon in Surah 74:32, "Nay, verily by the Moon," Yusuf Ali comments, "The moon was worshipped as a deity in times of darkness." (fn. 5798, pg. 1644)
- Muhammad commanded his followers to participate in these pagan ceremonies while the pagans were still in control of Mecca. (Yusuf Ali, fn. 214, pg. 78.)

*"...the whole of the [pagan] pilgrimage was spiritualized in Islam..."* (Yusuf Ali: fn. 223 pg. 80)

- Al-Lat, al-Uzza and Manat are called "the daughters of Allah". Yusuf Ali explains in fn. 5096, pg. 1445, that Lat, Uzza and Manat were known as "the daughters of God [Allah]".
- The stars were used as pagan symbols of the daughters of Allah.
- **The Qur'an at one point told Muslims to worship al-Lat, al-Uzza and Manat in Surah 53:19-20.**
- Those verses have been "abrogated" out of the present Qur'an. They were called "The Satanic Verses."
- The Arab tribes gave the Moon-god different titles: Sin, Hubul, Ilumquh, Al-ilah.
- The title "al-ilah" (the god) was used for the Moon-god.
- The word "Allah" was derived from "al-ilah."
- The pagan "Allah" was a high god in a pantheon of 360 deities worshipped at the Kaaba.
- Allah was only one of many Meccan gods in the Kaaba.
- The Muslims placed a statue of Hubul on top of the Kaaba, at that time Hubul was considered the Moon-god by the Arabs.
- The Kaaba was the "house of the Moon-god" and the name "Allah" eventually replaced that of Hubul as the name of the Moon god.
- They called the Kaaba the "house of Allah."

*"Historians like Vaqqidi have said Allah was actually the chief of the 360 gods being worshipped in Arabia at the time Mohammed rose to prominence. Ibn Al-Kalbi gave 27 names of pre-Islamic deities...Interestingly, not many Muslims want to accept that Allah was already being worshipped at the Ka'bah in Mecca by Arab pagans before Mohammed came. Some Muslims become angry when they are confronted with this fact. But history is not on their side. Pre-Islamic literature has proved this."* (G.J.O. Moshay, Who Is This Allah? Dorchester House, Bucks, UK, 1994, pg. 138)[viii]

The word Allah never appears in the Hebrew nor Greek scriptures as a name for God. In fact, the only time it appears in the Hebrew Scriptures, it is an "Oak tree". "And Joshua wrote these words in the book of the law of God, and took a great stone, and set it up there under an oak, that was by the sanctuary of the LORD" (Josh 24:26 KJV). Strongs # 427 Hebrew: 'allah (al-law') variation of 424, oak, terebinth.

Then shall ye know that I am the LORD, when their slain men shall be among their idols round about their altars, upon every high hill, in all the tops of the mountains, and under every green tree, and under every thick oak, the place where they did offer sweet savor to all their idols (Ezek 6:13 KJV).

**Allah, in Hebrew, refers to an IDOL. In Arabic, it is the Moon god.**

All false religions began in ancient Sumer with Nimrod. All archaeologists now agree that the first civilization was in the Fertile Crescent, particularly at Shinar. Shinar is the Biblical name for Iraq. The other name for a region Iraq where the God of Israel confused the languages of the people is the very place where the tower of Babel was going to be built, it is called Babylon. Literally and symbolically this name used for the last empire spoken of in the Bible and this last empire is Islam since these are the regions now occupied by Muslims.

Allah is AL-ILAH, which is related to Enlil, Baal, Baili, and to many other false gods. So Allah, contrary to popular belief, was not invented by Muhammad the Muslim prophet but, in fact, existed before his birth. In an allegory, a poem was written which centered on Gilgamesh, another name for Nimrod. The goddess is addressed and scolded for trying to kill Gilgamesh as follows:
Tammuz, the lover of thy youth.
Thou causest to weep every year.
The bright-colored Allahu bird thou didst love.
Thou didst crush him and break his pinions.
(Frazer, J G, The Golden Bough, Vol. IX, Unabr.Edition, The Scapegoat, Lond, pg. 371).

The name Allah is believed to be originated from at least 2300 BC. Allah's root is LIL, shortened to IL from Enlil. So Allah really evolved from Enlil to Lil and then IL. The Bible refer to Baal as a pagan god, or in Hebrew Ba'il meaning "the god". In Arabic it would be Al-Ilah and in Aramaic Alaha.

There is an inscription in stone from Al-Ula in Northern Arabia, circa 500 BC, just 1000 years before Muhammad was born. In the same Semitic language dialect, and in the same time frame, are two other names of the gods- Mar-Allah, meaning Lord-god, and Adar'IL, a Sardonic contraction using the root form of the name for the god from Sumer, LIL. The god Allah was exported by Nabonidus into Northern Arabia in the 6th century BC.

In pre-Islamic times, Allah was known as, "Lord of this house", the god called, Hubal, the house being Ka'ba. This was the derivation of Ba'al or ha Ba'al. It was to Hubal that the Meccans prayed for food, protection and provision; this is clearly seen in the Qur'an where even Muhammad said in Sura 106, to pray to him.
"For the protection of the Quraysh" (106:1)
"Their protection during their trading caravans in the winter and the summer" (106:2-3)

It may be interesting to note that Muhammad, in the early Meccan period, never spoke about Abraham or the God of Abraham, Yahweh. Muslims in desperation try to point out that Abraham is mentioned during the Meccan period, but the Surahs they present as evidence are disputed to be later Surahs revealed in Medina.

It may come as a surprise to many people that it was Nimrod who was deified and later became Molech, Baal and Allah. It was often the custom of pagans to kiss their deities statues such as we read in the Bible; 1 Kings 19:18 "Yet I have left me seven thousand in Israel, all the knees which have not bowed unto Baal, and every mouth which hath not kissed him."

**Persians worshipped Allah**

In 520 B.C. Darius, King of Persia built his citadel in a city called Allanush (derived from Allah). Darius grand headquarters was named Allanush, in honor of Allah (Olmstead, A T, History of Assyria, Scribner, NY, 1923). Allah wasn't an Arabic invention because he is found in Persia also. The Persians were pagans, so once again it is proven realistically that Islamic ideas of Allah aren't factual or based on history.

It will be astonishing to learn that a reference to a King Vikramadity inscription that was found in the Ka'ba temple in Mecca, proves beyond doubt that the Arabian Peninsula was a part of his Indian Empire". It is quite possible that this was, indeed, a Hindu Temple. Hindus worship many deities and the Ka'ba of pre-Muhammad's time did house at least 360 deities. (Reproduced by Muslim Digest, July to Oct. 1986 pages. 23-24) (Article written by Mr. P.N. Oak at N-128, Greater Kailas 1, New Delhi 14, India and distributed from Durban, South Africa)

"The text of the crucial Vikramaditya inscription, found inscribed on a gold dish hanging inside the Kaaba shrine in Mecca, is found recorded on page 315 of a volume known as "Sayar-ul-Okul" treasured in the Makhtab-e-sultania (library) in Istanbul, Turkey."

Rendered in free translated English, the inscription says, "Fortunate are those who were born (and lived) during King Vikrama's reign. He was a noble, generous, dutiful ruler, devoted to the welfare of his subjects."
"...The book also contains an elaborate description of the ancient shrine of Mecca, the town and the annual fair known as OKAJ which used to be held every year around the Kaaba temple in Mecca. This should convince many Muslims that the annual Hajj of the Muslims to the Kaaba is not an Islamic specialty, but a mere continuation of an earlier pre-Islamic congregation." "...It might come as a stunning revelation to many that the word "ALLAH" could possibly be derived from the Sanskrit language. In Sanskrit, Allah, Akka and Amba are synonyms. They signify a goddess. The term Allah forms part of Sanskrit chants invoking goddess Durga, also known as Bhavani, Chandi and Mahishasuramardini. The Islamic word Allah for God is therefore could possibly be ancient Sanskrit appellation retained and continued by Islam. The word Allah could mean in ancient Sanskrit mother goddess."

25

Muhammad did, indeed clean the Ka'ba of several gods but took the god Allah the chief god of Kaaba (shrine in Mecca) for his choice to be worshipped. This in itself is the concept of not only creating a religion but a god that does actually exist. Now the symbol of that god-moon god has become the symbol of Islam. The religious rituals continue in Islam with a pre-Islamic god with the concept of One god borrowed from Judeo-Christian faith.

**Islam is the mixture of pre-Islamic paganism and twisted Biblical stories.**

**Allah has no son but three daughters**

Muslims criticize Christians who believe that Jesus Christ is the Son of God which is the heart of the Gospel and the core belief of Christianity. In reality, Christians never have had made any attempt to make any physical connection of Jesus Christ with God of this universe. It is purely a Spiritual relationship since Jesus was born by the Spirit of God as the Qur'an confirms Jesus' super natural birth by the virgin Mary, also call Jesus Ruuallah (Spirit of God).

Now in the sixth month the angel Gabriel was sent by God to a city of Galilee named Nazareth, [27] to a virgin betrothed to a man whose name was Joseph, of the house of David. The virgin's name *was* Mary. [28] And having come in, the angel said to her, "Rejoice, highly favored *one*, the Lord *is* with you; blessed *are* you among women!" [29] But when she saw *him*, she was troubled at his saying, and considered what manner of greeting this was. [30] Then the angel said to her, "Do not be afraid, Mary, for you have found favor with God. [31] And behold, you will conceive in your womb and bring forth a Son, and shall call His name JESUS. [32] He will be great, and will be called the Son of the Highest; and the Lord God will give Him the throne of His father David. [33] And He will reign over the house of Jacob forever, and of His kingdom there will be no end." [34] Then Mary said to the angel, "How can this be, since I do not know a man?" [35] And the angel answered and said to her, **"*The* Holy Spirit will come upon you, and the power of the Highest will overshadow you; therefore, also, that Holy One who is to be born will be called the Son of God.** [36] Now indeed, Elizabeth your relative has also conceived a son in her old age; and this is now the sixth month for her who was called barren. [37] For with God nothing will be impossible." [38] Then Mary said, "Behold the maidservant of the Lord! Let it be to me according to your word." And the angel departed from her. (Luke 1:26-38; Matthew 1:18-25).

The doctrine of the Judeo-Christian faith about God is absolutely monotheistic in its essence and in its religious practices. "Hear, O Israel: The LORD our God, the LORD *is* one!" (Deuteronomy 6:4). "You are the God. You alone, of all the kingdoms of the earth." (2 Kings 19:15). "The foremost is, 'Hear, O Israel! The Lord our God is one [hen] Lord; "(Mark 12:29) "This is eternal life, that they may know You, the only [monos] true God" (John 17:3) "Now to the King eternal, immortal, invisible, the only [monos] God" (1 Timothy 1:17) "For there is one [hen] God, *and* one mediator also between God and men, *the* man Christ Jesus," (1 Timothy 2:5).

Even Mohammed borrowed the concept of Monotheism from the Jews and Christians of his day.

As history proves it with great authenticity that Mohammad was not born in a family who worshipped one god, and at the same time he was never raised in an environment of a monotheistic god. Mohammed might have been continued to worship diverse multiple deities if it had not been his close contact with his first wife, Khadija, who was a Jewess, and Warqa bin Naufal, an ebonite Christian, who was cousin of Khadija and later on his contact with three Jewish tribes of Medina.

At the time of Muhammad, Allah was the chief god with three daughters Allat, Manat and Al-Uzza.

## THE DIFFERENCE BEWEEN ALLAH AND GOD OF THE BIBLE

| THE GOD OF THE BIBLE (Yahweh) | THE GOD OF THE QURAN (Allah) |
|---|---|
| The Bible teaches that God is not only the transcendent creator, but also God who is approachable.<br>"*Am* I a God near at hand," says the LORD, "And not a God afar off?" (Jeremiah 23:23)<br><br>"Let us then with confidence draw near to the throne of grace, that we may receive mercy and find grace to help in time of need" (Hebrews 4:16).<br><br>The Bible teaches that we can approach God with confidence and boldly.<br><br>The God of the Bible is knowable.<br>That's why Abraham was called "the friend of God." (Jeremiah 24:7; 31:34; Hebrews 8:11<br>Moses knew God's ways (Psalm 103:7).<br><br>**The God of the Bible is close and personal.** | The Qur'an teaches that Allah is the transcendent creator, all-powerful and all-knowing.<br>He knows who you are; in fact, many Muslims believe he has fatalistically determined your thoughts, words and deeds – good and evil – and even your eternal destiny, which is why Muslims so often say, "**If Allah wills it.**" So, Allah does indeed know you.<br><br>Allah is not truly personal, knowable, or approachable.<br>Muslim call Allah Great (Allahu Akbar), but he is far away who is not approachable.<br><br>A famous Islamic scholar by the name of Al-Ghazali said that Muslims who try to know Allah end up understanding that he cannot have known him, and that it is absolutely impossible to know Allah.<br>**Allah is distant and unknowable.** |
| He creates only good<br>Genesis 1; 1 Timothy 4:4; James 1:17<br>"Every good gift and every perfect gift is from above, and comes down from the Father of lights, with whom there is no variation or shadow of turning." | He creates good and evil<br>(Sura 4:78; 3:54)<br>"Wherever you may be, death will overtake you, even if you should be within towers of lofty construction. But if good comes to them, they say, "This is from Allah "; and if evil befalls them, they say, "This is from you." Say, "All [things] are from Allah." So what is [the matter] with those people that they can hardly understand any statement?" |
| **The Bible depicts him more God of love and mercy than judgmental.**<br><br>God of the Bible, on the other hand, loves all people (John 3:16).<br>His love is not a response to our goodness, but in spite of our lack of goodness. He | **The Qur'an depicts him more judgmental than gracious.**<br><br>The Qur'an teaches that Allah loves those he chooses to love and hates those he chooses to hate. It appears his love or hate is in response to human behavior. "Allah loves not those |

| | |
|---|---|
| proved His love for us in that while we were still sinners, Christ died for us (Rom. 5:8). The apostle John wrote, "Herein is love, not that we loved God, but that He loved us and sent His Son to be the propitiation for our sin" (1 John 4:10). Even though God hates sin, He loves the sinner and takes no pleasure in punishing him (Ezekiel 18:23).<br><br>**His love for all people is unconditional.** | that do wrong," says the Qur'an (Surah 3:140), neither does he love "him who is treacherous, sinful" (Surah 4:107). "Those who reject faith and do wrong – Allah will not forgive them nor guide them to anyway – Except the way of Hell, to dwell therein forever. And this to Allah is easy (4:168-169; 5:49 and 40:10. Other types of people Allah hates: Transgressors (2:190). Ungrateful and wicked creatures (2:276). Those who reject faith (3:32; 30:45). Those who do wrong (3:57, 140; 42:40). The arrogant, the vainglorious (4:36; 16:23; 31:18; 57:23). Those given to excess (5:87). Wasters (6:141; 7:31). Treacherous (8:58). |
| **God does not change** (Malachi 3:6; James 1;17) "For I *am* the LORD, I do not change; Therefore you are not consumed, O sons of Jacob. | **Allah changes his mind frequently.** "And when We substitute a verse in place of a verse - and Allah is most knowing of what He sends down - they say, "You, [O Muhammad], are but an inventor [of lies]." But most of them do not know." (Sura 16:101; 13:39; 17:86; 87:6-8). Muslims claim that Quran is a perfect book that has its eternal tablets in heaven and little by little Allah dictated Quranic verses to Muhammad. At the same time, Allah canceled the had dictated and gave Muhammad a better verse. So Allah changed his mind and even made necessary changes in his so to speak document-an eternal tablet per say which seems to be variable document rather than an eternal one. |
| **The Bible speaks about a God whom we can have a Paternal relationship.** God can be called Abba Father. "For you did not receive the spirit of slavery to fall back into fear, but you have received the Spirit of adoption as sons, by whom we cry, "Abba! Father!" (Rom. 8:15) | **In Islam, the relationship is more like that of a Master to a slave.** In fact, that's what Islam means: to submit as a master to a slave, and a Muslim is one who submits. In Islam, the relationship is a one-way street: Allah says, and a Muslim does. One of the most common names for Muslim men and boys is Abdullah, which literally means "slave of God." |
| **God leads people to the path of righteousness.** (Psalm 23:3; | **Allah leads people to the right path as well as to the wrong path.** |

| | "He whom Allah leads, he indeed is led aright, while he whom Allah sends astray - they indeed are losers. Already have We urged unto hell many of the jinn and humankind, having hearts wherewith they understand not, and having eyes wherewith they see not, and having ears wherewith they hear not. These are as the cattle - nay, but they are worse! These are the neglectful." (Sura 7:178-179; 18:17) |
|---|---|
| **God cannot lie.**<br>In hope of eternal life, which God, that cannot lie, promised before the world began; (Titus 1: 2)<br><br>"God *is* not a man, that He should lie, Nor a son of man, that He should repent. Has He said, and will He not do? Or has He spoken, and will He not make it good? | **Allah can tell a lie deceives.**<br>*"They plot and plan, and Allah, too plans, but the best of planners"* (Surah 8: 30)<br>*"And they (the Jews) planned and Allah (also) planned, and Allah is the best of planners." (Surah 3:54).*<br><br>The word translated "plan" by most English translations of the Qur'an is actually the Arabic word *"makr"* meaning *"To practice deceit or guile or circumvention, practice evasion or elusion, to plot, to exercise art or craft or cunning, act with policy, practice stratagem."*<br><br>The word for deception/deceiver/scheme is *makr*. The lexical sources define the term as: **Miim-Kaf-Ra** = To practice deceit or guile or circumvention, practice evasion or elusion, to plot, to exercise art or craft or cunning, act with policy, practice stratagem. *makara* vb. LL, V7, p: 256<br><br>An early Islamic commentator Qurtubi observed that some scholars have considered the words 'best of schemers' to be one of God's beautiful names. Thus one would pray, 'O Best of Schemers, scheme for me!' Qurtubi also reports that Mohammad used to pray, 'O God, scheme for me, and do not scheme against me!' (Qurtubi, IV, pp. 98-99; cf. Zamakhshari, I, p. 366)." (Ibid., p. 166).<br><br>In fact, the Quran states that Allah actually raises wicked individuals to deceive and scheme: *"Even so have we placed in every city, ringleaders of its wicked ones, **to*** |

| | scheme therein (liyamkuroo): but only against themselves shall **they scheme (yamkuroona)!** and they know it not." (S. 6:123)<br><br>**Moreover, the Qur'an calls Allah a liar, because he has no problem using guile,** "*kayd* ", in Surahs 7:182-183 and 68:45.<br><br>**The Bible calls Satan the deceiver:** "*And the great dragon was thrown down, the serpent of old who is called the devil and Satan, who deceives the whole world; he was thrown down to the earth, and his angels were thrown down with him.*" *(Rev 12:9)*<br><br>**It also calls Satan a liar:** "*You are of your father the devil, and you want to do the desires of your father. He was a murderer from the beginning, and does not stand in the truth because there is no truth in him. Whenever he speaks a lie, he speaks from his own nature, for he is a liar and the father of lies.*" *(John 8:44)* |
|---|---|
| **God wants that the believers stay faithful unto death:** "Be faithful until death, and I will give you the crown of life" (Revelation 2:10). | **Allah demands that Muslims fight for him even unto death:** "Whoso fights in the way of Allah, be he slain or victorious, on him We shall bestow a vast reward" – Surah 4:74 |
| **God promises a heaven that will be a wonderful place because there won't be any pain, suffering, grief, sin or evil.** And I heard a loud voice from heaven saying, "Behold, the tabernacle of God *is* with men, and He will dwell with them, and they shall be His people. God Himself will be with them *and be* their God. [4] And God will wipe away every tear from their eyes; there shall be no more death, nor sorrow, nor crying. There shall be no more pain, for the former things have passed away." [5] Then He who sat on the throne said, "Behold, I make all things new." And He said to me,[b] "Write, for these words are true and faithful." (Revelation 21:3-5) | **Allah promises a heaven a place of sexual pleasure.**<br>"As for the righteous, they shall surely triumph. Theirs shall be gardens and vineyards, and **virgins with big breasts** for companions: a truly overflowing cup." (Surah 78:31).<br>"...They will sit with **bashful, dark-eyed virgins**, as chaste as the sheltered eggs of ostriches." (Surah 37:40-48).<br>"...They shall recline on couches ranged in rows. To **dark-eyed houris** (virgins) we shall wed them..." (Surah 52:17-20).<br>"...We created the **houris (the beautiful women) and made them virgins, loving companions** for those on the right hand... " (Surah 56:7-40). |

| When we get to heaven, there will be no marriage. "For in the resurrection they neither marry nor are given in marriage, but are like angels of God in heaven" (Matthew 22:30). | "In each there shall be **virgins chaste and fair... Dark eyed virgins** sheltered in their tents whom neither man nor Jinn will have touched before..." (Surah 55:70-77). "Round about them will serve **boys of perpetual freshness.**" (Surah 56:17). "In them will be **bashful virgins** neither man nor Jinn will have touched before. Then **which of the favors of your Lord will you deny?**" (Surah 55:56-57)<br><br>There are quotes from the Hadith that are too graphic. The reader might have uneasy feelings. That's why it is apt to narrate in the endnotes.[ix] |

## SUMMARY:

God of the Bible is the God of love and compassion. The Bible tell us that "Whoever does not love does not know God, because God is love" (1 John 4:8).

The Bible teaches that we can call him "Abba Father" (Romans 8:15). In Islam it is more like a slave or servant-master relationship. As a slave, a Muslim is bound to observe his/her religious duties at certain times. One must face a particular direction even knowing the reality that god is everywhere. A Muslim is obliged to recite his/her prayers in Arabic even knowing that Allah is all-knowing. Allah-god of Islam brings nothing but religious slavery. But God of the Bible brings freedom. It is a freedom to worship in one's native language, facing any direction at any time. This freedom is only through Jesus Christ. The Bible tells us: "So if the Son sets you free, you will be free indeed" (John 8:36). "It is for freedom that Christ has set us free" (Galatians 5:1).

# CHAPTER THREE

---

# THE TRUTH ABOUT
# THE PROPHET OF ISLAM
# MUHAMMAD

[15] "Beware of false prophets, who come to you in sheep's clothing but inwardly are ravenous wolves. [16] You will recognize them by their fruits. Are grapes gathered from thorn bushes, or figs from thistles? [17] So, every healthy tree bears good fruit, but the diseased tree bears bad fruit. [18] A healthy tree cannot bear bad fruit, nor can a diseased tree bear good fruit. [19] Every tree that does not bear good fruit is cut down and thrown into the fire. [20] **Thus you will recognize them by their fruits.** (Matthew 7:17-20-The Holy Bible)

# CHAPTER THREE

# THE TRUTH ABOUT THE PROPHET OF ISLAM

Muslims regard Muhammad as the perfect role model for mankind who **is** an ideal husband, father and politician, an embodiment of honesty, wisdom, and mercy. He is the last prophet and even call him the "seal of the prophets." On the other hand, his critics have a completely different view about Muhammad after keenly studying the Islamic sources equally. Some have said that Muhammad was an evil and barbaric manipulator who contrived his religion to satiate his lust for power, sex, and money. He was a terrorist. So what is the truth about this man?

The main source of information about Muhammed comes from Hadith and other Islamic resources like the biography written by Ibn Ishaq and later continued by Ibn Hashim.

The Islamic sources depict Muhammad's life with the good as well as the bad side of his character. That's why Muslims should be open and honest to accept the truth without overlooking the dark side of his character and teaching. The Islamic sources speak for itself. It has nothing to do with a vicious attempt by non-Muslims who dare to do a character assassination of Muhammad. I believe people in general are honest and open to accept a good moral, and inspiring sayings of any person, regardless of his background, without any predisposition or prejudice.

The Islamic history discloses that before Islam, Muhammad was known as, "SADIQ-the righteous one" and "AMIN-trustworthy." Apart from these titles, he was a generous, compassionate person. For example, the event of placing the black stone in the Holy Kaaba, excites Muslims to believe how their prophet was respected among different tribes in his home town and how he was able to bring peace and harmony in that given situation.

The legend goes like this:
It had rained heavily and continuously for a long period, and the water poured down towards the Holy Kaaba in Masjid-ul-Haram, the big mosque in Mecca, The Kaaba was in the lower section of Mecca. It had become old and dilapidated.
So the rebuilding was started. The work progressed well enough until al-Hajar-ul-Aswad, the Black Stone, was to be put back in its place.
Each quarter of the Kaaba was being built by one leading family of Quraish - the big and prominent tribe of Mecca. Each family of Quraish felt the honor of placing the Black Stone belonging to it.
The disagreement became deeper, and led to a lot of argument, shouting and abuse. The members of each big family thought that this would lead to war. None of them were willing to change their position. They regarded it as a great insult if they didn't have that special honor of putting the Black Stone back in its place.

One member stood up and said, "I have a suggestion, let us wait till tomorrow and see who enters the Masjid-ul-Haram first in the morning; then let him decide". All agreed, since that sounded like a good suggestion.

They anxiously waited until the next morning to see who was the first to come and enter Kaaba. Suddenly they heard footsteps heading towards them. It was Muhammad, the son of Abdulla. Everyone, of course, knew, loved, admired and respected Muhammad. So with a loud voice, everyone said, "Here comes Al-Amin" and the voice echoed through the place over and over again.

He was surprised to hear that title with which they called him. He was told about what the people of Quraish were fighting for. It was all silent for a while. Everyone thought his family was going to be favored. Their hearts were beating hard and they were getting anxious and impatient.

Muhammad put his robe on the floor, took the sacred Black Stone and put it in the center of the robe and said. "The chief of each family will take one corner of the robe and lift it together". With that, each understood a marvelous example of justice in sharing the honor. It showed how Muhammad's intelligence far exceeded those around him. It also showed his great capacity to solve difficult problems for such ease.

When the robe with the Black Stone was lifted to a reasonable height, Muhammad took the Black Stone and put it in its proper place by his own hands. None felt insulted and each had his share of the privilege and honor.

This is how Muhammad, the Prophet of Islam succeeded in uniting the ever-fighting and ignorant Arabs with his honesty, justice and noble character.

The Islamic history and traditions tell that when Muhammed dispatched troops, he would tell them; "Do not kill a child, nor a woman, nor an old man, nor obliterate a stream, nor cut-down a tree..." (Sunan Al-Bayhaqi). He asked to "show mercy to whatever is on earth, then He who is in heaven will show mercy to you" (Abu Dawud). Muhamad taught that "The strongman is not the one who is strong in wrestling, but the one who controls himself in anger" (Bukhari). "Visit the sick, feed the hungry, and free the captives" (Bukhari). The believers who show the most perfect faith are those who have the best character and the best are those who are best to their wives" (Tirmidhi). This is just a few selections from traditions that shows that Mohammed did do and say some good things. Any good moral person might do and say the same kind things as did Muhammad.

However, Islamic history very vividly and explicitly delineate a rather different picture as well. For example, how Muhammad dealt with the tribe called Qurayza who had sided with the Meccans during the Battle of the trench.

In AD 627, Muhammad committed an atrocity against the last remaining major tribe of Jews in Medina called the Qurayza that numbered about 300-600 men and pubescent boys, which he beheaded and enslaved the women and children. Ibn Ishaq says that the number may have been as high as 800-900 and their property was divided among the Muslims. What makes this incident even worse is that there was only certain member of the tribe that had sided with the Meccans, and this is confirmed heavily by the vast majority of Islamic history. It shows the climax of cruelty and broadness of brutality done to so many innocents lives by the so called merciful and benevolent prophet.

According to wikiIslam, the use of assassination to achieve political/religious goals has been important throughout the history of Arabia and Islamic expansion, and the very word "assassin" has Arabic roots (حشاشين).

This list contains the results and reasons for the targeted killings and assassinations ordered or supported by Prophet Muhammad, as well as the primary sources which mention these incidents.

**List of Killings:**

| No. | Name | Date | Reason(s) for Ordering or Supporting Killing | Result | Notable Primary Sources |
|-----|------|------|------|------|------|
| 1 | 'Asma' bint Marwan | January 624 | Kill 'Asma' bint Marwan for opposing Muhammad with poetry and for provoking others to attack him | Asma' bint Marwan assassinated | Ibn Hisham & Ibn Ishaq, Sirat Rasul Allah<br><br>Ibn Sa'd, Kitab al-tabaqat al-kabir, Volume 2 |
| 2 | Abu 'Afak | February 624 | Kill the Jewish poet Abu Afak for opposing Muhammad through poetry | Abu Afak assassinated | Ibn Hisham & Ibn Ishaq, Sirat Rasul Allah<br><br>Ibn Sa'd, Kitab al-tabaqat al-kabir, Volume 2 |
| 3 | Al Nadr ibn al-Harith | After Battle of Badr March 624 | According to Mubarakpuri, Al Nadir was captured during the Battle of Badr. A Qur'an verse was revealed ordering the execution of Nadr bin Harith, he was one of | Nadr bin Harith beheaded by Ali | Qur'an 83:13<br><br>Ibn Hisham & Ibn Ishaq, Sirat Rasul Allah |

| | | | two prisoners who were executed and not allowed to be ransomed by their clans because he mocked and harassed Muhammad and wrote poems and stories criticizing him | | |
|---|---|---|---|---|---|
| 4 | Uqba bin Abu Muayt | After Battle of Badr March 624 | Uqba bin Abu Muayt was captured in the Battle of Badr and was killed instead of being ransomed, because he threw dead animal entrails on Muhammad, and wrapped his garment around Muhammad's neck while he was praying | Uqba bin Abu Muayt beheaded by Asim ibn Thabbit or Ali | Sunan Abu Dawud no. 2680 (with commentary from Awnul Mabud 3/12)<br><br>Sahih Bukhari 1:9:499<br><br>Ibn Hisham & Ibn Ishaq, Sirat Rasul Allah<br><br>Tabari, Volume 9, The last years of the Prophet |
| 5 | Ka'b ibn al-Ashraf | September 624 | According to Ibn Ishaq, Muhammad ordered his followers to kill Ka'b because he "had gone to Mecca after Badr and inveighed | Ka'b ibn al-Ashraf assassinated | Bukhari 5:59:369, Sahih Muslim 19:4436 |

| # | Name | Date | Reason | Outcome | Sources |
|---|---|---|---|---|---|
| | | | against Muhammad. He also composed verses in which he bewailed the victims of Quraysh who had been killed at Badr. Shortly afterwards he returned to Medina and composed amatory verses of an insulting nature about the Muslim women" | | |
| 6 | Abu Rafi' ibn Abi Al-Huqaiq | December 624 | Kill Abu Rafi' ibn Abi Al-Huqaiq for mocking Muhammad with his poetry and for helping the troops of the Confederates by providing them with money and supplies | Abu Rafi assassinated | Bukhari 4:52:264, Bukhari 5:59:370, Bukhari 5:59:371, Bukhari 5:59:372 and more Ibn Hisham & Ibn Ishaq, Sirat Rasul Allah Tabari, Volume 7, The foundation of the community |
| 7 | Khalid ibn Sufyan | 625 | Kill Khalid bin Sufyan, because there were reports he considered an attack on Medina and that | Khalid ibn Sufyan assassinated | Musnad Ahmad 3:496 Abu Dawud, book 2 no.1244[ |

| | | | | | |
|---|---|---|---|---|---|
| | | | he was inciting the people on Nakhla or Uranah to fight Muslims | | Ibn Hisham, Sirat Rasul Allah<br><br>Tabari, Volume 9, The last years of the Prophet |
| 8 | Abu 'Azzah 'Amr bin 'Abd Allah al-Jumahi | March 625 | Behead Abu 'Azzah 'Amr bin 'Abd Allah al-Jumahi because he was a prisoner of War captured during the Invasion of Hamra al-Asad, that Muhammad released once, but he took up arms against him again | Abu 'Azzah beheaded by Ali | Tabari, Volume 7, The foundation of the community |
| 9 | Muawiyah bin Al Mugheerah | March 625 | Kill Muawiyah bin Al Mugheerah, because he was accused by Muhammad of being a spy. He went to Uthman (his cousin) for shelter, and Uthman arranged for his return to Mecca, but he stayed too long in Medina. After Muhammad heard he was still in Medina, | Muawiyah bin Al Mugheerah captured and executed | Ibn Hisham & Ibn Ishaq, Sirat Rasul Allah |

| | | | | | |
|---|---|---|---|---|---|
| | | | he ordered his death | | |
| 10 | Al-Harith bin Suwayd al-Ansari | March 625 | Kill Al-Harith bin Suwayd because according to some Islamic traditions, Allah revealed Qur'an 3:86-8, which indicated that those who reject Islam after accepting it should be punished. Al-Harith bin Suwayd was a Muslim who fought in the Battle of Uhud and killed some Muslims, he then joined the Quraysh and left Islam. After being threatened with those verses, Al-Harith sent his brother to Muhammad to ask for his forgiveness. | Conflicting reports 1. Muhammad allowed his return but then decided to kill him. Al-Harith was beheaded by Uthman Allah revealed Qur'an 3:89 and Al-Harith repented and "became a good Muslim" | Qur'an 3:86-88 Ibn Hisham & Ibn Ishaq, Sirat Rasul Allah |
| 11 | Abu Sufyan | 627 | Amr bin Umayyah al-Damri sent to assassinate Abu Sufyan | 3 polytheists killed by Muslims | Tabari, Volume 7, The foundation of the community |

| | | | | | |
|---|---|---|---|---|---|
| | | | (Quraysh leader) | | |
| 12 | Banu Qurayza tribe | February–March 627 | Attack Banu Qurayza because according to Muslim tradition he had been ordered to do so by the angel Gabriel. One of Muhammad's companions decided that "the men should be killed, the property divided, and the women and children taken as captives". Muhammad approved of the ruling, calling it similar to God's judgment, after which all male members of the tribe who had reached puberty were beheaded | Muslims: 2 killed Non-Muslims: 1. 600-900 beheaded (Tabari, Ibn Hisham) 2. All Males and 1 woman beheaded (Hadith) | Qur'an 33:26, Qur'an 33:09 & 33:10 Abu Dawud 38:4390 Bukhari 4:52:68, Bukhari 4:57:66 and more Tabari, Volume 8, Victory of Islam |
| 13 | Abdullah ibn Ubayy | December 627 (during Invasion of Banu Mustaliq) | Kill Abdullah ibn Ubayy, who was accused by Muhammad of slandering his family by spreading false | Muhammad calls off assassination and says to Umar "if I had had him (Abdullah bin Ubai) killed, a large number of | Bukhari 5:59:462, Bukhari 5:59:462 Ibn Hisham, Sirat Rasul Allah |

41

| | | | rumors about Aisha (his wife). His son offered to behead him | dignitaries would have furiously hastened to fight for him" Later he reveals a Quran verse forbidding Muslims from attending the funeral of disbelievers and "hypocrites" | |
|---|---|---|---|---|---|
| 14 | Al-Yusayr ibn Rizam | February 628 | Kill Al-Yusayr ibn Rizam because Muhammad heard that his group was preparing to attack him | 30 killed by Muslims | Tirmidhi no. 3923  Ibn Hisham & Ibn Ishaq, Sirat Rasul Allah |
| 15 | Eight men from 'Ukil | February 628 | Kill 8 men who came to him and converted to Islam, but then apostatized, killed one Muslim and drove off with Muhammad's camels | Muslims: 1 killed Non-Muslims: 8 tortured to death | Qur'an 5:33-39  Bukhari 1:4:234,  Bukhari 5:59:505,  Bukhari 7:71:623 and more |
| 16 | Rifa'ah bin Qays | 629 | To kill Rifa'ah bin Qays, because Muhammad heard they were allegedly enticing the people of Qais to fight him | 1 beheaded, 4 women captured by Muslims | Ibn Hisham & Ibn Ishaq, Sirat Rasul Allah  Tabari, Volume 8, History of Islam |

| | | | | | Bukhari 5:59:582, |
|---|---|---|---|---|---|
| 17 | Abdullah bin Khatal | During/ after Conquest of Mecca (Jan 630) | Kill Abdullah bin Khatal for killing a slave and fleeing, as well and for reciting poems insulting Muhammad | 2 Muslims execute him, after finding him hiding under the curtains of the Kaaba | Bukhari 3:29:72 Ibn Hisham & Ibn Ishaq, Sirat Rasul Allah Ibn Sa'd, Kitab al-tabaqat al-kabir, Volume 2 |
| 18 | Fartana | During/ after Conquest of Mecca (Jan 630) | Kill Fartana (a slave girl of Abdullah ibn Khatal), because she used to recite poems insulting Muhammad | Fartana is killed | Abu Dawud 14:2678 Ibn Hisham & Ibn Ishaq, Sirat Rasul Allah Ibn Sa'd, Kitab al-tabaqat al-kabir, Volume 2 |
| 19 | Quraybah | During /after Conquest of Mecca (Jan 630) | Kill Quraybah (a slave girl of Abdullah ibn Khatal), because she used to recite poems insulting Muhammad | Quraybah converts to Islam and is pardoned | Abu Dawud 14:2678 Ibn Hisham & Ibn Ishaq, Sirat Rasul Allah Ibn Sa'd, Kitab al-tabaqat al-kabir, Volume 2 |
| 20 | Huwayrith ibn Nafidh | During/ after Conquest of Mecca (Jan 630) | When Muhammad's daughters were fleeing Medina, he stabbed their camels, causing injuries. He was a poet who "disgraced and abused" Islam | Huwayrith ibn Nafidh killed by Ali | Ibn Hisham & Ibn Ishaq, Sirat Rasul Allah |

43

| | | | | | |
|---|---|---|---|---|---|
| 21 | Miqyas ibn Subabah | During/ after Conquest of Mecca (Jan 630) | Miqyas killed a Muslim who accidentally killed his brother, and escaped to Mecca and became an apostate by embracing polytheism | Miqyas killed | Ibn Hisham & Ibn Ishaq, Sirat Rasul Allah |
| 22 | Sarah | During/ after Conquest of Mecca (Jan 630) | Kill Sarah, because Muhammad claimed that she used to molest him while he was in Mecca | Conflicting reports:<br><br>1. Ibn Ishaq reports that she embraced Islam but was killed later, during the time of Umar<br>2. Tabari reports she was killed | Ibn Hisham & Ibn Ishaq, Sirat Rasul Allah<br><br>Tabari, Volume 8, History of Islam |
| 23 | Harith ibn Hisham | During/after Conquest of Mecca (Jan 630) | Kill Harith ibn Hisham, reason unknown | According to Ibn Sa'd, Zubayr ibn Abi Umayyah and Harith ibn Hisham both sought refuge in a Muslim relative's house, the relative pleaded with Muhammad for mercy, so he pardoned them on | Ibn Hisham & Ibn Ishaq, Sirat Rasul Allah<br><br>Ibn Sa'd, Kitab al-tabaqat al-kabir, Volume 2 |

| | | | | | |
|---|---|---|---|---|---|
| | | | | the condition they embrace Islam | |
| 24 | Zubayr ibn Abi Umayyah | During/ after Conquest of Mecca (Jan 630) | Kill Zubayr ibn Abi Umayyah, reason unknown | See above result | Ibn Hisham & Ibn Ishaq, Sirat Rasul Allah |
| 25 | Habbar Ibn al-Aswad bin Ka`b al-`Ansi | During/ after Conquest of Mecca (Jan 630) | Kill Habbar ibn al-Aswad because he was a "liar", he claimed he was a Prophet | Habbar ibn al-Aswad killed | Bukhari 5:59:662, Bukhari 4:56:817 Ibn Hisham & Ibn Ishaq, Sirat Rasul Allah Tabari, Volume 9, The last years of the Prophet Ibn Sa'd, Kitab al-tabaqat al-kabir, Volume 2 |
| 26 | Ikrimah ibn Abu Jahl | During/after Conquest of Mecca (Jan 630) | Kill Ikrimah ibn Abu Jahl, because he was hostile to Muhammad like his father Abu Jahl | Conflicting reports 1. Ibn Ishaq says, his wife "became a Muslim and asked for immunity for him and the apostle gave it" 2. Tabari says he was "eliminated" | Ibn Hisham & Ibn Ishaq, Sirat Rasul Allah Tabari, Volume 8, History of Islam |

45

| | | | | | |
|---|---|---|---|---|---|
| 27 | Wahshi ibn Harb | During/ after Conquest of Mecca (Jan 630) | Kill Wahshi ibn Harb, for killing Muhammad's uncle during the Battle of Uhud | Wahshi ibn Harb pardoned by Muhammad after he asks for forgiveness and offers to convert to Islam | Ibn Sa'd, Kitab al-tabaqat al-kabir, Volume 2 |
| 28 | Ka'b ibn Zuhayr ibn Abi Sulama | During/after Conquest of Mecca (Jan 630) | Assassinate Ka'b ibn Zuhayr ibn Abi Sulama for writing satirical poems about Muhammad | Ibn Ishaq wrote that Muhammad said "Leave him alone, he has become a repentant Muslim after the disposal of his past.", so he was pardoned | Ibn Hisham & Ibn Ishaq, Sirat Rasul Allah |
| 29 | Al-Harith bin al-Talatil | During/ after Conquest of Mecca (Jan 630) | For mocking Muhammad through poetry | Al-Harith bin al-Talatil is killed by Ali | Ibn Hisham & Ibn Ishaq, Sirat Rasul Allah |
| 30 | Abdullah ibn Zib'ari | During/ after Conquest of Mecca (Jan 630) | Kill Abdullah ibn Zib'ari, for writing insulting poems about Muhammad | Abdullah ibn Zib'ari repents and converts to Islam, so Muhammad pardoned him | Ibn Hisham & Ibn Ishaq, Sirat Rasul Allah |
| 31 | Hubayrah | During/ after Conquest of Mecca (Jan 630) | Kill Hubayrah, for mocking Muhammad through poetry | Tabari Volume 39 states, Hubayrah "ran away when Mecca was conquered, and died in Najran as an infidel" | Tabari, Volume 39, Biographies of the Prophet's companions and their successors |
| 32 | Hind bint Utbah | During/ after Conquest of | Kill Hind bint Utbah (wife of Abu Sufyan) for | Tabari said, Hind "swore allegiance and became a | Abu Dawud 33:4153 |

| | | | | | |
|---|---|---|---|---|---|
| | | Mecca (Jan 630) | cutting out the heart of Muhammad's uncle Hamza after he died, during the Battle of Uhud | Muslim.", she was pardoned by Muhammad | Tabari, Volume 8, History of Islam |
| 33 | Amr ibn Jihash (convert to Islam) | During the Invasion of Banu Nadir (Aug 625) | According to Ibn Kathir and Ibn Ishaq, Muhammad said to Yamin bim Umayr, about Amr ibn Jash "Have you seen the way your cousin has treated me and what he proposed to do?" Muhammad accused him of trying to assassinate him | Amr ibn Jihash is assassinated after a Muslim offers a reward for his killing | Ibn Hisham & Ibn Ishaq, Sirat Rasul Allah |
| 34 | King or Prince of Dumatul Jandal | October 630 | Attack the chief of Duma for Jizyah and booty | 1 killed, 2 taken captive | Abu Dawud 19:3031  Ibn Sa'd, Kitab al-tabaqat al-kabir, Volume 2  Tabari, Volume 9, The last years of the Prophet |
| 35 | Umaiya bin Khalaf Abi Safwan | Unknown | Kill Umaiya bin Khalaf, Muhammad's reason is unknown. But | Umaiya bin Khalaf killed by Bilal | Bukhari 4:56:826 |

| | | | Bilal wanted to kill him for torturing him | | |
|---|---|---|---|---|---|
| 36 | Blind man's wife/ concubine | Unknown | Muhammad supported this killing because the women insulted him | Blind Muslim kills his wife/concubine | Abu Dawud 38:4348 <br><br> Sunan al-Nasai no. 4081 |
| 37 | Ibn Sunayna | Unknown | Muhammad reportedly ordered his followers to "kill any Jew that falls into your power", Muhayissa heard this and went out to kill Ibn Sunayna (a Jew) | Ibn Sunayna killed by Muhayissa | Abu Dawud 19:2996 <br><br> Ibn Hisham & Ibn Ishaq, Sirat Rasul Allah |
| 38 | Abdullah ibn Sa'ad | Unknown | Kill Abdullah ibn Sa'ad, because he became an apostate (left Islam) and fled to Mecca. He also claimed that he was the one who wrote the Qur'an and started to mock Muhammad, which made him angry | A misunderstanding lead to his pardoning. Abdullah ibn Sa'ad was brought in front of Muhammad and offered his loyalty, Muhammad upheld his hand to indicate that his followers should kill him, but the Muslims thought he pardoned him. He said "Was not there a wise man among you who would | Abu Dawud 38:4346 <br><br> Ibn Hisham & Ibn Ishaq, Sirat Rasul Allah |

| | | | | | |
|---|---|---|---|---|---|
| | | | stand up to him when he saw that I had withheld my hand from accepting his allegiance, and kill him?" | | |
| 39 | Ibn an-Nawwahah | Unknown | According to Ibn Kathir, Muhammad once said about Ibn an-Nawwahah "I would have cut off your head, if it was not that emissaries are not killed" because he claimed Musaylimah was a Prophet, so Abdullah ibn Masud killed Ibn an-Nawwahah when he was no longer an emissary | Abdullah ibn Masud beheads Ibn an-Nawwahah | Abu Dawud 14:2756 Tabari, Volume 10, Conquest of Arabia |
| 40 | Blind Jew | Unknown | Muhammad's followers kill a blind Jew for throwing dust at his face | Blind Jew killed by Sa'd ibn Zayd | Ibn Hisham & Ibn Ishaq, Sirat Rasul Allah Tabari, Volume 7, The foundation of the community |
| 41 | Nameless spy | Unknown | Kill a man Muhammad | Salama bin Al-Akwa chases and | Bukhari 4:52:286 |

| | | | suspected of being a spy | kills the suspected spy | |
|----|----------------|----------|-----------------------------------------------------------------------------|----------------------------------|--------------------------------------------|
| 42 | Man from Aslam tribe | Unknown | Kill a man from the Aslam tribe for Adultery | Man from Aslam tribe stoned to death | Abu Dawud 38:4414 |
| 43 | Kinana ibn al-Rabi | July 628 | Torture Kinana ibn al-Rabi to find location of allegedly hidden treasure | Kinana ibn al-Rabi beheaded | Ibn Hisham & Ibn Ishaq, Sirat Rasul Allah |

This list speaks very loudly to convince any rationale mind that Muhammad moved from moderate form of Islam to a militant form of Islam. The Quran, so called, revealed in Mecca has a more moderate tone as compared to the Quran revealed in Medina which is militant at best. For example, the Meccan version of the Quran tells that there is no compulsion in religion (2:256), whereas the Medinan version will speak of fighting and killing of infidels until there is only one god, Allah and Muhammad his messenger.

Muslims revere their prophet Mohammed so highly. When they address him, they often add these words: "Peace be upon him." It is very interesting that the followers of Islam send peace on their prophet whereas Jesus Christ gives or sends peace to His followers. Jesus Christ doesn't need any peace. He is the source and personification of peace. He is called the Prince of Peace. Jesus said, "Peace I leave with you; my peace I give you. I do not give to you as the world gives. Do not let your hearts be troubled and do not be afraid." (John 14:27).

About seven centuries before the birth of Jesus Christ, Isaiah the prophet prophesied about the glorious coming of Jesus Christ. He told about the uniqueness of His virgin birth and about His glorious names. The Bible says, "For unto us a child is born, unto us a son is given: and the government shall be upon his shoulder: and his name shall be called Wonderful, Counsellor, The mighty God, The everlasting Father, **The Prince of Peace**" (Isaiah 9:6). Jesus, who is the personification of Peace, does not need any peace since He Himself is the source of peace. He gives peace to the troubled lives, and brings peace among the nations of the world once people are willing to accept Him and yield to His wonderful teachings.

Personally, I have no problem, if Muslims want to send peace to their prophet, it is their way to venerate their prophet. Who knows that it might be essential or crucial for Muhammad to receive this kind of wishes from his followers since peace is needed for troubled lives, to those who are living in confusion and even uncertainty about future and eternity!

When it comes to the historical truthfulness about Muhammad, much is known about the life of Muhammad. In 1851, the French scholar Ernest Renan wrote that Muhammad lived "in the full light of history." Muhammad's first biographer was Muhammad ibn Ishaq (704-773 A.D.) who wrote "Sirat Rasul Allah", a work which has not survived. No finished biography of Muhammad appeared until 150 years after his death in Arabia. However, Muslims, as well as others, have disregarded the historical facts. They have continually striven to turn this man

[Mohammed] into an imaginary superhuman being, a sort of God in human clothes, and have generally ignored the ample evidence of his humanity.[x]

## The early life of Mohammed

According to Muslim tradition, Muhammad was born in Mecca on April 20, 570 A.D. Shiites say he was born on April 26th. Some Islamic traditions even tell that he was born on Friday. At the time Muhammad was born, Muhammad's father Abdullah (slave of Allah) was the chief of the pagan worshipping tribe of Quraish, the tribe that controlled Kaaba. The branch of the Quraish tribe Muhammad belonged to was known as the Beni Hashem. Muhammad's father was 'Abd Allah ibn 'Abd al-Muttalib, of the family of Hashim (Shaiba ibn Hashim). 'Abd Allah means "slave of Allah". His father died soon after his son's birth--while he was out on a trading expedition. Muhammad was orphaned early in his life after his mother Amina died when he was six years old. He was raised by his grandfather Abdul Muttalib, the chief of the Quraish tribe, and his uncle Abu-Talib. Earlier, at about age of five, while in the care of a Bedouin nurse named Halima, Muhammad became subject to epileptic fits at very early age.

At the age of nine, the boy Muhammad was taken on a merchandising expedition into Syria. While away from Arabia, he saw the sacred places of the Jews. During this time Muhammad became acquainted more with both Jews and Christians. He heard many Biblical stories which would have caused Muhammad to write the things in the Koran about Judeo-Christian history, and theology without any proper understanding as Muhammad did not possess an intellect befitting a historian. It has also been thought that Muhammad could not read or write. In fact, the Qur'an says, Muhammad was illiterate (Ummi) in Surah 7:157. These Qur'an (Koran) entries are marred with gross errors and inattention to detail. Muslims consider Muhammad to be an illiterate in order to prove that Quran is a miracle. While some Islamic sources support the notion that Muhammad was literate since he was hired by Khadija to take care of her business.

It was while with his grandfather and uncle that Muhammad learned to exercise power, to fast, and to pray at certain specified times of the day. The Quraish tribe prayed to idols at sunrise, noon, and at sunset; and they faced the direction of the Black Stone idol and the Kaaba.

At the age of 20, Muhammad was hired by a wealthy Jewish woman named Khadija (or Khadijah) to manage her late husband's caravan business. When Muhammad was 25, he married Khadija, who was then 40 years old. Khadija's cousin, Waraqah Ibn Naufal (aka: Neufel), a monk in the heretical Nestorian Christian Ebonite sect, presided over their marriage ceremony. The Muslims need to appreciate and admire this reality that the marriage of their prophet was officiated by a Christian. Muhammad stayed faithful to his wife until her death. He did not enter into any polygamous relationship while being married to Khadija. Six children were born to them two sons, both of them died young, and four daughters whose names were Rockeya, Kolthum, Zeinale, and Fatima. But only one survived to adulthood; his beloved daughter Fatima.

The marriage to Khadija, proved very fortunate to Muhammad. Muhammad suddenly became equal to the richest men in Mecca. While married to Khadija, Muhammad did not marry any other wife. However, after she died, Muhammad married many wives, slaves, captives, even his own adoptive son, Zaid's wife, and the child bride, Aisha. She herself has narrated that she was nine years old when Muhammad married her. But the betrothal took place when she was six years old.

**Muhammad is said to been characterized by his love of three things: "Women, Perfume, and Fine Clothes."**

Muslim scholar and statesman Ali Dashti gives the following list of the women in Muhammad's life:

| | |
|---|---|
| 1. Khadija | 12. Hend |
| 2. Sawda | 13. Asma (of Saba) |
| 3. Aisha | 14. Zaynab (of Khozayma) |
| 4. Omm Salama | 15. Habla |
| 5. Halsa | 16. Asma (of Noman) |
| 6. Zaynab (of Jahsh) | 17. Mary (the Christian) |
| 7. Jowayriyi | 18. Rayhana |
| 8. Omm Habiba | 19. Omm Sharik |
| 9. Safiya | 20. Maymuna |
| 10. Maymuna (of Hareth) | 21. Zaynab (a third one) |
| 11. Fatema | 22. Khawla |

| Name of Bride | Age at marriage | Comments |
|---|---|---|
| Khadija bint khawilad | 40 | Twice widowed before |
| Sauda Bint Zama | 50 | Widow |
| Aisha bint Abu Bakr | 9 | Started living with the prophet at the age of 6. Muhammad was 53 years old. |
| Hafsa Bint Umar bin Khattab | 22 | Widow |
| Zainab bint Khuzaima | 30 | ? |
| Umm-I-Salma bint Abu Umayia | 26 | Widow |
| Zainab Bint Jahash | 38 | Widow |
| Juwaeria Bint Harith | 20 | Widow |
| Umm-I-Habiba bint Abu Sufyan | 36 | Widow |
| Marya Qibtiya bint Shamun | 17 | Virgin, Egyptian Christian |
| Safia bint Hayi bin Akhtab | 17 | Widow |
| Raihana bint umru bin hanafa | ? | ? |
| Maimuna bint Harith | 36 | Widow |

The Quran sets limit for men to marry four wives only if they can afford. While Muhammad married more than twenty. Muslims boast that Muhammad was given a special privilege of marrying as many wives he could.

The Christian apologist Ravi Zacharias has well states that Muhammad violated the laws of the Old Testament; the laws he made or received from his god Allah, and the laws of the land where he was living. Such man cannot be an ideal man for humanity who make alteration of laws in order satisfy his own lust, greed and power.

Muhammad's childhood name was not Ahmad, meaning "the praised one", but Amin, closer to his mother's name Amina meaning trustworthy. Muslims use ninety-nine names for Muhammad. There is a proverb that a beloved child has many names. When people adore someone, admire something or venerate some deity, spontaneously, out of love and respect, the names emerge. There is nothing wrong in giving names to someone, but there must be a criterion, which would correlate with the character and name. Muhammad means the "praised one" or the one who is praised.

## Mohammed had Forty-Two Encounters with Spirits

Muhammad had close connections with Arabs known as Henefites. Henefites rejected idol worship and were searching for true religion. They looked to the Jews and Christians as being close to what they were looking for. The Henefites abandoned their idols and would retreat to the caves of Mecca for meditation and prayer.

In 610, Muhammad had forty-two encounters with the spirits when, supposedly he got his first revelation in the cave of Hira at the age of 40. It would be very appropriate and important to document different writings which are related to this event. It provides deeper insight about Muhammad's first revelation, and at the same time many other subsequent revelations, that he got.

The Mishkat-ul-Massabih, Vol. IV, pp.356-357 narrates Muhammad's first revelation as reported by Aisha, Muhammad's favorite wife:
"The first revelation which began to be revealed to the Apostle of Allah, was a correct dream in sleep. He did not see a dream but it came like the morning dawn. Thereafter loneliness became dear to him and he used to seclude himself to the cave of Hira and engaged therein in deep devotion (and it is divine service) for many nights before he went to his house and provided himself with food. Then he would return to Khadija and take provision for the like of them (nights) until the truth came unto him while he was in the cave of Hira."

The angel appeared before him and said, "Read." He said, "I cannot read." He narrated: Then he took me and pressed me hard till there came great exhaustion on me; thereafter he let me off and said, "Read." I replied, "I cannot read." Then he took me and pressed me hard for the second time until there appeared a great exhaustion on me; thereafter he let me off. He said, "Read." I said, "I cannot read."

Sahih Bukhari's account about the first revelation of Muhammad is:
"Narrated 'Aisha: (the mother of the faithful believers) The commencement of the Divine Inspiration to Allah's Apostle was in the form of good dreams which came true like bright day light, and then the love of seclusion was bestowed upon him. He used to go in seclusion in the cave of Hira where he used to worship (Allah alone) continuously for many days before his desire to see his family. He used to take with him the journey food for the stay and then come back to (his wife) Khadija to take his food like-wise again till suddenly the Truth descended upon him while he was in the cave of Hira. The angel came to him and asked him to read. The Prophet replied, "I do not know how to read."

The Prophet added, "The angel caught me (forcefully) and pressed me so hard that I could not bear it any more. He then released me and again asked me to read and I replied, 'I do not know how to read.' Thereupon he caught me again and pressed me a second time till I could not bear it any more. He then released me and again asked me to read but again I replied, 'I do not know how to read (or what shall I read)?' Thereupon he caught me for the third time and pressed me, and then released me and said, 'Read in the name of your Lord, who has created (all that exists) has created man from a clot. Read! And your Lord is the Most Generous." (al-'Alaq 96:1-3) Then Allah's Apostle returned with the Inspiration and with his heart beating severely. Then he went to Khadija bint Khuwailid and said, "Cover me! Cover me!" They covered him till his fear was over and after that he told her everything that had happened and said, "I fear that something may happen to me." Khadija replied, "Never! By Allah, Allah will never disgrace you. You keep good relations with your Kith and kin, help the poor and the destitute, serve your guests generously and assist the deserving calamity-afflicted ones."

Khadija then accompanied him to her cousin Waraqa bin Naufal bin Asad bin 'Abdul 'Uzza, who, during the Pre-Islamic Period became a Christian and used to write the writing with Hebrew letters. He would write from the Gospel in Hebrew as much as Allah wished him to write. He was an old man and had lost his eyesight. Khadija said to Waraqa, "Listen to the story of your nephew, O my cousin!" Waraqa asked, "O my nephew! What have you seen?" Allah's Apostle described whatever he had seen. Waraqa said, "This is the same one who keeps the secrets (angel Gabriel) whom Allah had sent to Moses. I wish I were young and could live up to the time when your people would turn you out." Allah's Apostle asked, "Will they drive me out?" Waraqa replied in the affirmative and said, "Anyone (man) who came with something similar to what you have brought was treated with hostility; and if I should remain alive till the day when you will be turned out then I would support you strongly." But after a few days Waraqa died and the Divine Inspiration was also paused for a while.

Narrated Jabir bin 'Abdullah Al-Ansari while talking about the period of pause in revelation reporting the speech of the Prophet "While I was walking, all of a sudden I heard a voice from the sky. I looked up and saw the same angel who had visited me at the cave of Hira' sitting on a chair between the sky and the earth. I got afraid of him and came back home and said, 'Wrap me (in blankets).' And then Allah revealed the following Holy Verses (of Qur'an): 'O you (i.e. Muhammad)! wrapped up in garments!' Arise and warn (the people against Allah's Punishment), up to 'and desert the idols.' (al-Mudathir 74:1-5) After this the revelation started coming strongly, frequently and regularly." (Sahih Bukhari 1.3)

After having a keen observation of the narration of the first revelation of Muhammad, it is very sad to know that the spirit (jinn) (as Muslims believe supposedly Gabriel) was so hard on Muhammad. Even the angel choked him.

The truth of the matter is that it is very cruel act what the jinn did. The spirit forced Muhammad to read while Muhammad was persistent in telling him that he was illiterate. It is also very odd that an angel was so ignorant in knowing that Muhammad was unable to read and still it was forcing an illiterate to read. If an angel had been sent from God who knew that Mohammed was illiterate, most likely the angel simply had asked Muhammad to listen and repeat the message from God because God had known that Muhammad was illiterate. The Bible says, that God is all-knowing God. He even knows the end from the beginning. Here God of the Bible says that "I make known the end from the beginning, from ancient times, what is still to come. I say: My purpose will stand, and I will do all that I please" (Isaiah 46:10).

54

In the Bible, whenever an angel appeared to a person and brought the message from God, it was so gentle, joyful and a peaceful experience; whereas, the demonic activity to a person has always been a very frightening, depressing, and with different uncontrollable physical demonstrations. That's why, after Muhammad's encounter with the spirit at the Cave, Muhammad was very distressed, and he even wanted to commit suicide, "I shall go to some high mountain cliff and cast myself down there from so that I may kill myself and be at rest. I went off with this mind, but when I was in the midst of the mountains I heard a voice from heaven saying, 'O Muhammad, thou art God's apostle and I am Gabriel.' (*At-Tabari: "Tarikh al-Rasul Wa al-Muluk.", Leiden, 1991, I, p. 1152*).

After having his first encounter with the spirit which was very frightening, depressing, and physically tormenting, Muhammad himself said, *"Woe is me – poet or possessed."*[xi]

**A lengthy passage from the Hadith, volume 1, book 1, chapter 1, shows that Muhammad himself believed he was under demonic influence.**

There are many accounts in the Bible which tell how God sent angels to bring a message to mankind. God always chose to speak directly with His chosen prophets (as it is recorded in the Old Testament). He also sent his angels to convey his message to his prophets or ordinary people. The prophets were always so certain of receiving the word from God. Muhammad is the only and the first prophet that proclaimed his prophetic words came from an angel – and one that he first thought was demonic. "Muhammad's doubts are troubling," wrote Mark Gabriel, "for what major prophet doubts the source of his prophetic revelation? . . . Certainly, no major prophet in the Bible attributes God's revelation to demons, as Muhammad believed . . . ."[xii]

**After this visitation, Muhammad thought he had been visited by Satan and that he was possessed by a demon, so much so, that he wanted to commit suicide. He thought he was crazy and wanted to die.[xiii]**

Without a shadow of doubt, someone with reasonable reasoning and simple logic can come to the conclusion that Mohammad's first encounter with the spirits and his reaction does not convince the reliability of him as a true prophet, so much so, his right to earn the title of "seal of the prophets in reference to the prophets of Judeo-Christians faith is far from absolute reality. He can be in the zone of the prophets which Jesus mentioned in Matthew 24:24 (Jesus said, "For there shall arise false Christs, and false prophets, and shall shew great signs and wonders; insomuch that, if it were possible, they shall deceive the very elect.), but in the group of the true prophets like Abraham, Moses, David.... is not a very fitting beginning at all.

**Confirmation of Prophet hood:**

Khadija reassured him with these words: "Rejoice, O son of my uncle, and be of good heart! Verily by Him in whose hand is Khadija's soul, I have hope that thou wilt be the prophet of these people." Muhammad did not receive words of reassurance from Allah but from a woman. He considered Khadija's words to be a reliable confirmation of the visitation and his calling, even though later revelations from Allah disclosed that women were only half as intelligent as men and could not be relied upon because they were often deceivers.

In hadith 3:826, Muhammad is quoted as saying, "'Isn't the witness of a woman equal to half of that of a man?' The woman said, 'Yes.' He said, 'This is because of the deficiency of a woman's mind.'" If this was Muhammad's opinion of the mental capacity of women and, according to the traditions of Islam, he only spoke that which was revealed to him by Allah, then how could he trust the witness of a woman who was not even present during his visitation?

This dubious beginning for Muhammad's prophet hood was further complicated by what followed or did not follow. Unlike the prophets of old where God revealed His Word to them on a regular basis and confirmed the word that was already spoken. Allah did not reveal himself again to Muhammad through Gabriel for three years. Once again Muhammad became depressed and suicidal.

Some reliable sources make it very vivid to believe that Waraqa bin Naufal died two years after Muhammad got his first revelation, without becoming a Muslim. Waraqa bin Naufal was a poet and he had immense familiarity with the Old and New Testament. He helped Muhammad to formulate a text which would later become Qur'an, the Holy book for Muslims. The early Surahs, or chapters are long that get shorter and shorter subsequently. The text was a product of Muhammad's supposed revelation with the mixture of biblical information of Waraqa bin Naufal. Waraqa bin Naufal as being Khadija's cousin had been mentoring and training Muhammad with the biblical information ever since Muhammad got acquaintance with Khadija. Since Waraqa bin Naufal was a poet, he formulated the text in a poetic form which certainly help to memorize easily. After the death of Waraqa bin Naufal, no revelation was coming forth for a long time, which was causing Muhammad to be depressed to the point of his suicidal attempts. As he received revelations in the years following, his wives believed the visions were authentic because Muhammad would frequently go into trances or convulsions – a state of being that Jesus attributed to demon possession. (Matthew 12:22; 17:14-18.)

Unlike Moses and other prophets before him, Muhammad never had a personal encounter with the God of this universe. "Narrated Aisha: 'Whoever claimed that (the Prophet) Muhammad saw his Lord, is committing a great fault, for he only saw Gabriel in his genuine shape in which he was created covering the whole horizon (hadith 4:457).'" At one point Muhammad even claimed to have communicated with the dead and on numerous occasions, changed Allah's revelations to suit himself. Jesus also spoke to the dead, but He did so because He had power over death as demonstrated in the resurrection of Lazarus. (John 11.).[xiv]

## Preaching of New Faith Starts

Muhammad proclaimed Allah as the one true god and rejected the idol worship of Mecca for at least 13 years. During this time, Khadijah, his first wife, and his first convert died. Few listened to Mohammed's message and animosity grew against him as he confronted the idol worshippers and preached his religion to Mecca. Abu Talib his uncle and his tribe, the Hashim, protected him during this early Meccan period.

The locals intensified their mockery of Muslims and made life particularly difficult for some of them. Although Muslims today often use the word "persecution" to describe this ordeal (justifiably, in some cases), it is important to note that the earliest and most reliable biographers (Ibn Ishaq and al-Tabari) record the death of only one Muslim during this period, an older woman who died from stress.

This fact is a source of embarrassment to modern apologists, who do not like to admit that Muslims were the first to become violent at Mecca and that Muhammad was the first to resort to militancy... and at a later time, when it was entirely unnecessary.

To deal with this unpleasant truth, sympathetic narratives of the early Meccan years usually exaggerate the struggle of the Muslims with claims that they were "under constant torture." They may also include apocryphal accounts that are unsupported by earliest and most reliable historians.

Modern storytellers and filmmakers (such as those behind 1976's *The Message*) have even been known to invent fictional victims of Meccan murder, either to dramatize their own tale or to provide justification for the "revenge killings" that followed. But, in fact, the only Muslim whose life was truly in danger was that of Muhammad - after 13 years of who allowed him to mock the local religion.

[Muhammad's chief adversary] *Abu Sufyan, with other sundry notables, went to Abu Talib and said: "You know the trouble that exists between us and your nephew, so call him and let us make an agreement that he will leave us alone and we will leave him alone; **let him have his religion and we will have ours.**"* (Ibn Ishaq 278)

In 619 Khadijah, his first wife and his first convert, and his uncle Abu Talib died. Abu Talib headed the Hashim clan, which Mohammed was a member. The new leader of the Hashim tribe his uncle Abu Lahab refused to protect Mohammed. It is of great interest to note that the Quran, the holy book of Islam, does not mention Muhammad's birth, his father or his mother, or any of his ancestors. The only ones who are mentioned in the Quran are Abu Lahab, Muhammad's uncle, and his wife. In Surat Al-Lahab both were destined to hell fire because Abu Lahab refused to support Muhammad and ridiculed him. (Surat Al-Lahab 111:1-5).[xv]

During the next 3 years Mohammed would fear for his life. He sought refuge and protection in nearby cities from those seeking his life.

**Migration to Medina**

The Muslim calendar is dated from the Hegira, when Mohammed fled to Medina to escape persecution. The Christian calendar is also dated from a journey, but it was not a journey to flee persecution. Christ willingly made the journey from Heaven to earth, and when his time had come, willingly went to the cross to die at the hands of his enemies. -- Robert C. Shannon, 1000 Windows, (Cincinnati, Ohio: Standard Publishing Company, 1997).

The Muslim calendar tells about his prophet who migrated to prevent persecution, and to save his life. The Christian calendar tells about Jesus who willingly, voluntarily, and so sacrificially entered into to a world where he knew he will be rejected, and eventually condemn to the cross. He came not to save his life, but to give his life and in doing so he saves the lives of millions from eternal damnation.

In 621 during the Hajj, Arab tribes from the city of Yathrib later to be called Medina, came for the annual pilgrimage. They met Mohammed and thought him to be a prophet and invited him to their city to bring peace and settle disputes between the warring tribes. Yathrib (Medina) was founded by three Jewish tribes and the idea of monotheism was familiar to the Arab tribesmen. The Arabs of Medina had been told by Jewish tribesmen about the coming Messiah who would one day conquer the world including the Arabs. The Arab tribes hoped to find this individual before the Jews. Meeting Mohammed, they thought he was the one.

The following year, the situation became intolerable for the Muslims and in June 622 they made what has become known as the Hijra or flight. In small groups, the 150 Muslims of Mecca left for the city of Medina, 280 miles to the north. When word reached those of Mecca about the escape to Medina they tried to kill Mohammed. Mohammed and Abu Bakr were able to sneak out of the city and escape to Medina by another route on September 622.

In Medina, the warring Arab tribes submitted to Mohammed's leadership and prophet-hood. But the Jewish tribes rejected his claims of prophet and ridiculed his revelations. With most of the new arrivals from Mecca were without work and they needed to earn a living. Ghazu, or caravan raiding, was the way tribes would prevent one tribe from becoming too powerful. The Muslims in Medina began to rob the caravans heading toward Mecca. This is where the Muslim doctrine of Jihad was created.

With their caravan business while being threatened, Meccans respond with one thousand soldiers at the battle of Bedr March 624, while the Muslims fielded 300 warriors. The battle went to the Muslims. Mohammed proclaimed that his victory was a sign from Allah and his status in Medina was magnified. The lack of enthusiasm by one of the Jewish tribes caused them to be expelled by the victorious Muslim army. The direction of prayer was also changed from Jerusalem to Mecca since the Jews rejected Mohammad's prophet-hood.

Exactly one year later Mecca amassed 3000 soldiers at the battle of Uhud and the Muslims fielded 1000 soldiers. The battle did not go as planned. The Muslims were defeated by Meccans who then retreated back to Medina. Disheartened, the Muslims blamed the second Jewish tribe as conspirators against their cause. Their homes and possessions were confiscated, and they were expelled from the city in 626 AD.

The Meccans in the hope of ending the caravan raids by the Muslims assembled 10,000 soldiers to attack the city of Medina in the year 627. After a siege of two weeks in the hot sun, they are unable to penetrate the fortress-like city. They returned to Mecca. After this unsuccessful attack, Mohammed and the Muslims attacked the last remaining Jewish tribe. The tribe surrendered to the mercy of Mohammed. The men were killed and the women and children were sold into slavery.

The Muslims, then begin to consolidate their power with the surrounding Arab tribes and cities. Mecca began to feel the economic impact of its trading losses as Mohammed's power grew in the north. They reluctantly signed the 10 year Hudaybiah peace agreement with Mohammed and the Muslims in March 628. Muslims were allowed to return to Mecca and worship at the Kaaba once a year. The people of Mecca would leave their city so the Muslim could come and worship. Muhammad agreed to recognize the local gods in addition to Allah. This delighted the Meceans who generously extended their welcome. This agreement was based on the revelation he got that would become "the Satanic verses" in the Quran later. Muhammad's treatment of trickery and his dealings, full of deception, caused him to change his mind about accepting the Meceans gods along with Allah. Many of his own followers started to question his integrity since his earlier message was crystal clear to them that is: "There is no god but Allah, and Muhammad is his messenger." His own followers started to lose faith in him. In this situation, he claimed that Satan inspired him and had spoken through him. To please his followers, Muhammad refused to recognize the Meceans' gods (**Tabari 1192, Quran 22:52 & 53:19-26**). Indeed, it was based on deception. Muhammad was skillful in deceiving his followers and others who were at war with him.

Someone with a sense of logic and open mindedness might wonder that to what degree or measure Muhammad got his revelation from Satan and from his Allah. There were many Qur'anic verses that sound quite inspired by Satan. In this case, Muhammad's prophet hood is really in jeopardy, and the truth about his religion has many question marks which Muslims prevent and overlook examining. It also frustrates and infuriates them if someone likes to ask questions about the reliability of Muhammad's prophet hood and the authentication of his revelation.

Anyhow, two years later, in January 630, Mohammed led 10,000 warriors to Mecca and nullified the treaty of Hudaybiah because Muslims had been killed. The city submits to Mohammed and his warriors and accepts him as prophet. Mohammed goes to the Kaaba and destroys the 360 idols in the temple. From Mecca, the "Muslims" wage Jihad on the surrounding cities, forcing them to accept Islam as their religion and Mohammed as their prophet.

**Muhammad's Reaction to Criticism:**

After the battle of Badr, the people of Medina were horrified that they had given refuge to such a blatant criminal and his followers in their city. Many began protesting the presence of such violent and murderous people in their city. In a free society like Pre-Islamic Arabia, the poets acted as society's conscience and were free to criticize, satirize and examine the actions of people. The two most famous poets of this kind were Abu 'Afak; an extremely old and respected poet and Asma bint Marwan, a young mother with the gift of superb verse.

Muhammad was enraged at the criticism of Asma Bint and Abu Afak. When he heard the verses composed by Asma Bint Marwan he was infuriated and screamed aloud, "Will no one rid me of this daughter of Marwan!" That very night a gang of Muslims set out to do the dirty deed. They broke into the poets' house. She was lying in her bedroom suckling her newborn child, while her other small children slept nearby. The Muslims tore the newborn infant off her breast and hacked it to pieces before her very eyes. They then made her watch the murder of all four of her children, before raping and then stabbing her repeatedly to death. After the murder when the Muslims went to inform the Prophet, he said *"You have done a service to Allah and his Messenger, her life was not worth even two goats!"*

A month later the distinguished and highly respected Abu Afak, who was over a hundred years old and renowned for his sense of fairness, was killed brutally in the same manner as he slept. Once again the Prophet had commented that morning *"Who will avenge me on this scoundrel!"*

This shows us exactly how much the tolerant and peace loving Prophet respected life. Muslims claim that Mohammed was extremely gentle and loved children. Indeed, the horrifying way he had Asma Bint Marwan's five infants slaughtered certainly attests to this "loving" side of the Prophet.[xvi]

**Death of Muhammad**

Mohammed made his final Hajj in 632 and died unexpectedly 3 months later in June. His friend and father in law Abu Bakr (Father of Aisha) succeeded him as leader of the Muslims.

## Muhammad ask Forgiveness

Idolatry:

[Guillaume said:] "The only authentic story of Muhammad's early years is contained in an unpublished manuscript of his biographer Ibn Ishaq. It reads as follows:
I was told that the apostle of Allah said, as he was talking about Zayd son of 'Amr son of Nufayl, 'He was the first to upbraid me for idolatry and forbade me to worship idols. I had come from al-Ta'if along with Zayd son of Haritha when we passed Zayd son of 'Amr who was in the highland of Mecca. Quraysh had made a public example of him for abandoning his religion, so that he went out from their midst. I sat down with him. I had a bag containing meat which we had sacrificed to our idols -- Zayd b. Haritha was carrying it -- and I offered it to Zayd b. 'Amir -- I was but a lad at the time -- and I said, "Eat some of this food, my uncle." He replied, "Surely it is part of those sacrifices of theirs which they offer to their idols?" When I said that it was, he said, "Nephew mine, if you were to ask the daughters of 'Abd al-Muttalib they would tell you that I never eat of these sacrifices, and I have no desire to do so." Then he upbraided me for idolatry and spoke disparagingly of those who worship idols and sacrifice to them, and said, "They are worthless: they can neither harm nor profit anyone," or words to that effect.' The apostle added, 'After that I never knowingly stroked one of their idols nor did I sacrifice to them until God honored me with his apostleship." (*A. Guillaume, Islam, pp. 26-27,* emphasis mine)

Most Muslims, however, deny that Muhammad had ever committed idolatry. But Guillaume noted that early pious Muslims really have no reason to create such stories, nor for them to pass down such traditions, if there is no truth in these reports.

Muhammad asking Forgiveness of his past and future sins is mentioned in al-Fath Sur 48:2 & Muhammad 47:19. Whereas, Jesus was sinless throughout his life even the Roman centurion made this bold statement about Jesus' spinelessness in Luke 23:47, The **centurion**, seeing what had happened, praised God and said, "Surely this was a righteous man."[xvii]

## Muhammad is uncertain about Heaven

Muhammad was not sure if he was going to heaven himself:
The Prophet said, "By Allah, though I am the Apostle of Allah, yet I do not know what Allah will do to me." Hadith vol. 5, no. 266

Surah 46:9 I don't know what will happen with me or you so how can I tell you if you will go to heaven or not.

It is so sad and strange to say that Muslims are following a man who did not know if he was going to heaven or not. Once a person is not sure about his going to heaven, how could he intercede for his followers? For this very fact, Muslims sends blessings upon him and prayers every day for the forgiveness of their prophet. Jesus, on the other hand, has the power to forgive sins. He even said with great certainty that "Jesus said unto him, I am the way, the truth, and the life: no man cometh unto the Father, but by me" (John 14:6).

## After Mohammad

Abu Bakr received the title "Caliph" or successor of Mohammed. There was a struggle for who would succeed Mohammad. Some felt Ali the cousin and son-in-law (the husband of Fatima, Mohammed's daughter) deserved the position. However, Muhammad's father-in-law, and close friend Abu Bakr became the first caliph or leader of the Islamic faith. Under Abu Bakr, Islam's power in the Arabian Peninsula was completed. In 634 AD Abu Bakr died and was succeeded by Umar (Omar), the 2nd Caliphate.

Umar advanced the Muslim armies against Syria and Palestine. In 637 A D, the armies of Byzantium lost control of Jerusalem to Islam.

Uthman, the 3rd Caliph, succeeded Umar. Uthman ordered a complete revision of the Quran, which would cause a mutiny. He was killed and his death was considered justified because the mutineers claimed he ceased to be a Muslim. Following Uthman, there was a struggle between rival factions of Islam about who was the rightful successor to lead Islam.

Ali the 4th Caliph, Mohammad's son-in-law and husband of Fatima, succeeded Uthman. Not everyone accepted him as rightful Caliphate. War broke out between the rival groups. This succession was short lived, when he was killed 2 years later. The **Shi'a** (Party of Ali) mourned the death of Ali, and his two sons Imam Hasan and Imam Hussain (grandsons of Mohammed) during the month of Muharram. Ali is revered as a saint by the Shi'a who are in majority in Iran and Iraq. The Shi'a feel Ali was the rightful successor to Mohammed and don't recognize the three earlier Caliphs. The Sunnis accept Ali and the first three caliphates as legitimate.

Thomas Carlyle, a Scottish historian (1795-1881), wrote concerning Muhammad: **Can it be possible that so many creatures have lived and died for something which must be regarded as a tragic fraud?**

# WHAT DOES THE QURAN SAYS ABOUT JESUS?

## QURANIC TEACHING ABOUT JESUS

The Quran gives more preeminence to Jesus than Muhammad. Jesus is mentioned 25 times as compared to Muhammad who is mentioned only 4 times.

The Quran in 19:21 says that Jesus as a **revelation for mankind** and a mercy from God, and it is a thing ordained.

The Quran also says very clearly that Jesus, son of Mary, illustrious in the world and the Hereafter, and one of those brought near unto God (Qur'an 3:45). So we may keep our duty to God and obey Jesus (Qur'an 3:50; 43:61).

Both the Bible and the Quran says that Jesus was born as a faultless (sinless) man.

"He (Archangel Gabriel) said (to Mary): I am only a messenger of thy Lord, that I may bestow on thee a faultless son" (Qur'an 19:19).

The Hadith (traditions of Islam) also says that all the children of Adam are touched by Satan at their birth, except Jesus, son of Mary.

The Bible says about Jesus: "For it was fitting that we should have such a high priest, holy, blameless, unstained, separated from sinners, exalted above the heavens" (Hebrews 7:26).

Once Jesus directly asked to the Jews, "Which of you convicts me of sin? If I tell the truth, why do you not believe me? He who is of God hears the words of God; the reason why you do not hear them is that you are not of God" (John 8:46).

## ATTRIBUTE OF JESUS ACCORDEING TO SURAH 3:45-55
[And mention] when the angels said, "O Mary, indeed Allah gives you good tidings of a word from Him, whose name will be the Messiah, Jesus, the son of Mary - distinguished in this world and the Hereafter and among those brought near [to Allah].
He will speak to the people in the cradle and in maturity and will be of the righteous."

She said, "My Lord, how will I have a child when no man has touched me?" [The angel] said, "Such is Allah; He creates what He wills. When He decrees a matter, He only says to it, 'Be,' and it is.
And He will teach him writing and wisdom and the Torah and the Gospel
And [make him] a messenger to the Children of Israel, [who will say], 'Indeed I have come to you with a sign from your Lord in that I design for you from clay [that which is] like the form of a bird, then I breathe into it and it becomes a bird by permission of Allah. And I cure the blind and the leper, and I give life to the dead - by permission of Allah. And I inform you of what you eat and what you store in your houses. Indeed, in that is a sign for you, if you are believers.
And [I have come] confirming what was before me of the Torah and to make lawful for you some of what was forbidden to you. And I have come to you with a sign from your Lord, so fear Allah and obey me.

Sahih International

62

Indeed, Allah is my Lord and your Lord, so worship Him. That is the straight path."

But when Jesus felt [persistence in] disbelief from them, he said, "Who are my supporters for [the cause of] Allah?" The disciples said," We are supporters for Allah. We have believed in Allah and testify that we are Muslims [submitting to Him].

Our Lord, we have believed in what You revealed and have followed the messenger Jesus, so register us among the witnesses [to truth]."

Surah 3:54
And the disbelievers planned, but Allah planned. And Allah is the best of planners.
[Mention] when Allah said, "**O Jesus, indeed I will take you and raise you to Myself and purify you from those who disbelieve and make those who follow you superior to those who disbelieve until the Day of Resurrection.** Then to Me is your return, and I will judge between you concerning that in which you used to differ.

## According to The Quran Jesus is:

➢ Kalmatullah-Word of God (3:45; 4:171; 3:39)

➢ Ruhullah-Spirit of God

➢ Messiah-the promised one

➢ Jesus spoke when he was very small (about 2 days old)

➢ Jesus Created bird from clay and breathe into. This shows that Jesus gives life.

➢ Jesus cured blind and the lepers

➢ Jesus Raised dead

➢ Jesus went to heaven

➢ Jesus is still alive while Muhammad is dead and buried in a grave in Medina

➢ Jesus will come again while Muhammad will be judged according to the works he did in life.

**QUESTION: HOW DID GOD CREATE THIS UNIVERSE?** The Bible vividly tells that God created this universe with His Word. In the beginning God created the heavens and the earth. [2] The earth was without form, and void; and darkness *was* on the face of the deep. And the Spirit of God was hovering over the face of the waters.

[3] Then God said, "Let there be light"; and there was light.

Indeed, through His WORD. Word is creation or creator? If Word is creator, then Jesus is creator since Jesus is Word. Muslims believe that Jesus is a word rather than the Word. In spite of all this, Muhammad is not given that honor.

## A COMPARISON BETWEEN JESUS AND MOHAMMAD

The Muslims revere Mohammed as the greatest of prophets, and even call him the seal of prophets. An honest and realistic comparison of Mohammed with Jesus demonstrates that Jesus has far greater character, teaching, and miracles than Mohammed ever did. Truthfully speaking, there is no comparison between Jesus and Muhammad, but for the sake of those who try to elevate their prophet, they must know the truth and that might help them come out of the deception.

| Jesus | Mohammad |
|---|---|
| **Jesus was born of virgin Mary.** Even The Qur'an testifies In the Bible the prophet Isaiah predicts the virgin birth [Isa 7:14] Matthew confirms the virgin birth. [Matt 1:18-25] | **Mohammad had a normal common birth.** His father Abdullah died before his birth and his mother Amina died when he was six. Islamic traditions present very odd and dubious presentations about Muhammad's birth in order to delineate his miraculous birth that lack solid ground. |
| **Jesus as a child knew monotheistic God. (Luke 2:39-42)** | **Muhammad was an idol worshipper before his supposedly call of a prophet hood of a monotheistic god (Bukhari vol. 6. p. 452)** Allah commanded Muslims to observe the pagan customs right alongside the Arab pagans and their 360 idols. Some of these practices included kissing the black stone: Narrated 'Abis bin Rabia: 'Umar came near the Black Stone and kissed it and said **"No doubt, I know that you are a stone and can neither benefit anyone nor harm anyone. Had I not seen Allah's Apostle kissing you I would not have kissed you."** (*Sahih al-Bukhari* 2:667) |
| **Jesus was born sinless; He lived a sinless life.** Jesus asserted his sinless ness. John 8:46 - **"Can any of you prove me guilty of sin?** If I am telling the truth, why don't you believe me?"  Matthew 27:4, 19; John 9:16;1 Peter 2:22; 2 Cor. 5:21, 1 John 3:5, Heb. 4:15. Even Quran confirms the sinless life of Jesus in Surah 19:19; 3:45). Sahih Al-Bukhari Hadith, Hadith 4.506, narrated by Abu Huraira: The Prophet said, "When any human being is born, Satan touches him at both sides of the body with his two fingers, except Jesus, the son of Mary, whom Satan tried to touch but failed, for he touched the placenta-cover instead." Sahih Al-Bukhari Hadith, Hadith 4.641 Narrated by Said bin Al Musaiyab: Abu Huraira said, "I heard Allah's Apostle saying, 'There is none born | **Muhammad was sinful.** "Therefore have patience; God's promise is surely true. Implore forgiveness for your sins, and celebrate the praise of your Lord evening and morning." **(Surah 40:55)** "We gave you a glorious victory so that God may forgive you your past and future sins ...." **(Surah 48:1,2; cf. 47:19, 21;)** Muhammad prayed for forgiveness 70 times a day. Bukhari vol. 8 # 319 Mohammad also prayed for forgiveness of his sins, Bukhari vol. 9, #482: "...O Allah! Forgive me the sins that I did in the past or will do in the future, and also the sins that I did in secret or in public. Further, Mohammad even acknowledged harming or cursing people unjustly.          From Sahih Muslim, volume 4, "The Book of Virtue and |

64

| | |
|---|---|
| among the off-spring of Adam, but Satan touches it. A child therefore, cries loudly at the time of birth because of the touch of Satan, except Mary and her child." | Good Manners, and Joining the Ties o Relationship, chapter MLXXV "He upon whom Allah's apostle invoke curses whereas he in fact did not deserve i it would be a source of reward and mercy fo him". |
| Mohammad was touched by Satan and sinned like all of us? Many times in the Quran, Mohammad is reminded of repenting his sins. | Hadith #6287 - "Abu Juraira reporte Allah's Messenger as saying, "O Allah, I an a human being and for any person amongs Muslims upon whom I hurl malediction o invoke curse or give him whipping make it source of purity and mercy." |
| **Jesus Himself was the divine revelation.** Jesus knew His mission (Luke 19:10) | **Muhammad doubted whether the revelation he received was divine o demonic.** With this perplexity, he wa suicidal on numerous occasions. |
| **Jesus' words never change.** "Heaven and earth will pass away, but My words will by no means pass away" **(Matthew 24:35).** | **Muhammad's words change.** "And when We substitute a verse in place of a verse - and Allah is most knowing of what He sends down - they say, "You, [O Muhammad], are but an inventor [of lies]." But most of them do not know." (Surah 16:101) |
| **Jesus confronted Satan with confidence.** He even cast out demons from so many people. Even today, Satan and demons tremble at the name of Jesus Christ. (Matthew 8:16,32; 9:33; Mark 1:34,39; 5:8; 9:25; 7:26; Luke 4:35, 41; 8:29) | **Muhammad was afraid of Satan.** Mohammed felt that he was demon possessed. And he was so afraid of Satan that many times he was asking refuges from Satan (Surah 114:1-6). Muhammad was visited by Jinn (Genies, or demons) who promised to promote Islam (Surah 46:29-31; 72:1-15) |
| **Jesus intercedes for His people. (Romans 8:34; Hebrews 7:25; 4:14-16)** | **Muhammad incapacitates in interceding for others.** Because he did not know even his own fate being afraid of what Allah will do to him. |
| **Jesus had compassion toward sinners. Go and sin no more** (John 8:2-11) At dawn He (Jesus) appeared again in the temple courts, where all the people gathered around him, and he sat down to teach them. The teachers of the law and the Pharisees brought in a woman caught in adultery. They made her stand before the group and said to Jesus, "Teacher, this woman was caught in the act of adultery. In the | **Muhammad was harsh towards sinners.** From the Hadith of Abu Dawud, #4428 "Buraidah said: "A woman of Ghamid came to the Prophet and said: "I have committed fornication", He said: "Go back". She returned and on the next day she came to him again, and said: "Perhaps you want to send me back as you did to Maiz b. Malik. I swear by Allah, I am pregnant." He |

65

Law Moses commanded us to stone such women. Now what do you say?" They were using this question as a trap in order to have a basis to accuse Him.

But Jesus bent down and started to write on the ground with His finger. When they kept on questioning him, he straightened up and said to them, "If any one of you is without sin, let him be the first to throw a stone at her." Again he stooped down and wrote on the ground.

At this, those who heard began to go away one at a time, the older ones first, until only Jesus was left, with the woman still standing there. Jesus straightened up and asked her, "Woman, where are they? Has no one condemned you?" "No one sir", she said. "Then neither do I condemn you," Jesus declared. "Go now and leave your life of sin."

said to her: "Go back". She then returned and came to him the next day. He said to her: "Go back until you give birth to the child." She then returned. When she gave birth to the child she brought the child to him, and said: "Here it is! I have given birth to it." He said: "Go back, and suckle him until you wean him." When she had weaned him, she brought him to him with something in his hand which he was eating. The boy was then given to a certain man of the Muslims and he (the prophet) commanded regarding her. So a pit was dug for her, and he gave orders about her and she was stoned to death. Khalid was one of those who were throwing stones at her. He threw a stone at her. When a drop of blood fell on his cheek, he abused her. The prophet said to him: "Gently, Khalid. By Him in Whose hand my soul is, she has repented to such an extent that if one who wrongfully takes an extra tax were to repent to a like extent, he would be forgiven". Then giving command regarding her, prayed over her and she was buried.""

**Jesus showed love and His enemies and taught his disciples to do the same.**
In Luke 9:54, 55 Jesus rebuked His disciples when they wanted to destroy a town that rejected Him. Also, in Luke 22:52, Jesus' disciples started to fight against those that came to arrest Jesus, He stopped them, and healed a man injured in the fight.
"You have heard that it was said, '**Love your** neighbor and hate **your** enemy.' But I tell you: **Love your enemies** and pray for those who persecute you, (Matthew 5:43-44)

**Muhammad hated his enemies. His followers still follow his pattern.**
Mohammed told his followers to aggressively make war on non-Muslims: 9:5, 29. Surah 9 was one of the last Surahs given by Muhammad. Initially, when Muhammad's group was weak, he ordered his followers to try to get along with other people. After the Muslims became powerful, he ordered them to spread Islam by force. Abu Bakr, Umar, and Uthman continued his wars of aggression. A few of Muhammad's actions include:

The massacre of approximately 800 Jewish male captives: (noted in Surah 33:26).

He ordered the execution of 10 people when he took Mecca. Three of these people were slave girls who had previously made fun of Muhammad. Refer to "The Life of Mohammad", pages 551 and 552.

He attacked the Jewish city of Khaibar where he took one of the Jewish leaders and tortured him to force him to tell where some

| | buried money was. After the man refused t[ talk, and was near death, Mohamma[ ordered that his head be cut off. Refer t[ "The Life of Mohammad", page 515. |
|---|---|
| **Jesus preached against violence.** Jesus said, "He who lives by the sword will die by the sword" (Matt. 26:52) | **Muhammad preached violence.** It has beer narrated on the authority of Abdullah b 'Umar that the Messenger of Allah said: I have been commanded to fight agains[ people till they testify that there is no god bu[ Allah, that Muhammad is the messenger o[ Allah, and they establish prayer, and pay Zakat and if they do it, their blood and property are guaranteed protection on my behalf except when justified by law, and their affairs rest with Allah. (Muslim Book 1, Hadith 33) <u>Muhammad ordered 65 military campaigns and raids in his last 10 years.</u> (Ibn Ishaq). |
| **Jesus said, "Let He who is without sin cast the first stone" (John 8:7)** | **Muhammad stoned women for adultery.** A woman who became pregnant confesses to Muhammad that she is guilty of adultery. Muhammad allows her to have the child, then has her stoned. The description is graphic: "Khalid b. Walid came forward with a stone which he flung at her head and there spurted blood on the face of Khalid and so he abused her" (**Sahih Muslim 17.4206** cf. **Bukhari _4.56.829;_ Muslim 17.4207, 4207; Bukhari 7.63.196; Ibn Ishaq 970**). **Islamic Law: "The stone shall not be so big so as to kill the person by one or two strikes neither shall it so small that it cannot be called a stone" The victim is intended to suffer.** |
| **Jesus prohibited stealing.** Jesus said, you shall not steal" (Matthew 19:18) | **Muhammad permitted stealing from unbelievers.** _"We were in the company of the Prophet at Dhul-Hulaifa. The people felt hungry and captured some camels and sheep (as booty) ..."_ Muhammad said that Allah would always provide sustenance for those who believe in him. Stealing from non-Muslims was a legitimate means of fulfilling Allah's promise. (Bukhari 44:668) |
| **Jesus said "Thou shalt not bear false witness."** (Matthew 19:18) | _**Muhammad permitted lying (Taqiyya).**_ _"And they (the disbelievers) schemed, and Allah schemed (against them): and Allah is_ |

67

| | |
|---|---|
| | *the best of schemers.*" The Arabic word used here for scheme (or plot) is *makara*, which literally means 'deceit'. If Allah is supremely deceitful toward unbelievers, then there is little basis for denying that Muslims are allowed to do the same. *"He who makes peace between the people by inventing good information or saying good things, is not a liar.*" Lying is permitted when the end justifies the means. Bukhari (49:857) |
| **Jesus said "If someone strikes you on the right cheek, turn to him the other also." (Matthew 5:39)** | Muhammad said "If then anyone transgresses the prohibition against you, transgress ye likewise against him." (Qur'an 2:194; 5:48) |
| **Jesus said "Blessed are the peacemakers, for they will be called Sons of God." (Matthew 5:9)** | *Muhammad encouraged Jihad* *"Whoever cheerfully accepts Allah, Islam and Muhammad is entitled to enter Paradise. But there is another act which elevates the position of a man in Paradise to a grade one hundred times higher, Jihad in the way of Allah! Jihad in the way of Allah!" (Sahih Muslim 20:4645)* |
| **Jesus said "Love your enemies and pray for those who persecute you." (Matthew 5:44)** | **Muhammad said "And fight them until there is no more persecution and religion is only for Allah." (Qur'an 8:39)** |
| **Jesus preached against divorced (Matt. 5:31-32). Jesus taught about the monogamous relationship that was divinely intended from the beginning (Matthew 19:5, 6)** | **Muhammed made divorce very simple and easy for men by simply saying Talaq three times. He even preached to have polygamous relationship with four wives at the same time (Quran 4:3). He allowed temporary marriage with compensation (mut'a) (Surah 2:230; Bukhari vol. 7, p.7)** Surah 2:230, which unambiguously states that a divorced Muslim couple can reconcile if and only if the wife marries another man, has sexual relationship with him, and then he divorces her. |
| **Jesus was crucified for the sins of the world.** | **Muhammad advocated crucifying others.** Indeed, the penalty for those who wage war against Allah and His Messenger and strive upon earth [to cause] corruption is none but that they be killed or crucified or that their hands and feet be cut off from opposite sides |

| | or that they be exiled from the land. That i for them a disgrace in this world; and fo them in the Hereafter is a great punishmen (5:33; Sahih Muslims 16:4131). |
|---|---|
| **Jesus gave himself as a sacrifice for all mankind (John 1:29; 10:18).** No one takes it from Me, but I lay it down of Myself. I have power to lay it down, and I have power to take it again. This command I have received from My Father." (John 10:18) | **Muhammad died of unexpected illness, as he was poisoned according to his ow account** (Bukhari vol. 5, p.510) |
| **Jesus rose from the dead on the third day and ascended into heaven. (Luke 23 & 24 1 Cor. 15:1-3; Surah 4:157; 3:45)** The Bible as well as secular history testifies about the death and resurrection of Jesus. | **Mohammad was buried in Medina on third day after his death. (Al-Tabari vol 9, p.208)** Millions of Muslims visit his tomb each year |
| **Jesus judged men and women according to grace and His work on the Cross.** (Thief on the Cross) | **Muhammad judged men and women according to their obedience to him and Allah.** (Surah 9:5; 9:29; Persian Poet) |
| **Jesus is the Prince of Peace (Isaiah 9:6-7).** Jesus forbade violence and preached throughout his life (Matt. 5:44; Luke 6:27; 1 Thess. 5:15) | **Mohammed was the prophet of war.** He commanded peace when he was weak (Surah 2:256; 109:1-6; 6:107-109), but violence when he grew stronger (Surah 9:29; 2:216; 8:39; 9:5; 5:51). |
| **Jesus' aim was voluntary CONVERSION (Acts 3:19).** Jesus preached FAITH (John 6:29,35). Jesus said, "Believe and live!" (John 6:47; 11:25-26). Jesus won followers by miracles and unconditional love. | **Mohammed's method was COMPULSION; this method is still practiced adherently** Muhammed practiced FORCE; Muhammed said to the masses, "Convert or die!" He won a following by military victory and/or forced conversion. |
| **Jesus forbade adultery (Matt. 5:28)** | **Muhammad married his adopted son's wife, allowed temporary marriages (Surah 33:37; 4:24)** |
| **Jesus heard from God.** He began his ministry with boldness, (Mark 1:14-15). Jesus received his calling from God directly. Jesus received his commission in the daylight. (Matt. 3:17). | **Muhammad heard from God angel Gabriel.** He terrified, was uncertain, and wanted to commit suicide (Qur'an 74:1-5) Muhammad received his words in the darkness of a cave. |
| **Jesus claimed to be God (John 8:24; 8:58) as well as a man.** Jesus claimed to be the way, the truth, and the life (John 14:6). Jesus explicitly | **Muhammad claimed to be a man.** |

| | depicts the attributes of God with His glorious sayings and marvelous miracles. | |
|---|---|

| | |
|---|---|
| Jesus is the Creator and Sustainer of the Universe. (Colossians 1:1-23) He Himself is the Judge. (2 Timothy 4:1; John 522) | Muhammad did not know his eternal destiny. (Bukhari vol. 5 #266; vol. 2 #413; vol. 8 #805 Muslim vol. 1 #398, #402) |
| Jesus shed His own blood on the Cross. | Muhammed shed other people's blood. |
| Jesus performed many miracles. This includes healing people, calming a storm with a command, and raising people from the dead. (Luke 3:9-10). Even Quran mentions about the miracles of Jesus (Surah 3:45-55) | Muhammad did not perform any miracle. (Surah 29:49) Muhammad's only alleged miracle was the Quran. The book that is so disorderly, and full of contradictions |
| Jesus caused a blind to see (Luke 18:35-43) | Muhammad caused a seeing person blind (Bukhari vol. 8, p. 520). He turned away from a blind man (Surah 80:1-10) |
| Jesus healed the lame to walk (Matthew 9:2-8) | Muhammad made the walking lame (Bukhari vol. 8, p. 520) |
| Jesus healed withered hands (Matthew 12: 10-13) | Muhammad taught to cut off the hands. "Cut off the hands of thieves, whether they are male or female, as punishment for what they have done-a deterrent from God: God is almighty and wise." 39 "But if anyone repents after his wrongdoing and makes amends, God will accept his repentance: God is most forgiving and merciful." (Quran 5:38). |
| Jesus raised the dead (John 11:1-45) | Muhammad had the living killed (Ibn Hashim p. 466; Bukhari vol. 5, p. 248). |
| Jesus fulfilled biblical prophecy about being the Messiah. | Mohammad did not fulfill any biblical prophecy except the ones about false teachers (Matt. 24:24). |
| Jesus voluntarily laid his life down for others | Mohammad saved his own life many times and had others killed. |
| Jesus owned no slaves | Muhammad owned slaves. |
| Jesus spoke well of women. Jesus healed women, forgave women, and encouraged women. The New Testament teaches that husbands should love their wives and not be harsh with them: Col. 3:19, Eph. 5:25, that men and women are equal in Christ - Gal 3:28, that they should be treated with respect - 1 Pet 3:7. | Muhammad viewed men superior to women. Muhammad said women were 1/2 as smart as men (Hadith 3:826; 2:541), that the majority in hell will be women (Had. 1:28,301; 2:161; 7:124), and that women could be mortgaged. |

| | Mohammed commanded his male follower to beat their disobedient wives. He gave me the right to beat their wives who persistentl disobeyed them.<br>Surah 4:34 "As those you fear may b rebellious admonish, banish them to thei couches, and beat them."<br><br>The above verse was revealed in connectio with a woman who complained t Mohammad that her husband slapped her o the face, which was still marked by the slap At first Muhammad said to her "Get eve with him", but then added 'Wait until I thin about it". Later on the above verse wa revealed, and Muhammad added, 'We (H and the woman) wanted one thing, Alla wanted another.<br><br>The Hadith also said much about women: Mohammed said that women are generall so evil, that they will make up the majority of people in to hell. Continuing wit Bukhari, Vol. 1, #301: "O women! Giv alms, as I have seen that the majority of the dwellers of Hell-fire were you (women) They [women] asked, "Why is it so, C Allah's Apostle?" He replied, "You curse frequently and are ungrateful to you husbands."<br>Bukhari Vol. 1, #28: "The Prophet said, " was shown the Hell-fire and the majority o its dwellers were women who were ungrateful." It was asked, "Do they disbelieve in Allah?" (or are they ungrateful to Allah?), he replied, "They are ungrateful to their husbands and are ungrateful for the favors and the good done to them...."<br><br>Sahih Muslim says they are the minority in Paradise: Volume 4, #6600: "Imran Husain reported that Allah's messenger said: Amongst the inmates of Paradise the women would form a minority." |
|---|---|
| **Jesus' last words were about forgiveness:** "Father forgive them, for they do not know what they are doing." Luke 23:34. (He said while dying on the cross at Calvary after being betrayed and sentenced to die for no legitimate reason). | **Muhammad's last words were about hatred.** "May Allah curse the Jews and Christians for they built the places of worship at the graves of the prophets." Bukhari, Vol. 1, #427 [Muhammad had been |

71

| | poisoned years earlier by a Jewish woman whose husband was killed by the Muslims and the poison had slowly worked its effect. He said this while dying in the arms of his wife Aisha]. |
|---|---|
| **Jesus was a religious and spiritual leader.** He came to restore spiritual relationship of people with God. Jesus saved an estimated of 3000 on the Day of Pentecost alone from the eternal damnation. He has saved millions of people throughout the ages from the flames of hell fire. | **Muhammad was a religious, political and military leader.** Muhammad killed an estimated 3000 people including 700 Jews of Banu Qurayza tribe in Medina. Sadly, Muhammad has pushed millions of people to the flames of hell fire. |
| **Jesus' religion is known as forgiveness and love.** | **Muhammadan religion is known as submission and fear.** |
| **Jesus never forced his followers to continue believing (John 6:31-69)** **People are free to accept Jesus' message or reject it (Luke 10:10, 11)** | **Muhammad forced his follower to continue believing** ("whosoever changes his Islamic religion, then kill him" Hadith al-Bukhari, vol. 9, Bk. 84, No. 57). It is so contradictory to the Qur'anic teaching that says that there is no compulsion in religion (Surah 2:256). It is very devious and deceptive. People are forced to accept Muhammad's message (Surah 9:29) |
| **Jesus' disciples were killed for their faith** (Acts 12:2; 2 Timothy 4:7). A martyr in Judeo-Christian faith is the one who die for his faith. Christian and Jewish martyr says, "I will die for what I believe | **Mohammed's disciples killed for the faith;** A martyr in Islam is the one who dies while killing infidels (Surah 9:123; 66:9; 9:29). A Muslim martyr says, "you will die for what I believe. |
| **None of Jesus' apostle led armies (Luke 9:52-56)** | **All of the Caliphs who followed Muhammad led armies.** (Abu Bakr, Umar, Uthman, Ali, Muawiyya, the Umayyads, the Abbasids, etc.) Presently self-proclaimed Caliph called Abu Bakr Baghdadi is leading a ferocious army called ISIS. According to a prominent Palestinian leader called Ismail Haniyeh, "we love death like our enemies love life." |
| **Jesus guarantees heaven for his people.** (John 14:2; 1 John 5:12. Jesus said to a dying thief on the cross, "Today, you will be with on in Paradise" (Luke 23:43) | **Muhammad guarantees hell for his people for an unspecified period** (Surah 19:71-72). This should be scary for people and especially for Muslims who are promised to start their eternity by entering into hell and no one knows for how long? |

## SUMMARY:

Jesus is unique in his birth, the sinless life he lived, the majestic message he preached, the mighty miracles he did, the sacrificial death he died on the cross, the resurrection from the dead, and in his glorious coming back. Even Muslims believe that Jesus will come back. All three monotheistic-faith in the world are waiting for the coming of Jesus Christ who will bring ultimate peace on this earth. Jesus came even for the first time to bring peace and he is the one who will bring ultimate peace when he comes the second time. The Bible says, "Therefore, having been justified by faith, we have peace with God through our Lord Jesus Christ, through whom also we have access by faith into this grace in which we stand, and rejoice in hope of the glory of God" (Romans 5:1-2). Someone has said very wisely that "when you are at peace with God, you will be at peace with yourself, and when you are at peace with yourself you will be at peace with other." This kind of real peace only Jesus can bring. Jesus is the one who gives assurance for eternity.

# CHAPTER FOUR

---

# THE TRUTH ABOUT
# THE HOLY BOOK OF ISLAM
# THE HOLY QURAN

I have read many books, but the Bible reads me.
Karl Barth

# CHAPTER FOUR
## TRUTH ABOUT THE HOLY BOOK OF ISLAM
## THE HOLY QURAN

The Qur'an is the holy book of Muslims who consider it as the most sacred book and the final revelation to mankind. It is the focal point of their faith and religious practices. According to Muslims, The Qur'an is the <u>greatest wonder</u> among the wonders of the world . . . This book is <u>second to none</u> in the world according to the unanimous decision of the learned men in points of diction, style, rhetoric, thoughts and soundness of laws and regulations to shape the destinies of mankind (Hadith (Mishkat III, pg. 664). According to the testimony of Quran itself, it is "Mother of Books" (Surah 43:3-4).

The word, "Qur'an", comes from the Arabic verb, *qara'a* meaning "to recite", "to read". According to Mohammed, he was commanded, when a spirit asked three times in the cave of Hira, was *"to qara'a"* or read. Mohammad replied, "What shall I read"? Thus, the word for Mohammad's revelation is known as the Qur'an.[xviii]

The Qur'an is about 80% of the New Testament in length. The Qur'an contains 114 chapters, or surahs that are arranged from longest to shortest. The document is quite repetitive, and disorganized. It is neither chronological nor topical. The verses jump from one subject to another which cause confusion. Contrary to the Qur'an, the Bible is arranged in chronological order. It begins with the Book of Genesis and ends with the Book of Revelation. Dr. Lehman Strauss wrote in the introduction of his book, the book of The Revelation, pages 17,18: One careful reading of the Bible will convince anyone that this inspired volume forms a complete cycle. Genesis is the book of commencement; Revelation is the book of consummation. Revelation is an excellent finish to the divine library.

**Genesis - The commencement of Heaven and earth (1:1)**
**Revelation - The consummation of Heaven and earth (21:1)**

**Genesis - The entrance of sin and the curse (3:1-19)**
**Revelation - The end of sin and the curse (21:27; 22:3)**

**Genesis - The dawn of Satan and his activities (3:1-7)**
**Revelation - The doom of Satan and his activities (20:10)**

**Genesis - The tree of life is relinquished (2:9; 3:24)**
**Revelation - The tree of life is regained (22:2)**

**Genesis - Death makes its entrance (2:17; 5:5)**
**Revelation - Death makes its exit (21:4)**

**Genesis - Sorrow begins (3:16)**
**Revelation - Sorrow is banished (21:4)**

The first book of the Bible knows no completion apart from the last book of the Bible, and all the rest of the sixty-four books in between are dependent upon each other. Not one book in the Bible is an independent contribution to be divorced from the other books.[xix]

According to Robert C. Douglas, the Qur'an is a document that presents Muslims and non-Muslims with a host of perplexities. According to Muslim tradition it must be read in Arabic if someone wants to experience the real message it contains. But Qur'anic Arabic is a difficult language, even for native born Arabic speakers.

The Qur'an, in the Arabic is written in rhyme prose, *saj*, a style similar to the prose used by the *kāhins*, or soothsayers of Arabia.[xx]

A word within the text is taken to title the chapters of the Qur'an. The word for the title does not related to the subject manner in the chapter (surah), from which it is derived. The titles have names such as "The Cow" (Surah 2), "Women" (Surah 4), "The Bee" 16 (Surah 16).

Dr. Labib Mikhail has highlighted that there are strange names for sections of the book in the Qur'an, which Muhammad claimed is the book of Allah and that the same identical book also exists in heaven. It is difficult to understand why Allah would name the chapters of his book like Surat Al-Baqarah (Number 2) The Cow, Surat Al-Nahl (Number 16) The Bee, Surat Al-Naml (Number 27) The Ant, Surat Al-'Ankabut (Number 29) The Spider, Surat Al-Fil (Number 105) The Elephant, even after evil spirits like Surat Al-Jinn (Number 72) The Jinn.

Quran has no sequence, no chronology or history, no pattern, no geography, no biography, no prophecy, just verses in a jumbled, mixed-up fashion. A chapter will contain different subjects all jumbled up in a haphazard manner within the chapter. The chapter which comes first, is just because, it is the longest in length, followed by the next longest and so forth, and finally the shortest chapter. One surah might say something reasonable, but another will be the opposite, in complete contradiction. The entire Quran is supposed to be from Allah, but it is as though different Allahs (gods) or authors, wrote the different chapters or even parts of the chapter due to the varying styles, fashions, words used, patterns, and content. Only the story of Joseph is a complete story. It has many literary defects such as None chronological, Endless repetitions, Jumps from one topic to the next, Inconsistencies in grammar, law, and theology.

According to Al-Kindi, a Christian polemicist employed in the Caliphal court (830 A.D.):
*"The result of all of this [process by which the Qur'an came into being] is patent to you who have read the scriptures and see how, in your book, histories are all jumbled together and intermingled; an evidence that many different hands have been at work therein, and caused discrepancies, adding, cutting out whatever they like or disliked. Are such, now, the conditions of a revelation sent down from heaven?"* (Muir 1882:18-19, 28).

The German secular scholar Salomon Reinach in his rather harsh analysis states that:
*From the literary point of view, the Quran has little merit.*
*Declamation, repetition, puerility, a lack of logic and coherence*
*strike the unprepared reader at every turn. It is humiliating*
*to the human intellect to think that this mediocre literature*
*has been the subject of innumerable commentaries, and*
*that millions of men are still wasting time in absorbing it."* (Reinach1932:176)

Carlyle confessed that it was "as toilsome reading as I ever understood; a wearisome, confused jumbled, crude, incondite. Nothing but a sense of duty could carry any European through the Quran."

# The History of the Qur'an

Muhammad claimed that the angel Gabriel transmitted the entire Qur'an to him from Allah while in a sequence and series of revelation starting from the first revelation in the Hira Cave. At first Muhammad feared he had been overtaken by a "Jinn", a troubling spirit. But Muhammad's wife, Khadijah, encouraged him that his visions were indeed from God and that he had been chosen as his special messenger. Amr ibn Sharhabil says Muhammad mentioned to his wife Khadijah that he feared he was possessed by demons and wondered whether others might consider him possessed by jinn (Pfander 1910:345). He says, (Muhammad), "When I went into seclusion I heard a voice. By Allah I feared that something wrong was going to happen."[xxi]

The Qur'an was revealed to Mohammad during 23 years and even though the time span between the Qur'an and the Bible compare 23 years with 1500, is very short and still there are so many contradictions in the Qur'an. The Qur'an itself declares that Allah said to Muhammad: "We have rehearsed it to you in slow, well-arranged stages, gradually" (*Surah 25.32*).

According to the Islamic history and the traditions passed to Muslims over the years, it seems that there happened strange experiences to Muhammad while he was receiving revelation from Allah, who was dictating a book that would later become the Qur'an. First the spirit forced Muhammad to read who was illiterate. Once the spirit realized that Muhammad was illiterate, then, asked him to memorize the revelation. Sometimes, he would faint, foam at the mouth and tremble at times. The book *True Guidance Part IV*, records the *Hadiths* regarding the way Mohammad received his revelations,

"The authoritative *Hadith* (Tradition) relate that Muhammad used to faint whenever revelations came to him. It is claimed he used to act like a drunkard (Al-Sirah al-Nabawiya, by Ibn Hisham; chapter on how the revelation came). In his book, *Al-Qur'an al-Majid*, Darwaza claims that Muhammad was taken out of this world. Abu Huraira says that "whenever Muhammad received revelation, he was overwhelmed by trembling." Another account says: "He became distressed, foaming at the mouth and closing his eyes. At times he snorted like a young camel" (Ahmad b. Hanbal I, 34, 464, VI. 163).... Umar b. al-Khattab said: "When revelation descended upon Muhammad, one could hear it near his face like the humming of bees" (Ahmad b. Hanbal, I. 34).[xxii]

After getting the first revelation from the "angel" there was a period of silence for about three years. During this period, Mohammad was distressed and often thought about committing suicide, wishing to throw himself off the mountains of Hira or Qubays. Muhammad fell into solitude, separated from himself from the people. It is told that even Khadijah said to him, "Does it not seem that your Lord is displeased with you?" Dismayed and frightened, he returned to the mountain and the cave of Hira. He wanted to ask God about the cause of this divine displeasure.

Some reliable sources make it very vivid to believe that Waraqa bin Naufal died two years after Muhammad got his first revelation, even without becoming a Muslim. Waraqa bin Naufal was a poet and a Nestorian priest (heretic sect of Christianity) and he had immense familiarity with the Old and New Testament. He helped Muhammad to formulate a text which would later become Qur'an, the Holy book for Muslims. The early Surahs, or chapters are long while subsequent chapters become shorter. The text was a product of Muhammad's supposed revelation with the mixture of biblical information from Waraqa bin Naufal. Waraqa bin Naufal was Khadija's cousin, who had been mentoring and training Muhammad with the biblical information from the time Muhammad became acquaintance with Khadija. Since Waraqa bin Naufal was a poet, he formulated the text in a poetic form which certainly helps to memorize easily. After the death of Waraqa bin Naufal, no revelation was forth coming for a long time, which was causing Muhammad to be depressed to the point of his suicidal attempts.

Upon the death of Waraqa bin Naufal, Muhammad got his first revelation and three years of silence, the depression to the point Muhammad contemplated suicide, leads to many doubts concerning he revelation he received. It leads to many question marks.

In Biblical history, we find that the prophets were sure and peaceful when they received a revelation from God. It is undeniable that there were moments of fright and bewilderment after having a visitations and encounters with angelic beings. It is quite a natural and normal phenomenon for human being to some sort of strange feelings after an encounter with super natural or paranormal beings. The God of the Bible spoke to His true spokesmen in such a way that there was a peace in their hearts and that the recipients when receiving the message. But when it comes to Muhammad, how he got his revelations are so strange.

According to the Qur'an, the unbelievers of Mohammed's day rejected the Qur'an because it was composed of old stories and myths.

*But the unbelievers say, "This is nothing but a lie which he has plagiarized, and others have helped him do it...Tales of the ancients, which he has caused to be written; and they are dictated before him morning and evening."* (Surah 25:4-5)

It is quite clear from the very beginning, people have questioned the reliability of the Qur'an. It is not a "revelation" brought down out of heaven to Muhammad, but ideas derived previously existing stories.

It is a taboo for Muslims to ask questions about the Qur'an and the character of Muhammad in Islam. Muslims believe that in questioning about Allah, Qur'an, and the character of Muhammad can cause someone to lose faith. That's why people are forced blindly to follow every precept. It is ipso facto that if there is a prevention of probing and concealing in questioning, there might be an absolute intention to cover up or hide something which must be uncovered. Once people are truthful, there is no need to hide anything and everything must be transparent in bringing the absolute truth on the stage. When the non-Muslims challenge the truthfulness of Islam, then the Muslims become so angry and aggressive. It is very hard for them to swallow this bitter pill of probing the Qur'an and Muhammad. But with the attitude of oppression and aggression, the lies might be covered up for some time, but eventually the truth triumphs. It is so hard to believe that the people have been told so many lies. This is the same that Satan does who is called the "Father of Lies." But it is very important that people come to know the truth. Jesus said, "And ye shall know the truth, and the truth shall make you free" (John 8:32). The reality of fallacy and falsity brings bondage, whereas the truth breaks the shackles of bondage and opens doors of spiritual freedom in knowing and serving the almighty God with an awesome relationship which is hard to imagine and difficult to express.

**The question about the sources of the Qur'an is crucial to whether Islam is true or false.**

The noisy and an out of tune trumpet which the Muslims have been playing in their attempt to promote their book over the Bible, and in proving the supremacy of their book is: One can't rely on the Bible, because there are so many different versions. For them, The Bible is corrupted since it does not correspond with the Qur'an. To verify the validity of the Qur'an, they must make every possible attempt to nullify the authenticity and reliability of the Bible. The different versions of the Bible do not convey a different message, but the same message. Of course, there are also many English versions of the Qur'an which are so different in expression, but they want to bring the same foundational message. The versions might be different in expression, but original text of the Bible in Hebrew and Greek is the same. There are thousands of Greek and Hebrew biblical manuscripts. When Christian scholars encounter any doubt about the text in different languages, they consult with the original manuscripts.

Speaking truthfully, **In The Qur'an Allah has commanded Muhammad and the doubting believers to refer to the Christians and Jews for Consultation.**
*"If thou wert in doubt as to what We have revealed unto thee, then ask those who have been reading the Book from before thee: The Truth hath indeed come to thee from thy Lord: so be in no wise of those in doubt." (Surah 10:94)*

*"And We sent not (as Our messengers) before thee other than men whom We inspired - Ask the followers of the Remembrance if ye know not!" (Surah 16:43).*

It is very odd that The Qur'an encourages Muhammad and his followers to verify the teaching of Islam from the Books of the Jews (Torah) and the Christian (Gospels) but at the same time how it could claim the corruption of these scriptures which must be the source and standard of verifying the scripture of Islam (Qur'an). It is quite logical that the truth must verify the truth. No one dare to verify the truth with falsity. The prophet of Islam was convinced about the truthfulness of the Scriptures which came before him. That's why, he was asked and he himself encouraged others to consult with the Scriptures of the Jews and the Christians. If Allah, the god of Islam encouraged Muhammad to so do, then undoubtedly, Allah was convinced that the scriptures before Muhammad would have been reliable. Otherwise, Muhammad might have been warned strongly about the corruption of the previous scriptures and could have told him to nullify every previous scripture. But Muhammad had no doubt about authenticity of the previous scriptures.

If someone claimed that at the time of Muhammad, the scriptures of the Jews and the Christians were authentic and reliable and could have been the source of verification, but later declared the corruptions of these scriptures had taken place. If this argument is substantial for the Muslims, then, the Muslims lose the battle before it starts since after Muhammad, the Jews and the Christian have been following the same Scriptures with the evidence of the ancient manuscripts which were in existence before and after Muhammad.

It is important to note that the questioning of the authenticity and the reliability of the Bible started as the Muslims started questioning the authenticity of the Qur'an after finding contradicts in its content itself and in relating to its narratives found in the Biblical text.

In 1064, Ibn-Khazem was the first to charge that the Bible had been corrupted and it is falsified. This charge was to defend Islam against Christianity because Ibn-Khazem came upon differences and contradiction between the Bible and the Quran. Believing, by faith that the Quran was true, the Bible must then be false. He said, "Since the Quran must be true it

80

must be the conflicting Gospel texts that are false. Prior to Ibn-Khazem and even after, Muslims scholars believed the authenticity and the reliability of the Bible.

For Muslims, The Qur'an has been protected by the people who have memorized it over the centuries as it has passed from generation to generation in its pure form. It is very interesting to note here that there is a human effort and an attempt at work in protecting their scripture. On the other hand, when it comes to The Bible, God has preserved and protected His Eternal Word under so many difficult situations over the centuries.

Muslims believe that before the creation of the world, God had the exact words of the Arabic Koran inscribed in what is called the "mother of the book" or the "master tablet".

- In Quran 13:34 it says, "With Allah is the Mother of the Book."
- In 43:2 "And the enlightening scripture. We have rendered it an Arabic Quran, that you may understand. It is preserved with us in the original master (or mother book, as Yusuf Ali translates) honorable and full of wisdom." 43:2-4; Again in 85:22, "Indeed, it is a glorious Quran. In a preserved master tablet."

Muslims also believe that the Arabic text of the Quran, that we hold in our hands today is identical with this mother preserved master tablet right down to the very syllables and individual letters of the text. Maududi said, "The Qur'an - the book he gave to mankind - exists in its original text, without a word, syllable nor even letter having been changed." (Towards Understanding Islam, Maududi, p.58); **Abu Dhabi said,** "No other book in the world can match the Qur'an ... The astonishing fact about this book of ALLAH is that **it has remained unchanged, even to a dot, over the last fourteen hundred years.** ... No variation of text can be found in it. You can check this for yourself by listening to the recitation of Muslims from different parts of the world. (Basic Principles of Islam), Abu Dhabi, UAE: The Zayed Bin Sultan Al Nahayan Charitable & Humanitarian Foundation, 1996, p 4, Muslim). The Qur'an, on the other hand, exists exactly as it was revealed to the Prophet; not a word - nay, not a syllable of it - has been changed. It is available in its original text and the Word of God has been preserved for all time." (Towards ... Islam, Maududi, p.74f, Muslim). "The Qur'an contains the word of God. In it is preserved the divine revelation, unalloyed by human interpolation of any kind, unaffected by any change or loss to the original." (Towards Understanding Islam, Maulana Sayyid Abul A'la Maududi, p.11, 1993 Markazi Maktaba Islami, Muslim); "Not one letter has changed ... the protection of the Qur'an as a book" is an accurate prophecy that has been fulfilled. (Dr. Jamal Badawi, Cambridge University Debate, 1994, Muslim). "Two copies of the original Qur'an from the time of Uthman (pbuh) still exist today, one is in Istanbul and the other in Tashkent. Whosoever is interested, may compare the text of the Qur'an today from any part of the world with these two original copies, he will not find any discrepancy. "In other words: two of the copies of the Qur'an which were originally prepared in the time of Caliph `Uthman, are still available to us today and their texts and arrangement can be compared, by anyone who cares to, with any other copy of the Qur'an, be it in print or handwriting, from any place or period. They will be found to be identical." (Von Denffer, Ulum al-Qur'an, p 64).

At first glance, it sounds impressive and might be convincing that there is one Qur'an in Arabic which all the Muslims follow everywhere. However, when the matter goes through the scrutiny, crosses the boundaries of falsification into factual realization and as it enters sincere openness of rationalism, then the reality is completely different. Today's Arabic Qur'an is not a reliable guide to the original. Far from establishing the reliability of the Qur'an, the fact that only a single version is in existence today serves to underline its *unreliability*.

The Muslim scholars also have a difference view concerning the relatability of the Quran. Muslim Shabir Ally said in a televised debate in Atlanta GA, Oct. 19, 2000, **"It doesn't matter if the Qur'anic manuscripts are corrupted, or have evolved, as long as we have a picture of the true Jesus..."** (Televised Debate in Atlanta, Oct. 19, 2000). In the introduction to Dawood's translation of the Quran he said, "owing to the fact that the Kufic script in which the Quran was originally written contained no indication of vowels or diacritical points, variant readings are recognized by Muslims as of equal authority." (N.J. Dawood, The Koran, Middlesex, England: Penguin Books, 1983, p 10, introduction to Dawood's translation of the Koran). The International Journal of Islamic and Arabic Studies, in an article called, **"A Study of Seven Quranic Variants, said in 1989, "It is interesting to note that in scholarly Muslim journals, there is beginning to be a grudging acknowledgment of the fact that there are variant and conflicting readings on the text of the Quran"** [One example would be Saleh al-Wahaihu] (A Study of Seven Quranic Variants, International Journal of Islamic and Arabic Studies, Vol. V (1989), #2, pp. 1-57).

Non-Muslims, McClintock, and Strong say, "All Western and Muslim scholars admit the presence of variant readings in the text of the Quran" and "The Shiite Muslims claim that Uthman left out 25 percent of the original verses in the Quran for political reasons" (Dashti, 23 Years, p. 28; Mandudi, Meaning of the Quran, pp. 17-18; McClintock and Strong, Cyclopedia, V:152). Burton said, in his book, The Collection of the Quran, "The Muslin accounts of the history of the Quran texts are a mass of confusion, contradiction and inconsistencies" (Burton, The Collection of the Quran, p. 231). Since most Muslims believe that the Qur'an was revealed in seven forms, their mind thinks, "I wonder where the differences come, from if caliph 'Uthman eliminated six of those forms?" The scholars who are attributed with founding the madhabs could not agree on how to assess the Qur'an and Sunnah. Shafi'i said that the Qur'an alone can abrogate (cancel) the Qur'an and that the Sunnah alone can abrogate the Sunnah. However, the other three madhabs (Maliki, Habali and Hanafi) all said the Qur'an CAN cancel the Sunnah and the Sunnah CAN cancel the Qur'an. This means that some of the Qur'an that the followers of Shafi'i adhere to are considered as cancelled by the other madhabs! The supposed final revelation is unknowable, and so is the supposed eternal sharia. If the greatest Islamic scholars couldn't figure out the true sources, then what chance has the poor ordinary fellow have! Doesn't God love the ordinary fellow? Then why would He give a confusing book that they cannot follow? In fact, it also makes the 'preservation' of the texts to be a side issue in reality - but they want to keep it up front. ("Brother Mark, author of "The perfect Koran"). The Shorter Encyclopedia of Islam says, "One thing only is certain and is openly recognized by tradition, namely, that there was not in existence any collection of revelations in the final form, because, as long as he was alive, new revelations were being added to the earlier ones." (Shorter Encyclopedia of Islam, p 271). Guillaume points out that the Quran at first "had a large number of variants, not always trifling in significance" (Islam, p. 189). According to Professor Guillaume in his book, Islam, (pp. 191ff.), "some of the original verses of the Quran were lost." "That there are verses which got left out of Uthman's version of the Quran is universally recognized" (Shorter Encyclopedia of Islam, pp. 278-282; Guillaume, Islam, p. 191; Wherry, A Comprehensive Commentary on the Quran, pp. 110-111).

**There is a story of a follower of Muhammad named, Abdullah Sarh who would offer suggestions to Muhammad on how to rephrase the prophet's various revelations. Muhammad occasionally accepted the new version. Ali Dashti explains what happened:**

*"Abdullah renounced Islam on the ground that the revelations, if from God, could not be changed at the prompting of a scribe such as he. After his apostasy, he went to Mecca and joined the Qurayshites"* (Ali Dashti, *23 Years,* p. 98). Upon conquering Mecca Abdullah ibn Sarh, was one of the first people Muhammad killed.

When Muhammad died in AD 632, there was no complete written version of the Qur'an in existence. The immediate disciples did not have the entire document of the Qur'an whereas, some portions were memorized.

According to the authenticated traditions of Islam, it is very evident that discrepancies about different readings of the Qur'an arose even at the time of Muhammad. In the well-known book of traditions, the Mishkat-al-Musabih in the chapter called Fajail-ul-Quran we read: -

"Umr-ibn-al-Khatab said, 'I heard Hisham-ibn-Hakim ibn-Hijami reading Surah Furqan in a different way from that which I was accustomed to do; but the prophet had taught me this Surah. Then I wished to immediately forbid him, but allowed him to read to the end. Then I seized his dress, and took him to the prophet, and said, oh prophet of God; I heard this man reading Surah Furqan in another way; he read it differently from what you taught me. Then the prophet said to me, 'Let him go.' He then told him to read. He then read in the manner which I had heard. Upon that the prophet said; It has been revealed in this way.' Again, he said to me, 'Do you read also.' Then when I had read, he said, 'It was revealed in this way also; the Qur'an was revealed in seven readings, read it in the way which is easy to you'."

There are many traditions relating to the seven-fold reading of the Qur'an. The International Journal of Islamic and Arabic Studies, in an article called, **"A Study of Seven Quranic Variants, said in 1989, "It is interesting to note that in scholarly Muslim journals, there is beginning to be a grudging acknowledgment of the fact that there are variant and conflicting readings on the text of the Quran"** [One example would be Saleh al-Wahaihu] (A Study of Seven Quranic Variants, International Journal of Islamic and Arabic Studies, Vol. V (1989), #2, pp. 1-57). The Muslim scholars have tried in various ways to explain its significance, but without success. The differences which existed in the seven different readings of the Qur'an were certainly very serious. According to the tradition recorded by Nisai: 'Umr boldly accused Hisham of falsehood, and asserted that he had read many words in his recitation of the Qur'an which had never been learned from the prophet. In another tradition, recorded by Muslim states that Ibn-Kab, one of the most famous of the Qur'an readers, heard two men reciting the Namaz in a reading different from his own. Upon reference being made to the prophet, the latter pronounced both correct, "upon which," says Ibn-Kab "such a revolt arose in my heart as had not existed since the times of ignorance."

From these various traditions, it is clear that even during the lifetime of the prophet the Qur'an was being read in various conflicting ways. So, grave were the differences that quarrels soon arose; for the inhabitants of Hims stood by the reading of Al-Miqdad-ibn-al-Aswad; the Kufites by that of Ibn-Mas'ud; the Busrites by that of Abu-Musa, and so on. But it would be a mistake to suppose that these differences simply consisted in the recitation of the Qur'an in the various dialects of Arabia, as some would convince someone to believe; for there is ample evidence to show that the differences extended far deeper. Indeed, from the Itqan it is evident that 'Umr and Hisham, were both same tribe, the Quraish, so that a supposed difference of dialect does not account for the difference reading.[xxiii]

After the death of Muhammad, his followers continued to recite in various conflicting ways. At the same time, out of the memories of these recitations of the Qur'an the surahs were also written on palm-leaf stalks, thin white stones, bones, and leather.

According to the Mishkat, it is evident and apt to believe that there was a fear of losing the Qur'an partly or as a whole since many disciples who had memorized some portions of the Qur'an (Hafiz) were killed in the Battle of Yamama in 633. Umr requested Abu Bakr, the first Muslim ruler (caliph) to collect the Quranic material and to compile into one book. At first Abu Bakr objected by saying, *"How can I do a thing which the prophet has not done?"* But upon Umar's importunity, Abu Bakr ordered Zaid-ibn Sabit that the Qur'an should be written down, based on the recollection of Muhammad's surviving disciples. The first reaction of Zaid-ibn Sabit was very strong in collecting and compiling the Qur'an into a book. He said, *"By Allah, if you (Abu Bakr) had ordered me to shift one of the mountains (from its place) it would not have been harder for me than what he had ordered me concerning the collection of the Qur'an.* Zaid said to both of them, "How dare you do a thing WHICH THE PROPHET HAS NOT DONE?" Abu Bakr said, "By Allah, it is (really) a good thing. According to Zaid's own narrative, he said, "So I kept on arguing with him about it till Allah opened my bosom for that which He had opened the bosoms of Abu Bakr and Umar. So, I started locating Qur'anic material and collecting it from parchments, scapula, leaf-stalks of date palms and from the memories of men (who knew it by heart).

This task of collecting Quranic material and compiling into a book was completed in 634. The considerable care was taken - only readings supported by at least two witnesses were allowed. This version of the Qur'an, known as the Hafsah Codex (Hafsah was one of Mohammed's wife and the daughter of Umar, the second caliph of Islam), was undoubtedly the most accurate written text of the Qur'an ever produced, closer than any other version to the words of Muhammad.[xxiv]

## AUTHORIZED VERSION OF QUR'AN BY USMAN (Uthman)

Unfortunately, for Muslims the Hafsah Codex no longer exists. As Islam spread through military conquest during the following decades, it was noted that Muslim soldiers were reading different versions of the Qur'an. Here it would be appropriate to explain about the different versions of the expression that might exist as long as it conveys the same meaning. For example, when someone says about the death of a person in English language, he might say in different ways like: He died, he folded the pages of his life, he passed away, or he expired. All these different expressions convey the same meaning. But when it comes to the different readings or versions of Qur'an that became the matter of concern was that all of them were different in its content and message. These differences were so serious that the different groups regarded each other as heretics. In an effort to restore order, the Muslim leader, and the third caliph, Uthman ibn Affan, ruler from 644 to 656, ordered just four men to rewrite the entire Qur'an from memory. Not the best way to ensure reliable textual reproduction, especially in a context when large differences between different versions were provoking such hostility between different Muslim groups. No attempt was made by Uthman's scribes to adhere to the Hafsah Codex. Worse still, all other surviving manuscripts, including all existing copies of the Hafsah Codex, were collected, and burned.

This is not a biased historical reconstruction taken from ill-informed anti-Muslim propaganda. On the contrary, it's taken from the Hadith, a collection of sayings related to the life and teaching of Muhammad, regarded by Muslims as an important guide to interpreting the Qur'an and following the Muslim way of life. Here's the relevant section in full:

Hudhaifa bin Al-Yaman came to Uthman at the time when the people of Sham and the people of Iraq were waging war to conquer Arminya and Adharbijan. Hudhaifa was afraid of their (the people of Sham and Iraq) differences in the recitation of the Qur'an, so he said to Uthman, 'O chief of the Believers! Save this nation before they differ about the Book (Qur'an) as Jews and the Christians did before.' So, Uthman sent a message to Hafsah saying, 'Send us the manuscripts of the Qur'an so that we may compile the Qur'anic materials in perfect copies and return the manuscripts to you.' Hafsah sent it to Uthman. Uthman then ordered Zaid bin Thabit, Abdullah bin AzZubair, Said bin Al-As and Abdur Rahman bin Harith bin Hisham to rewrite the manuscripts in perfect copies. Uthman said to the three Quraishi men, 'In case you disagree with Zaid bin Thabit on any point in the Qur'an, then write it in the dialect of Quraish, the Qur'an was revealed in their tongue.' They did so, and when they had written four copies. One copy was kept in Medina. The three copies were sent to Baghdad, Basra, and Damascus. After Uthman sent copies to those locations, he ordered that all the other Qur'anic materials, whether written in fragmentary manuscripts or whole copies, must be burnt.

One must question honestly, where are those copies that were sent to Baghdad, Basra, and Damascus. These places have been under the control of Muslims since the dawn of Islam in those territories.

Caliph Uthman (Usman) wanted to eliminate this situation, but the way he did ensured the permanent corruption of the Qur'an by eliminating all checks and balances. He made an "official" version, and burned all others to prevent cross checking for errors and corruption; whereas, with the inspired word of the true God (YHWH) of Abraham, Isaac, and Jacob, creator of all, there is, the Bible. There are over 30,000 ancient Manuscripts, Codex's, fragments, and scrolls that permit checking for errors and corruption's and which make possible the correction of any corruption.

## THE QUR'AN IS A CORRUPTED DOCUMENT FROM IT VERY BEGINNING

The historical facts shed light in regards to the reliability of the Qur'an, without of shadow of doubt, it is not difficult to believe that there were different renderings of the Qur'an at the time of Muhammad. Following his death, this serious dilemma continued for his follower to decide what to believe to be the part of the Quranic canon or which portions must be rejected as not being part of the canon.

While Uthman made his best attempt in compiling an authorized version of the Qur'an by collecting all the older copies and burning them and sending the revised versions throughout the Muslim world, the dilemma of a corrupted Quran continues. Even though many Muslims might be committed to the orthodoxy of this belief that the Qur'an is a pure document, even though they might be familiar with the fact the Qur'an has been a corrupted document from its very origin. Undoubtedly, there are many Muslim scholars who are familiar and convinced with the corrupted Qur'an, but still they are keeping so many Muslims ignorant about the fact. There is also a sense of fear and intimidation which the Muslims have been carrying throughout the centuries. They are not allowed to pronounce any statement in regards to the Qur'an which is not in form of Islamic orthodoxy or traditional relevancy. Even when someone, other than

Muslims, attempts to make any statement contrary to the traditional views of Islam, it becomes a threat and danger to Islam. It is sad to say that the followers of Islam really live in slavery and ironed-bar prison of religion.

Muslim scholars have realized truthfully, sincerely, and honestly, that parts of the Quran were lost, perverted, and that there were many thousand variants which made it impossible to talk about the Quran. For example, As-Suyuti (died 1505), one of the most famous and revered of the commentators of the Quran, quotes Ibn 'Umar al Khattab as saying: "Let no one of you say that he has acquired the entire Qur'an, for how does he know that it is all? Much of the Qur'an has been lost, thus let him say, 'I have acquired of it what is available'" (As-Suyuti, Itqan, part 3, page 72).

A'isha, the favorite wife of the Prophet, says, also according to a tradition recounted by as-Suyuti, "During the time of the Prophet, the chapter of the Parties used to be two hundred verses when read. When 'Uthman edited the copies of the Qur'an, only the current (verses) were recorded" (73).

As-Suyuti also tells this story about Ubbay ibn Ka'b, one of the great companions of Muhammad:
This famous companion asked one of the Muslims, "How many verses in the chapter of the Parties?" He said, "Seventy-three verses." He (Uba) told him, "It used to be almost equal to the chapter of the Cow (about 286 verses) and included the verse of the stoning". The man asked, "What is the verse of the stoning?" He (Ubbay) said, "If an old man or woman committed adultery, stone them to death."

The Shia Muslims have constantly charged Uthman for eliminating the Quranic material which was favorable to Ali and his family. Some Muslim scholars even believe that twenty five percent of the Quranic material which reveals the supremacy of Ali over all three caliphs has been eliminated from the Qur'an.

Now when it comes to the background of Ali, he was and is not a heretic in Islam. He was cousin of Muhammad, and the son in law. Many see him even the victim of injustice done by three other caliphs prior to him. Ali was the fourth ruler (caliph) even though some Muslims acknowledge Ali to be the true successor after Muhammad.

Even though, it is up to Muslims to solve their dispute, but when it comes to the Qur'an, it is convincing that the Qur'an is a corrupted document. To cover up the corruption of the Qur'an, the Muslims made every baseless attempt to pronounce that the Bible has been corrupted!

## WHICH QURAN IS THE UTHMANIC QURAN?

The two copies the Qur'an, one in Tashkent (Uzbekistan) and the other in Topkapi (Turkey) are in existence. According to the Muslim tradition, the real Qur'an is the one which has blood stains of Uthman. However, since Uthman was murdered while reading the Qur'an, and the Muslims who believe his blood stains on that Qur'an, it's the real one. But the problem is the both copies that exist in the museums have blood stains!

The "Samarqand" codex which exists in Tashkent only begins with the seventh verse of Suratul-Baqarah and many intervening pages are missing. It has only 46 surahs (chapter) whereas the present Quran has 114 surahs. The whole text from Surah 43.10 has been lost.

What remains, however, indicates that it is obviously of great antiquity, being devoid of any kind of vocalization although here and there, a diacritical stroke has been added to a letter. Nonetheless, it is clearly written in Kufi script which immediately places it beyond Arabia in origin and of a date not earlier than the late eighth century. No objective scholarship can trace such a text to Medina in the seventh century. Its actual script is also very irregular. Some pages are neatly and uniformly copied out while others are distinctly untidy or imbalanced. On some pages the text is smoothly spread out while on others it is severely cramped and condensed. At times, the Arabic letter "kaf" is written uniformly with the rest of the text, at others it has been considerably extended and is the dominant letter. The manuscript may well be a composite text of portions from different original codices, alternatively different scribes were employed to transcribe it. It also has artistic illumination between some of the surahs with colored medallions. The very appearance of the text compared with the known development of the early scripts prevents a date earlier than one hundred and fifty years after Muhammad's death or a place of origin anywhere in Arabia.

The other famous manuscript is known as the "Topkapi" codex as it is preserved in the Topkapi Museum in Istanbul in Turkey. Once again, however, it is written in Kufi script, giving its date away to not earlier than the late eighth century. Like the Samarqand codex it is written on parchment and is virtually devoid of vocalization though it, too, has occasional ornamentation between the surahs. It was 46 surahs as well. It also appears to be one of the earliest texts to have survived but it cannot sincerely be claimed that it is an `Uthmanic original.

A comparison between these two codices in any event shows that they were not transcribed in the same place at the same time. The Topkapi codex has eighteen lines to the page while the Samarqand codex has between eight and twelve. The whole text of the former is uniformly written and spaced while the latter, as mentioned already, is often haphazard and distorted. They may well both be two of the oldest sizeable manuscripts of the Qur'an surviving but their origin cannot be taken back earlier than the second century of Islam.

The oldest surviving texts of the Qur'an, whether in fragments or whole portions, date not earlier than about a hundred and fifty years after the Prophet's death.[xxv]

The Qur'an found in 1972 in the Great Mosque of Sana'a, Yemen during the restoration of the mosque considered to be the oldest document of the Qur'an. Some of the fragments contradict the Qur'an that the Muslims hold today. The Yemeni Qur'an is actually older then the two Qur'ans from Tashkent and Topkapi. The scholars working on the Sana manuscript have discovered thousands of variations and flaws.

## Who corrupted the Qur'an?

Muslim source materials reveal some of these select people who are known to have created their unique version of the Qur'an. (Sahih Bukhari, Volume 5, Book 58, Number 150).

I heard the Prophet saying, "Learn the recitation of Qur'an from four persons:
(1) Abdullah Ibn Mas'ud,
(2) Salim (who was killed in the 633 CE battle), the freed slave of Abu Hudhaifa,
(3) Ubayy B. Ka'ab and
(4) Muadh bin Jabal."

So, a few select people close to Muhammad thought they knew the Qur'an and collected their personal version. These versions of the Qur'an became widely distributed and used. That is why Muslim soldiers were arguing and calling one another heretics.

After the "official" Qur'an was released and the order was given to burn all other versions, some very bad feelings erupted. The following information from Muslim sources is probably the most important information that tell about the people who actually knew Muhammad personally.

Let's begin with Mas'ud, who was asked to burn his personal version of the Qur'an. "How can you order me to recite the reading of Zaid, when I recited from the very mouth of the Prophet some seventy Surahs?" "Am I," asks Abdullah, "to abandon what I acquired from the very lips of the Prophet?" (Masahif" by Ibn abi Dawood, 824-897 AD, pp. 12, 14).

**Would Mas'ud accept the Qur'an of today as being pure since he refused to destroy his unique version**? Since Mas'ud did not want to have his unique version of the Qur'an destroyed, it is doubtful that Mas'ud would honestly accept that the Uthmanic version of the Qur'an is pure. It is important to ask, "Why did Mas'ud refuse to give in and destroy his version of the Qur'an?"

Mas'ud was a close companion and personal servant of Muhammad. The prophet Muhammad taught the Qur'an to Mas'ud in person. Due to his close relationship with Muhammad, Mas'ud would have had the confidence that he was qualified to create his unique version of the Qur'an. Mas'ud, moved to Kufa, Iraq where he completed his unique version of the Qur'an (commonly called the Kufan Codex). The unique Qur'an created by Mas'ud was completed years after the most important original manuscript (634 CE) that Hafsah kept until she died in 667 CE. Additionally, the Qur'an version created by Mas'ud did not have chapters 1, 113, and 114 that are in the "official" Qur'an of today. Is the Qur'an truly pure as believed by Muslims today?

Another unique Qur'an was created by Ubayy B. Ka'ab. He was a close companion of Muhammad and served as a secretary to Muhammad. Ubayy could recite much of the Qur'an, which he had learned from the prophet Muhammad.

Scholars have found that Ubayy's version differed from the "official" Qur'an with two additional chapters entitled: Surat Al-Khal and Surat Al-Afd. Since Ubayy was taught the Qur'an by the prophet Muhammad, why doesn't the "official" Qur'an contain the two additional chapters?

Ubayy died during the reign of Umar, which was before the "official" Qur'an was created by Uthman. Therefore, Ubayy did not have to witness that his version of the Qur'an was burned by Uthman's order. Since Ubayy created a unique version of the Qur'an and had learned from the mouth of the prophet Muhammad, would he have agreed with Mas'ud by refusing to give in and destroy his version of the Qur'an?"

Due to Uthman's decision to create an "official" version of the Qur'an, Ubayy's version of the Qur'an was destroyed. It is important to ask, "Is the Qur'an pure?"

Now consider the original Qur'an called the Hafsah Codex. Muslims leaders destroyed it immediately after Hafsah died. It is most important to ask, "Why did Hafsah not wish to have this most important original manuscript of the Qur'an to be burnt?"

The "official" Qur'an version of today comes from Zaid ibn Thabit, who was the youngest writing member. Zaid, being very young, outlived the older people who had spent more time with Muhammad. However, in the end it was Zaid's version of the Qur'an that was selected by Uthman for the "official" Qur'an version.

When Zaid ibn Thabit was asked to collect the fragmentary Quran from difference sources, his initial reaction was quite dramatic: *"Abu Bakr sent someone to call me when Yamama people were killed. Umar was there with him. Abu Bakr said: 'On the day of Yamama, Umar came to me and said that the reciters of the Quran were killed. He was afraid that others might be killed elsewhere. This indicates the loss of much of the Quran. He suggested that I command that the Quran be compiled.' I asked Umar: 'How would you do something that the Prophet of Allah did not do?' Umar kept telling me to think about it until Allah made my heart cheerful. I took on Umar's perspective. Abu Bakr said to me: 'We do not doubt that you are a wise young man. You used to write down the revelation for the Prophet of Allah. So, trace the Quran and compile it.' I said: 'By Allah, if they had chosen me to move the mountain from its place, it would have been easier than compiling the Quran. I argued: 'How would you do something the Prophet of Allah did not do?' He replied: "By Allah, this is good!' Therefore, I continued compiling it from palm branched, thin stones, and the chests of men. I found the end of Surah al-Tawba [9] with Abu Khuzaima al-Ansari. I did not find it with anyone other than him. The leaves (suhuf) were with Abu Bakr until he died; then they were handed down to Umar, then to Hafsah, Umar's daughter."* (1: pp. 47-48, citing al-Bukhari)

Muslims who had been close to Muhammad became righteously angry when Uthman insisted that only one version of the Qur'an be used.

Islamic sources show that the purity of the Qur'an from the days of Muhammad appears to have been compromised. If no variants existed, then no burning party would had been held. Muslims believe that seven versions of the Qur'an exist but that only Uthman's Qur'an is correct. So, Muslims disregard the "official" book burning party cited in Muslim source materials. However, it takes "blind faith" to believe and accept this viewpoint.[xxvi]

There were several versions of the Qur'an which are:
1.  Ibn Masud's Qur'an
2.  Ibn Kab's Qur'an
3.  Ali's Qur'an
4.  Zaid's Qur'an (Hafsah's Qur'an or the Caliph's, which was compiled under Uthman's order), without mentioning the seven renderings and the other probable copies like the Yemen's scripts which were found in the 70's...

The Arabic version of the Qur'an published in Turkey in 1908 is different from the standardized and canonized version of Cairo Quran in Egypt 1924. There was a great and critical need of standardizing the Quran at that time since there were 80 different copies of Quran in existence.

# Missing Verses in the Qur'an

Arthur Jeffrey gives the complete text of a chapter in Abu Ubaid's *Kitab Fada'il-al-Qur'an*, folios 43 and 44, concerning chapters that have been lost from the Koran.

Abu 'Ubaid al-Qassim. Sallam (154-244 AH) studied under renown scholars and himself became well known as a philologist, jurist, and Quranic expert. His chapter contains a list of Hadith on the missing verses of the Koran. According to these Hadith:

- 'Umar is recorded as saying that much of the Quran has disappeared.
- Ai'sha ways that surah 33 used to have 200 verses, but much of it has been lost.
- Ibn Ka'b says that Surah 33 had as many verses as surah 2 (i.e. at least 200 verses), and included the verses on stoning [NB: as the Surah 33 has 73 verses today.]
- 'Uthman also refers to the missing verses on the stoning of adulterers (several different Hadith all report this).
- Ibn Ka'b and al-Khattab differed over whether S. xxxlii:6 (*sic*) was part of the Koran or not.
- Several people (Abu Waqid al-Laithi, Abu Musa al-Ash'ari, Zaid b. Arqam, and Jabir b. 'Abdallah) remember an aya about humans being greedy which is not now in the Koran.
- Ibn Abbas confesses to hearing things and not knowing if they were part of the Koran or not.
- Abi Ayyub b. Yunus reports a verse that he read in A'isha's codex that is not now in the Koran, and adds that A'isha accused 'Uthman of having altered the Koran.
- ' Adi b. 'Adi comment on the existence of another missing verses, the previous existence of which was confirmed by Zaid ibn Thabit.
- 'Umar questioned the loss of another verse, and was informed by 'Abd ar-Rahman b. 'Auf that "It dropped out among what dropped from the Koran."

'Ubaid concludes the chapter by asserting that these verses were all genuine and used to be recited during prayers, but they were not passed down by the *savants* because they were considered extra, similar to verses contained elsewhere in the Quran.[xxvii]

## THE ABROGATION OF THE QUR'AN

The Muslims believe that the similar copy of the Qur'an exist in heaven. Allah dictated the Qur'an to Muhammad so that there would a copy of the same Qur'an on earth. It sounds quite good, but the reality speaks differently.

If Muhammad would have consistently told as he was receiving the revelation from God, then the Qur'an could have been regarded as coming from God. However, even the Muslims believe that there was abrogation of revelation. It means that Allah was sometimes sending completely different message or a message with an addition to the former revelation. It means that Allah changed his mind many times, and even made necessary changes in the book he already had.

The abrogation of Quranic verse concerning Jews and Christians:

*"Those who believe (in the Quran) and those who follow the Jewish (scriptures) and the Christians and the Sabaeans, - Any who believe in Allah and the Last Day, and*

*work righteousness, shall have their reward with their Lord: on them shall be no fear, nor shall they grieve.* " (Surah 2:62).

*"If only they had stood fast by the Law, the Gospel, and all the revelation that was sent to them from their Lord, they would have enjoyed happiness from every side. There is from among them a party on the right course: but many of them follow a course that is evil.* " (Surah 5:69).

These verses were abrogated by Surah 3:85 which says,

*"If anyone desires a religion other than Islam (submission to God), never will it be accepted of him; and in the Hereafter, he will be in the ranks of those who have lost (All spiritual good).* "

- Surah 9:29 abrogating Surah 2:109
- Surah 2:185 abrogating Surah 2:184
- Surah 9:36 abrogating Surah 2:217 and Surah 45:14

The classical abrogation can be exemplified by this event:

### The Marriage of Zainab bint Jahsh
Muhammad's third marriage is a story of great tragedy, filled with nothing but lust, and sensual desires.

The story began when Zayd ibn Haritha was kidnapped from his aristocratic family by some traveling Arabians who sold him to Khadija, the first wife of Muhammad, who in turn gave him as a present to her husband, Muhammad, to be his servant. But after Muhammad heard his calling to Islam, he freed Zayd and he adopted him for a son publicly, where he said, "Zayd is my son, I inherit him and he inherits me." Thereafter, he was called "Zayd, the son of Muhammad."

Later, he asked Zainab, his cousin on his father's side, to marry Zayd. She first refused because Zayd was homely. Furthermore, even though Muhammad adopted him publicly, he was considered by the majority of the Arabs as a slave. For this reason, she could not bring herself to love him, so she said to Muhammad, "If you insist on me marrying him, I will, but I'd rather marry you, not Zayd." Muhammad insisted that she marry Zayd, and so it was.

**To convince her to marry Zayd, a verse had to descend upon Muhammad from heaven that commanded Zainab and all the Muslims to obey him:**
"It is not fitting for a believer, man or woman, when a matter has been decided by Allah and his Messenger, to have any option about their decision; if anyone disobeys Allah and his Messenger, he is indeed on a clearly wrong path." (Surah *Al-Ahzab* (the Allies) 33:36.

Thus, Zainab married Zayd. Up to this point, the matter could seem logical despite all the coercion and duress that were imposed upon Zainab. But what happened thereafter was very peculiar, shocking and appalling.

The story goes on to tell us that one day Muhammad went to visit his adopted son Zayd. When he entered the house, Zayd was not home. Muhammad saw Zainab half naked as she was putting her clothes on. Muhammad desired her, but he was afraid to enter the house and commit adultery with her.

As he was leaving, he said to her, **"Praise be to Allah who changes hearts."**

Zainab smiled and later told Zayd about that visit and Muhammad's statement. Zayd went immediately to Muhammad and asked him: "Do you want me to divorce her for you?" Muhammad answered him: **"Hold unto your wife and fear Allah."** That was initially a noble stand on the part of Muhammad. However, what filled Muhammad's heart and soul was totally different than what his lips expressed, for he really desired her as was reported by Al-Zamkhashri: "The external appearance of Muhammad differed from what was inside him." Simply put, on the outside it appeared that Muhammad did not want Zayd to divorce Zainab. But his intentions were the opposite: for Muhammad fell in love with Zainab when he saw her half naked.

The Qur'an tells us that when Muhammad saw Zainab half naked, he fell in love with her, and wanted her as his wife. However, he hesitated because of what people would say about him, snatching the wife of his adopted son. But Muhammad's god came to reprimand him for his hesitation. Strangely, it was Allah who wanted the woman to leave her husband, and to violate all moral laws, so Muhammad could have her. And it's in plain sight in the Qur'an:
"Behold, thou didst say to whom who had received the grace of Allah and thy favor, 'Retain thou (in wedlock) thy wife, and fear Allah.' But thou didst hide in thy heart that which Allah was about to make manifest: thou didst fear the people, but it is more fitting that thou shouldst fear Allah. Then when Zayd had dissolved (his marriage) with her, with the necessary (formality), we joined her in marriage to thee." Surah *Al-Ahzab* (the Allies) 33:37

Little time passed between Surah 33:36, where Allah encouraged Zayd to stay married, and 33:37, where the god of Muhammad commanded Zayd to leave Zainab so Muhammad could marry her. What caused that god to change his mind? Was that god a toy in Muhammad's hand, so a new verse would come down to annul the verse that came before (the one that encouraged Zayd to keep his wife)? Did not Allah *command* Zayd to stay married to Zainab? Was his god unable to keep their house together? How could Muhammad's god find it easy to destroy a home, so Muhammad's desires could be met? Was that a god of justice and mercy?

During his lifetime, Arabs and Muslims criticized Muhammad's behavior, saying he married the divorcée of his own son, which was not legal. But for Muhammad to get out of such a predicament, "Gabriel" was ready to bring down a verse from his god, stating he had never adopted Zayd. Therefore, marrying Zainab would be legal:
"Muhammad is not the father of any of your men, but he is the Messenger of Allah, and the seal of the prophets: and Allah has full knowledge of all things." Surah *Al-Ahzab* (the Allies) 33:40)

This verse made it seem as though Muhammad had forgotten that he told the Muslims a short time before, "Zayd is my son, I inherit him and he inherits me." And it is obvious that he did not care that his actions were the cause of abolishing adoption in Islam (even to this day), just because of his lustful relation with Zainab.[xxviii]

Time and Time again, Muhammad violated the laws of his time, laws of the Bible, and even his own laws. Can this kind of man be trusted?

## Allah Changes his mind!

Muhammad communicated to his early followers in Mecca that the Qiblah, the physical direction of their prayers, should be toward Ka'bah. Once he migrated to Medina, he changed the direction toward Jerusalem, to please the predominant Jewish population in Medina. Then seventeen months later, Allah changed His mind the third time by commanding Muhammad to look toward Mecca and no longer toward Jerusalem. At first Muhammad told his followers to face Jerusalem in prayer. Then he told them since God was everywhere they could face any way they wanted. Then he changed his mind yet again and directed them to pray Mecca (Surah 2:115 versus 2:144). Many scholars believe that the changes in direction were dependent on whether he was trying to please the Jews or the pagans. (Morey, *The Islamic Invasion: Confronting the World's Fastest Growing Religion* [Harvest House Publishers, Eugene, Oregon 1992], p. 146)

## Change of verses according to time

Even for a time at Medina, he was moderate. In Surat al-Baqarah (The Cow) 2, verse 256, it states, **There is no compulsion in religion.** The right direction is henceforth distinct from error. And he who rejecteth false deities and believeth in Allah hath grasped a firm handhold which will never break. Allah is Hearer, Knower.

But it was very different after Muhammad's power was established. When the Muslims armies went forth to attack the surrounding tribes, or other nations, they offered them three options: **accept Islam, pay tribute, or die by the sword** (the Repentance Surat, verse 9: 29).

These stories and the host of many verses in the Qur'an cause even the Muslims to believe that there was abrogation of revelation from Allah on number of occasions.

This is very disgraceful act from a divine being that would change his mind from time to time so deceitfully. In this scenario, the revelation of this kind of divine being cannot be considered trustworthy and counted reliable.

Logically, when a human being changes his statement from time to time for the same situation, even though he has a tendency of doing so, the person is not considered to be a trustworthy person and simply speaking the person is called a liar.

Keeping the fact of abrogation in view, conclusively, it is appropriate to say that the Qur'an is not a book inspired by the God of Abraham, Isaac, and Jacob. Its sources are far from the source it claims for.

In surah 2:106 the Quran says, "We do not abrogate a verse or cause it to be forgotten except that We bring forth [one] better than it or similar to it. Do you not know that Allah is over all things competent?

In Surah 16:101, the Quran says, "And when We substitute a verse in place of a verse - and Allah is most knowing of what He sends down - they say, "**You, [O Muhammad], are but an inventor [of lies].**" But most of them do not know.

These verses distinctly show the DOCTRINE OR ISLAMIC THEOLOGY OF ABROGATION which means that Allah cancelled many verses in the Quran and added different verses. Now an intelligent mind with good and sound logic will question that what made Allah change his mind, and wasn't the initial verses of Allah any good? Why did Allah correct his own work?

The God of the Bible is presented as all wise who even knows the end from the beginning. The Bible says, "God is not a man, that he should lie; neither the son of man, that he should repent (change his mind): hath he said, and shall he not do it? or hath he spoken, and shall he not make it good?" (Numbers 23:19).

But it means that Allah, the god of Islam change his mind and correct himself. Can a person trust such kind god who makes mistakes, change his mind, and correct his own word he has spoken?

According to Surah 16:101, the people of Muhammad's day also had many question marks about his revelation as they realized many contradictions. They were not hesitant to say that Muhammad is an inventor of lies.

Once a person is inconsistent in what he says or promise is consider to be a liar. In the same manner, the prophet who is inconsistent in his revelation leave people with no choice other than considering him an inventor of lies. Either the god who is giving revelation inconsistently and unharmoniously is false or the prophet who is changing revelation presumably his god is acting in this way would be considered untruthful and unreliable.

## SOURCES OF THE QUR'AN

Muhammad was illiterate which is also debatable. He depended on oral information from Christians and especially from Jews. The corruption of oral transmission explains the inaccuracies of the stories. Historical errors include: Mary being the sister of Aaron (Surah 3:31ff), Haman being Pharaoh's minister (Surah.28:38), and the conflation of Gideon and Saul (Surah 2:250).[xxix]

Some of the sources of the Qur'an are:

### 1. The Holy Bible
It was estimated that about 170 quotations from the Holy Bible are present in the Qur'an.[xxx] There are names, events, and prophets in the Qur'an that has directly taken from the Bible. For example, the creation story in six day, Adam and Eve, Cain and Abel, Noah's flood, Lot, Abraham, the story of Abraham offering Isaac as a sacrifice, Moses, Pharaoh, David, Solomon and many other. However, often the stories in the Qur'an are corrupted and confused. Muhammad must have heard these stories from his Jewish friends in Medina, where he lived during the time he said he received most of the revelations which became the Qur'an. At the same time, Muhammad's wives who were Jewesses also had influence on Muhammad in providing the information about the Jewish religion. For example, his seventh wife, Raihana, and ninth, Safiyya, were Jewesses. His first wife, Khadija, had a Christian background. His eighth wife, Maryam, was part of a Christian sect. They undoubtedly shared with him much of the Old and New Testament literature, drama, and prophetic stories. Bishop Waraqa ibn Naufel (Khadija's Uncle) who was an Ebonite Bishop and well familiar with the Holy Bible, but at the same time, he belonged to the cult who denied the deity of Christ. Bishop Naufel provided Muhammad information about the Old and New Testament, but simultaneously, he imparted in him the erroneous teaching about Jesus Christ.

### Qur'anic and Biblical passages

Having hearts where with they understand not, and having eyes where with they see not, and having ears where with they hear not. (Surat al-A'raf [The Heights] 7:179).

Hear this now, O foolish people, Without understanding, Who have eyes and see not, And who have ears and hear not. (Jer. 5:21)

He is the First and the Last, and the Outward and the Inward; and He is the Knower of all things. (Surat al-Hadid [The Iron] 57:3)

I am the First and I am the Last; Besides Me there is no God. (Isa. 44:6)

Surat al-Ma'idah (The Table Spread) 5, Surat Maryam (Mary) 19, Surat al-Imran (The Family of 'Imran) 3, and several other Surahs that are full of New Testament references. The Qur'an mentions Jesus ninety-seven times, plus Zachariah and his son, John, along with the disciples of Jesus. This indicates that Muhammad knew much more than the average Arab of his time about the New Testament Scriptures.

There are 131 passages in the Qur'an in which the Bible is referred to as the Law, Psalms, and the Gospel. Furthermore, numerous passages in the Qur'an so closely parallel passages in the New Testament, which is six hundred years older that the Qur'an, that one can safely conclude that Muhammad borrowed some of the content of his "revelations" from the truly inspired text of the New Testament Scriptures.

And the dwellers of the Fire cry out unto the dwellers of the Garden; Pour on us some water or some of that wherewith Allah hath provided you. (Surat al-A'raf [The Heights] 7:50).

Then he cried and said, "Father Abraham, have mercy on me, and send Lazarus that he may dip the tip of his finger in water and cool my tongue; for I am tormented in this flame." (Luke 16:24)

And when Jesus son of Mary said: O Children of Israel Lo! I am the messenger of Allah unto you, confirming that which was (revealed) before me in the Torah, and bringing good tidings of a messenger who cometh after me, whose name is the Praised One. (Surat al-Saff [The Ranks] 61:6) . . .

The word which you hear is not Mine but the Father's who sent Me . . . But the Helper, the Holy Spirit, whom the Father will send in My name, He will teach you all things, and bring to your remembrance all things that I said to you. (John 14:24, 26)

### 2. The cultic and Heretic Teaching

It is intriguing and instructive to discover why Muhammad did not believe in the Trinity and the divinity or resurrection of Jesus Christ. To understand this, we must examine the prevalent deviant doctrines of Nestorians and his followers, sectarian Christians who migrated to Arabia 140 years before Muhammad's birth. Muhammad apparently drew his denials from their heresy.

There have been many heresies emerged from the very beginning of Christianity who proclaimed the false teaching about Jesus Christ which were non-scriptural and contrary to the apostolic creed. God inspired many of His apostles to write under the inspiration of the Holy Spirit in condemning the false teaching. For example, Arians denied that Jesus is equal to God the Father; Gnostics denied his humanity; where Nestorians denied the union of two natures.

Nestorius was patriarch of Constantinople from AD 428 to 431. Orthodox Christians believed, as per scriptural teaching, that Jesus had two natures, one divine and one human. Although the two were distinct, they were joined together in one person. Nestorius, however, insisted that in Christ Jesus both a divine and a human person acted in unity, but were not the one divine person with both a divine nature and a human nature.

## Muhammad & Nestorians

Most Christian scholars believe that Muhammad came in contact with Nestorians during his business travels to Damascus and Egypt with his uncle's caravans, then later with Khadija's caravans. The Nestorians established monasteries on the caravan routes and entertained travelers like Muhammad, frequently. Buhaira, a Nestorian monk, is recognized as one of the most influential men in Muhammad's knowledge of the Scriptures.

## The Gospel of Barnabas

One of the favorite sources used by Muslims to support their erroneous views of Christ and the Holy Bible is the spurious Gospel of Barnabas. Here in Acts, Barnabas is the friend of Paul (Acts 11:26). However, in the Gospel of Barnabas, he is Paul's bitter enemy. The Gospel of Barnabas is a false Gospel because:
(1). It counteracts "Pauline Christianity";
(2). Its Jesus denies that He is the Messiah; and
(3). Its Jesus prophesies the coming of Muhammad.
Yet, this eighteenth-century forgery is a false document from beginning to end.
Christians and Muslims should reject it because it contradicts both the Bible and the Qur'an.

## 3. Folkloric stories

There were numerous folk stories in circulation during the time of Muhammad. Muhammad borrowed many of these stories in compiling his book. It would be appropriate to document some these stories with their background. These stories emerged from the heretics. The history reveals that many heretics were expelled from the Roman Empire and migrated to Arabic before the time of Muhammad.

1. Muhammad told how the angel Gabriel took him on the winged animal, Al-Buraq, and showed him all the seven levels of heaven in one night. The tale and its details appear originally in The Secrets of Enoch, which predates Muhammad by four centuries.
2. The Seven Sleepers, or Companions of the Cave (Surah 18:8-26) is a story of Greek origin found in a Latin work of Gregory of Tours ('Story of Martyrs' 1:95) and was recognized by Christians as pious fiction.
3. The History of Mary (Surah 19:16-31, 66:12, 3:31-32&37-42, 25:37). Mary is said to be the sister of Aaron, the daughter of Imran (Hebrew *Amran* the father of Moses), and the mother of Jesus. The hadith tell us that Mary's mother was an aged, barren woman who promised to give her child to the temple if God gave it to her (from the *Protevangelium of James the Less*). The hadith also explain that the casting of rods mentioned in the Koran refers to when 6 priests were vying for who would raise Mary. They threw their rods into the river, only Zachariah's rod floated (from *the History of our Holy Father the Aged, the Carpenter (Joseph)*, and Arabic apocryphal book). Mary was denounced as an adulteress but pleaded her innocence (from *Protevangelium* a

Coptic book on the Virgin Mary), and gave birth under a palm tree that aided her (from *History of the Nativity of Mary and the Saviour's Infancy*)

4. The Childhood of Jesus – Jesus spoke from the cradle and created birds of clay which he then turned to life (Surah 3:41-43, 5:119), from *The Gospel of Thomas the Israelite* and *The Gospel of the Infancy* Ch. 1, 36, 46. Jesus was not really crucified (s. 4:156) in accordance with the heretic Basilides (quoted by Iraneus). The Koran erroneously thinks that the Trinity consists of father, mother, and son (s. 4:169, 5:77).

Some other stories from Christian or heretical writers: In the hadith *(Quissas al-Anbial)* God sends angels together dust to create Adam and Azrael brings it from every quarter (Ibn Athir via Abdul Feda). This is from the heretic Marconian who argued that it was an angel (the 'God of the law') who created people, not the true God. The balance of good and bad deeds (Surah 42:16, 101:5-6) is from the 'Testament of Abraham' and from the Egyptian 'Book of the dead.' Two New Testament verses are alluded to: (a) camel through the eye of a needle (S. 7:38, Mt. 19:24), God has prepared for the righteous things that eyes have not seen nor ears heard (Abu Huraira quoting the prophet in *Mishkat* of the Prophet, 1 Cor. 2:9).[xxxi]

**4. Ancient Zoroastrian and Hindu Beliefs**

Arabian and Greek historians tell us that much of the Arabian Peninsula was under Persian rule before and during Muhammad's life. Ibn Hisham tells us that the stories of Rustem, Isfandiyar and ancient Persia were told in Medina and the Quraish used to compare them with tales in the Koran (e.g. the tales told by Nadhr, son of al-Harith).

1. Ascent (*Miraj*) of the prophet (Surah 17:1) – There is a great variation in interpretation. Ibn Ishaq quotes A'isha and the prophet as saying this was an out of body journey. Muhyiad-Din [ibn al-'Arabi] agrees. But Ibn Ishaq also quotes the prophet saying that it was a literal journey. Cotada relates the prophet saying that it was a literal journey into the 7th heaven. In a Zoroastrian story the Magi send one of their number into heaven to get a message from God (*Ormazd*) (from a Pahlavi book *Arta Viraf Namak* – 400 B.H.) Also, the 'Testament of Abraham' tells of Abraham being taken up to heaven in a chariot.

2. Paradise – filled with houris (Surah 55:72, 56:22) – like the 'paries' in Zoroastrianism. The words 'houry', 'djinn', and 'bihist' (Paradise) are derived from Avesta or Pahlavi sources. The 'youths of pleasure' (*ghilunan*) are also in Hindu tales. The name of the Angel of death is taken from the Jews (in Hebrew two names are given, Sammael and Azrael, the latter was borrowed by Islam), but the concept of the angel killing those in hell was taken from Zoroastrianism.

3. Azazil coming from hell – in the Muslim traditions he worshiped God 1000 years in each of the 7 heavens before reaching earth. Then he sat 3000 years by the gates of paradise trying to tempt Adam and Eve and destroy creation. This is very similar to the Zoroastrian tale regarding their devil (*Ahriman*) in the book *Victory of God*. The peacock agreed to let Iblis into Paradise in exchange for a prayer with magical qualities (the *Bundahishnih*) - an association also noted by the Zoroastrians (Eznik in his book *Against Heresies)*.

4. The light of Muhammad was the first created thing (Qissas al-Anbia, Rauzat al Ahbab). The light was divided into 4, then each into 4. Muhammad was the first of the first divisions of light. This light was then placed on Adam and descended to the best descendent. This is virtually identical to the Zoroastrian view which described 4

97

divisions of light (*the Minukhirad, Desatir-i Asmani, Yesht* 19:31-37); the light was placed on the first man (*Jamshid*) and passed to his greatest descendent.
5. The Bridge *Sirat* is a concept from *Dinkart*, but it is named *Chinavad* by the Zoroastrians.
6. The concept that each prophet predicts the next prophet is from *Desatir-i Asmani* where each Zoroastrian prophet predicts the next one. Also, the openings of these books (i.e. the *Desatir-i Asmani*) is "In the name of God, the Giver of gifts, the Beneficent' which is similar to the opening of all the Surahs 'In the name of God the Merciful, the Gracious.'

How could Muhammad have learned these stories? *Rauzat al-Ahbab* tells us that the prophet used to talk to people from all over the region. Al-Kindi accuses the Quran of including foolish old-wives' tales. Also, in *Sirat-Rasul* we learn of the Persian, Salman, who advised Muhammad regarding the battle of the trench and was accused of helping compose the Koran. (The Koran mentions him, though not by name, in Surah 16:105).[xxxii]

## CONTRADICTIONS IN THE QUR'AN

The Muslims claim that the Qur'an is a pure and perfect document on the face the earth. The very same carbon copy of the Qur'an exists in heaven with Allah, god (Surah 85:21-22). If the Qur'an is a perfect book from Allah, then it should be free from any contradictory statement, and since God is thought to be all-knowing God who makes no mistake, so then his Word must be free from mistake. Of course, all verses must be taken in the context. It is an act of cruelty to pick some words or sentences and make it a contradictory statement without studying the entire context. It is certainly important that one shouldn't pull just few verses from here and there and make it a sharp weapon for the author to attack. But when it comes to the Qur'an, there are clear and evident contradictions.

In venerating a book, a person, or any object, one has the absolute right and freedom to say anything he or she likes, but to some extent and to some sort of reality must be well regarded with sufficient emotional attachment at the same time.

Ali Dashti, an Iranian author and a committed Muslim, commented that the errors in the Qur'an were so many that the grammatical rules had to be altered in order to fit the claim that the Qur'an was flawless. He gives numerous examples of these in his book, Twenty-three years: The Life of the Prophet Mohammed. (The only precaution he took before publishing this book was to direct that it be published posthumously.)"

Dashti writes:
"The Qur'an contains sentences which are incomplete and not fully intelligible without the aid of commentaries; foreign words, unfamiliar Arabic words, and words used with other than the normal meaning; adjectives and verbs inflected without observance of the concord of gender and number; illogical and ungrammatically applied pronouns which in rhymed passages are often remote from the subjects. These and other such aberrations in the language have given scope to critics who deny the Qur'an's eloquence...To sum up, more than 100 Qur'anic aberrations from the normal rules and structure of Arabic have been noted."

A contradiction occurs when one statement on a subject excludes the possibility of another. The first one here is a good example. In Surah 19:67, it states that man was created

98

out of nothing. In 15:26, man is created from clay. Since clay is something, we have a contradiction since "nothing" excludes the possibility of "clay." Both cannot be true.

The reality of abrogation (to do away with something, different or better) in the Qur'an has already been discussed which conveys the truth that the Quranic document is not trustworthy since Allah is changing his mind and even making the necessary changes in his own document in heaven.

The reality of abrogation is the fundamental and foundational facet of the contradictions in the Qur'an, which leads to many doctrinal, historical, cosmological, scientific, and even its contradictory statement with the Holy Bible.

| God's Words Don't Change | God's Words Do Change |
|---|---|
| [Yunus 10:64] Theirs are good tidings in the life of the world and in the Hereafter - **There is no changing the Words of Allah -** that is the Supreme Triumph. | [an-Nahl 16:101] **And when We put a revelation in place of (another) revelation, -** and Allah knoweth best what He revealeth- they say: Lo! thou art but inventing. Most of them know not. |
| [al-Kahf 18:27] And recite that which hath been revealed unto thee of the Scripture of thy Lord. **There is none who can change His words,** and thou wilt find no refuge beside Him. | [al-Baqarah 2:106] **Nothing of our revelation (even a single verse) do we abrogate or cause be forgotten, but we bring (in place) one better or the like** thereof. Knowest thou not that Allah is Able to do all things? |
| [al-Hijr 15:9] **Lo! We, even We, reveal the Reminder, and lo! We verily are its Guardian.** | [ar-Ra`d 13:39] **Allah effaceth what He will, and establisheth (what He will),** and with Him is the source of ordinance. |

## Historical Blunders in Qur'an:

In several Surahs of the Qur'an confuses Mary the mother of Jesus [Miriam in Hebrew] with Miriam the sister of Aaron and Moses, and daughter of Amram which is about 1400 years off. Ironically, Muhammad makes Moses Jesus' uncle even though they are hundreds of years apart from each other. One might ask how it is possible? Yes, it is possible once a person depends on non-factual and oral-traditions.

**Surah: 19:27-28** - "At length she brought (the babe) to her people, carrying him (in her arms), They said: "O Mary! Truly a strange thing has thou brought!" "O sister of Aaron, thy father was not a man of evil, nor your mother a woman unchaste!"

**Surah: 66:12** - And Mary, the Daughter of Imran, who guarded her chastity, and We breathed into (her body) of our spirit; and she testified to the truth of the words of her Lord, and of His revelations, and was one of the devout (servants).[xxxiii]

**Did Mohammad visit Al-Masjid Al-Aqsa (Surah 17:1)?**
The problem is that there was no Masjid Al-Aqsa nor any other masjid during the life of Mohammad since Islam entered Palestine after Omar bin El Khattab conquered Palestine after the death of the prophet. Al-Masjid Al-Aqsa was built almost sixty years after the death of Mohammad by Marwan bin Abdel Malik.

### Did Pharaoh use crucifixion (Surah 7:120-125)?

Pharaoh used crucifixion in dealing with the sorcerers - a practice which historical evidence gives no precedent to before the Babylonian Empire. This is once again a problem of historical compression.

### Did Samaritan help the Israelite to build the Golden Calf?

A Samaritan helped the Israelites build the golden calf, and it mooed after coming out of the fire.

In Surah 20:85-88, 95 we read:
"He [Allah] said, 'We have tempted thy people since thou didst leave them. The Samaritans has led them into error.' Then Moses returned...and we cast them [(gold) ornaments], as the Samaritan also threw them, into the fire.' (Then he brought out for them a Calf, a mere body that lowed; and they said, 'This is your god, and the god of Moses, whom he has forgotten.') ...Moses said, 'And thou, Samaritan, what was thy business?'"

Now here is the question, how can a Samaritan have led the Israelites astray at the time of Moses (approx. 1400 B.C.) when the city of Samaria was founded by King Omri about 870 B.C.? The Samaritans did not exist until after the exile of the Northern Kingdom of Israel and the resettlement of the area under King Sargon II in 722 B.C. with non-Israelites who then adopted a syncretism (mixture) between the religion of the Jews and their own polytheistic background. The Samaritans did not exist until 530 years after Moses. By this mistake alone, the Qur'an can be rendered unreliable and certainly not an inerrant work of God.

### Was Alexander the Great a devout Muslim and lived a long life? (Surah 18:89-98)

Alexander the Great was a devout Muslim and lived to a ripe old age.

Historical records however show that Alexander the Great died young at 33 years of age (b. 356 B.C. - d. 323 B.C.), and believed he was divine, forcing others to recognize him as such. In India on the Hyphasis River (now Beas) Alexander erected twelve altars to twelve Olympian gods. Once again, the Qur'an shows errors in historical and religious fact.

## Self-contradictory Quranic verses

### Which one is correct?

**Qur'an: 2:256: "Let there be no compulsion in religion:** Truth stands out clear from Error: whoever rejects evil and believes in Allah hath grasped the most trustworthy hand-hold that never breaks. And Allah heareth and knoweth all things,"

### OR

**Qur'an: 9:29:** Fight those who do not profess the true faith (Islam) till they pay the poll tax (jizya) with the hand of humility.

**Qur'an: 9:5:** Then, when the sacred months have passed, slay the idolaters wherever ye find them and take them captive, and besiege them and prepare for them each ambush....

**Qur'an: 47:4:** When you meet the unbelievers in the Jihad strike off their heads....

**Qur'an: 2:191:** And slay (kill) them wherever ye catch them, and turn them out from where they have turned you out such is the reward of those who suppress faith.

**Qur'an: 8: 65:** O Apostle! Rouse the believers to the fight...(against) unbelievers.

Very often apologetics claim that, Islam is a religion of peace and there is no compulsion. Yet, punishment of an apostate in Islam is, of course, death penalty.[xxxiv]

### What was man created from, water, blood, clay, dust, or nothing?

**Water:** "And He it is Who hath created man from water..." Surah 25:54
**Blood:** "Created man, out of a (mere) clot of congealed blood," (96:2).
**Clay:** "We created man from sounding clay, from mud molded into shape, (15:26).
**Dust:** "The similitude of Jesus before Allah is as that of Adam; He created him from dust, then said to him: "Be". And he was," (3:59).
**Out of Nothing:** "But does not man call to mind that We created him before out of nothing?" (19:67, Yusuf Ali). Also, 52:35).

"He has created man from a sperm-drop; and behold this same (man) becomes an open disputer! (16:4).

### Is it lawful to marry the wife of an adopted son or not?

It is permitted
> "Behold! Thou didst say to one who had received the grace of Allah and thy favor: "Retain thou (in wedlock) thy wife, and fear Allah." But thou didst hide in thy heart that which Allah was about to make manifest: thou didst fear the people, but it is more fitting that thou shouldst fear Allah. Then when Zaid had dissolved (his marriage) with her, with the necessary (formality), We joined her in marriage to thee: in order that (in future) there may be no difficulty to the Believers in (the matter of) marriage with the wives of their adopted sons, when the latter have dissolved with the necessary (formality) (their marriage) with them. And Allah's command must be fulfilled" (Surah 33:37),

> yet

> "It is forbidden Allah has not made for any man two hearts in his (one) body: nor has He made your wives whom ye divorce by Zihar your mothers: nor has He made your adopted sons your sons. Such is (only) your (manner of) speech by your mouths. But Allah tells (you) the Truth, and He shows the (right) Way. Call them by (the names of) their fathers: that is juster in the sight of Allah. But if ye know not their father's (names, call them) your Brothers in faith, or your maulas. But there is no blame on you if ye make a mistake therein: (what counts is) the intention of your hearts: and Allah is Oft-Returning, Most Merciful" (Surah 33:4-5).

### Is Allah the one Creator or Allah is the best one among many Creators?

Allah is "the best of creators"
> "Will ye call upon Baal and forsake the Best of Creators" (37:125).
> "Then we developed the drop into a hanging (embryo), then developed the hanging (embryo) into a bite-size (fetus), then created the bite-size (fetus) into bones, then covered the bones with flesh. We thus produce a new creature. Most blessed is GOD, the best Creator (23:14).

Allah alone is "the creator of all things"
> "GOD is the Creator of all things, and He is in full control of all things" (39:62).

**Will all Muslims go to Hell for some time or straight to Heaven?**

Every Muslim will go to Hell (for at least some time)

> *"By your Lord, we will certainly summon them, together with the devils, and will gather them around Hell, humiliated. Then we will pick out from each group the most ardent opponent of the Most Gracious. We know full well those who are most deserving of burning therein. Every single one of you must see it; this is an irrevocable decision of your Lord"* (Surah 19:68-71).

Since a Muslim has no assurance, that's why when a Muslim dies, the fellow Muslims send prayers of intercession for the dying soul to enter heaven. There is no assurance of salvation and no certainty of heaven, even Muhammad didn't have any assurance where he would go after his death; whereas Jesus said with a great confidence, He will go to his Father's house....... (John 14:1), To the dying thief on the cross once he made the confession of his sins, Jesus said to him, "Today you will be with me in paradise" (Luke 23:43). to his while another passage states that:

**One who dies in Jihad will go to Paradise immediately.**

The specific Hadith in which the number of virgins is specified is Hadith Al-Tirmidhi in the Book of Sunnah (volume IV, chapters on The Features of Paradise as described by the Messenger of Allah, chapter 21, About the Smallest Reward for the People of Paradise. The same hadith is also quoted by Ibn Kathir in his Quranic commentary (Tafsir) of Surah Al-Rahman:
"The Prophet Muhammad was heard saying: 'The smallest reward for the people of paradise is an abode where there are 80,000 servants and 72 wives, over which stands a dome decorated with pearls, aquamarine, and ruby, as wide as the distance from Al-Jabiyah [a Damascus suburb] to Sana'a [Yemen]."

> *"In the Gardens of Paradise, Facing one another on thrones, Round them will be passed a cup of pure wine; White, delicious to the drinkers, Neither they will have any kind of hurt, abdominal pain, headache, or sin, nor will they suffer intoxication from it. And with them will be chaste females, restraining their glances, with wide and beautiful eyes."* (37:40-48)

> *"Verily! The righteous will be in Paradise. Among Gardens and Springs; Dressed in fine silk and also in thick silk, facing each other, and We shall marry them to Houris with wide, lovely eyes."* (44:51-55)

> *"Verily, for those who fear Allah there will be Gardens in Paradise, filled with Delight. Enjoying in that which their Lord has bestowed on them, and the fact that their Lord saved them from the torment of the blazing Fire. The Lord will say: 'Eat and drink with happiness because of what you used to do'. They will recline with ease on thrones arranged in ranks. And We shall marry them to Houris with wide lovely eyes."* (52: 17-20)

> *"Reclining upon the couches lined with silk brocade, and the fruits of the Gardens will be near at hand. Then which of the Blessings of your Lord will you deny? Wherein will*

*be those houris, restraining their glances upon their husbands, whom no man or jinn has opened their hymens with sexual intercourse before. Then which of the Blessings of your Lord will you deny? In beauty, they are like rubies and coral. Then which of the Blessings of your Lord will you deny?"* (55:54-59)

*"Therein gardens will be fair wives good and beautiful; Then which of the Blessings of your Lord will you deny? Houris restrained in pavilions; Then which of the Blessings of your Lord will you deny? Whom no man has opened their hymens with sexual intercourse before. Then which of the Blessings of your Lord will you deny? Reclining on green cushions and rich beautiful mattresses. Then which of the Blessings of your Lord will you deny?"* (55:70-77)

*"...We created the houris and made them virgins, loving companions for those on the right hand...."* (56:37-40)

*"As for the righteous, they shall surely triumph. Theirs shall be gardens and vineyards, and high-bosomed virgins for companions: a truly overflowing cup."* (78:31-34)

Two points need to be noted. First, there is no mention anywhere in the Qur'an of the actual number of virgins available in paradise, and second, the dark-eyed damsels are available for all Muslims, not just martyrs. It is in the Islamic Traditions that we find the 72 virgins in heaven specified: in a Hadith (Islamic Tradition) collected by Al-Tirmidhi (died 892 AD) in the Book of Sunan (volume IV, chapters on The Features of Paradise as described by the Messenger of Allah [Prophet Muhammad], chapter 21, About the Smallest Reward for the People of Paradise, (Hadith 2687). The same hadith is also quoted by Ibn Kathir (died 1373 CE ) in his Quranic commentary (Tafsir) of Surah Al-Rahman (55), verse 72: "The Prophet Muhammad was heard saying: 'The smallest reward for the people of paradise is an abode where there are 80,000 servants and 72 wives, over which stands a dome decorated with pearls, aquamarine, and ruby, as wide as the distance from Al-Jabiyyah [a Damascus suburb] to Sana'a [Yemen]'."

## WHAT A DISCOURAGEMENT THERE WILL BE... IF THERE WON'T BE ANY VIRGIN AVAILABLE IN PARADISE?

Steve Keohane in his book called "True History of Islam, Mohammed and the Quran" has highlighted the fact that the famous passage that talk about the martyrs who die in Jihad will go straight to paradise and they will be given the seventy-two virgins is based on the word hur, which is an adjective in the feminine plural meaning simply "white."
Islamic tradition insists the term hur stands for "houri," which means virgin, but Mr. Luxenberg who teaches at the Saarland University in Germany insists that this is a forced misreading of the text. In both ancient Aramaic and in at least one respected dictionary of early Arabic, **hur means "white raisin."**[xxxv]

Logically speaking, as the God of Abraham, Isaac and Jacob has commanded in His Ten Commandments given through Moses stating that **"Thou shalt not kill"** (Exodus 20:13), how could the same God allow the one who kills innocent people to go straight to paradise and even give him favor of having seventy-two virgins by his side to satisfy his sexual desire endlessly. It is simply a lie from the pit of hell and with this lie, so many Muslims have been deceived, and especially young children (boys and girls) who have been brain washed, and their parents have been telling such kind of lies to their children with such serious and deep ignorance. <u>One should also wonder, if a young man who is martyr in Jihad will get seventy-two virgins, what about young suicide woman or small girl bomber? Islam teaches that the young girls and women who participate in Jihad will get the husband (s) of their choice.</u>

## Is Wine Good or bad?

Strong drink and ... are only an infamy of **Satan's handiwork**.
*"O you who believe, intoxicants, and gambling, and the altars of idols, and the games of chance are abominations of the devil; you shall avoid them, that you may succeed"* [(5:90), also 2:219].

Yet

In Paradise are rivers of wine
*"The allegory of Paradise that is promised for the righteous is this: it has rivers of unpolluted water, and rivers of fresh milk, and **rivers of wine** - delicious for the drinkers - and rivers of strained honey. They have all kinds of fruits therein, and forgiveness from their Lord. (Are they better) or those who abide forever in the hellfire, and drink hellish water that tears up their intestines?"* [(47:15), also 83:22,25].

How does Satan's handiwork get into Paradise?

## When did Pharaoh Command the Killing of the Sons of Hebrews?

When Moses was a Prophet and spoke God's truth to Pharaoh

*"We sent Moses with our signs and a profound authority. To Pharaoh, Haamaan, and Qaaroon. But they said, "A magician; a liar." And when he showed them the truth from us, they said, "Kill the sons of those who believed with him, and spare their daughters." Thus, the scheming of the disbelievers is always wicked"* (40:23-25)

**or**

When he was still an infant

"When we revealed to your mother what we revealed. Saying: `Throw him into the box, then throw him into the river. The river will throw him onto the shore, to be picked up by an enemy of Mine and an enemy of his.' I showered you with love from Me, and I had you made before My watchful eye" (20:38-39)?

## Was Pharaoh Drowned or Saved when chasing Moses and the Israelites?

He was Saved.

*"We delivered the Children of Israel across the sea. Pharaoh and his troops pursued them, aggressively and sinfully. When drowning became a reality for him, he said, "I believe that there is no god except the One in whom the Children of Israel have believed; I am a submitter." Too late! For you have rebelled already, and chose to be a transgressor. Today, we will preserve your body, to set you up as a lesson for future*

104

*generations."* Unfortunately, many people are totally oblivious to our signs" (10: 90-92),

He was drowned:

*"We supported Moses with nine profound miracles - ask the Children of Israel. When he went to them, Pharaoh said to him, "I think that you, Moses, are bewitched." He said, "You know full well that no one can manifest these except, obviously, the Lord of the heavens and the earth. I think that you, Pharaoh, are doomed." When he pursued them, as he chased them out of the land, we drowned him, together with those who sided with him, all of them"* (17:101-103; 28:40; 43:55).

## Will Non-Muslims enter Paradise or go to Hell?

Yes, Non-Muslims will enter Paradise:

*"Surely, those who believe, those who are Jewish, the Christians, and the converts; anyone who (1) believes in GOD, and (2) believes in the Last Day, and (3) leads a righteous life, will receive their recompense from their Lord. They have nothing to fear, nor will they grieve"* (Surah 2:62; 5:69).

No, Non-Muslims will not enter Paradise:

*"Pagans indeed are those who say that GOD is the Messiah, son of Mary. The Messiah himself said, "O Children of Israel, you shall worship GOD; my Lord and your Lord." Anyone who sets up any idol beside GOD, GOD has forbidden Paradise for him, and his destiny is Hell. The wicked have no helpers"* (Surah 5:72; 3:85).

## What is the punishment for adultery?

*"The adulteress and the adulterer you shall whip each of them a hundred lashes. Do not be swayed by pity from carrying out God's law, if you truly believe in GOD and the Last Day. And let a group of believers witness their penalty.* (24:2).

OR

*"Those who commit adultery among your women, you must have four witnesses against them, from among you. If they do bear witness, then you shall keep such women in their homes until they die, or until GOD creates an exit for them. The couple who commits adultery shall be punished. If they repent and reform, you shall leave them alone. GOD is Redeemer, Most Merciful"* **(Surah 4:15-16).**

## The punishment for women and men equal in Surah 24 but different in Surah 4?

## Moses and the Injil?

Jesus is born more than 1,000 years after Moses, but in Surah 7:157 Allah speaks to Moses about what is written in the Injil [the book given to Jesus].

## The event of worship of the golden calf:

The Israelites repented about worshipping the golden calf BEFORE Moses returned from the mountain

*"During his absence, Moses' people made from their jewelry the statue of a calf, complete with the sound of a calf. Did they not see that it could not speak to them, or guide them in any path? They worshipped it, and thus turned wicked. Finally, when*

105

*they regretted their action, and realized that they had gone astray, they said, "Unless our Lord redeems us with His mercy, and forgives us, we will be losers."* (7:148-149),

yet

They refused to repent but rather continued to worship the calf until Moses came back *They said, "We will continue to worship it, until Moses comes back."* (20:91).

Does Aaron share in their guilt? No [20:85-90], yes [20:92, 7:151].

**How long does it take to reach Allah?**
*"All matters are controlled by Him from the heaven to the earth. To Him, the day is equivalent to* **one thousand** *of your years"* (Surah 32:5, 70:4)

**OR**

*The angels, with their reports, climb to Him in a day that equals* **fifty thousand** *years"* (Surah 70:4)

**"Palm tree talking to Mary" (Surah 19:25).**
First of all, Bethlehem is a mountainous city where no palm trees grow anyway. Secondly, dates from a palm tree mature in the summer time not the cold winter of December. Thirdly Christ was born in a manger. Fourthly it takes a superman to be able to shake the trunk of a palm tree. A second interesting point about Mary is the story of the date palm speaking and offering its fruit to her (Surah 19:23). This legend is easily traced to similar legends found in the apocryphal "Protoevangelium of James" the "Pseudo-Matthew" and "the Gospel of the Nativity of Mary" all of which have been dated to the fourth to sixth centuries, and were again believed by the sects found in Arabia. (Information on Quranic sources may be found in Rev. W. St. Clair Tisdall's *The Religion of the Crescent*).

**Did the Jews believe Ezra is the Son of God (Surah 9:30)?**
The Jews believe that Ezra is the Son of God - the Messiah. This never has been a tenet of Judaism. This is a clear problem of distorted knowledge of other religions and historical fact.

**What is The Trinity?**
According to the Qur'an (Surah 5:116, 5:73-75) the Christians believe in "three Gods" - Father, Mother, and Son. This shows the influence of heretical 'Christian' sects in central Arabia at the time of Muhammad.
In contrast, Christianity has always distinctly stated that the Trinity is the Father, Son, and Holy Spirit. The teaching of the Qur'an on the Trinity has undoubtedly led to confusion among many Muslims on what the Bible (*and thus Christianity*) teaches about the Triune God.

## Scientific Errors in the Qur'an

**Is the earth flat or round? 88: 20**
The earth has been flattened. An obvious contradiction to simple science.

**Where does the sun set?**
Surah 18:86 claims that the sun sets in a spring of murky water.

**Why did Allah create Stars?**
**Quran-67:5:** And We have (from of old) adorned the lowest heaven (sky) with lamps, and We have made such (Lamps as) missiles to drive away Satan (Evils)...
**Quran-37:6-8:** We have indeed decorated the lower heaven (sky) with (in) the stars, (for beauty) and for guard against all obstinate rebellious Satan. So, they should not strain their ears in the direction of the Exalted Assembly but be cast away from every side.

*Thus, the stars are nothing but missiles to throw at devils so that they may not eavesdrop on the heavenly council. Heavenly council? Here Qur'an is actually talking/describing about falling (shooting) stars. Superstitious minds of Qur'an believed that the sky is the roof (seven firmaments) over the earth where kingdom of Allah situated and there in Allah's kingdom daily assembly (Allah and His Angels) sits to discuss how to run Allah's business on earth. So, Allah does not want Satan to listen Allah's secret conversation with His Angels (p. 1191of Maulana Yousuf Ali's Shanrnazul).*[xxxvi]

**Why were Mountains created?**

**(Qur'an- 21:31):** ...We have set on earth firm mountains, lest it should shake with them.
**(Quran-16:15):** And he has cast the earth firm mountains lest it shake with you...
**(Quran-31:10):** He created the heavens without supports that you can see, and has cast onto the earth firm mountains lest it shake with you...

*It is clearly understood that Quranic author was completely ignorant about the geological reasoning for existence of mountains. He saw that mountains are huge and heavy. So, He (Allah) thought mountains actually prevent Shaking (Earthquake) of the earth. Fact is, this particular reason for existence of mountains is a direct contradiction with modern geological knowledge. Geology proves to us that movement of tectonic plates, or earthquake itself causes mountains to be formed. Besides, we know very well that, every year several dozens of earthquakes happen on earth. Then what is the result of Allah's promise? Can we believe that, Mountains are there to prevent earthquake?*[xxxvii]

The Quran confesses very honestly that Satan threw some misunderstanding in the revelation given to Muhammad.

Sahih International
And We did not send before you any messenger or prophet except that when he spoke [or recited], Satan threw into it [some misunderstanding]. But Allah abolishes that which Satan throws in; then Allah makes precise His verses. And Allah is Knowing and Wise.

# CONFLICTS BETWEEN THE QURAN AND THE BIBLE:

These are JUST A VERY FEW of the major conflicts between the Quran and the Bible.

| The Quran | The Bible | Comment |
|---|---|---|
| ′ritten by Mohammed, but y compiled post-mortem by who claimed to have heard ammed speak, late 7th, early 8th ries AD. | Moses wrote around 1440 BC. The remaining Old Testament books were completed by 300 BC. Most of the OT Bible stood the test of 1500 years before Mohammed arrived. | The Quran is ultimate revisionism, refuting and redefining great Biblical truths that were already established for 700-2000 years. |
| He taught Adam all the names, presented them to the angels; He said: Tell me the names of if you are right. said: Glory be to Thee! we have nowledge but that which Thou aught us; surely, Thou art the ∨ing, the Wise. id: O Adam! inform them of names. Then when he had ned them of their names, He Did I not say to you that I surely ′ what is ghaib (unknown) in the ens and the earth and (that) I ′ what you manifest and what ıide? ↓when We said to the angels: ∶ obeisance to Adam they did ance. ä 2:31-34 | And out of the ground the LORD God formed every beast of the field, and every fowl of the air; and brought them unto Adam to see what he would call them: and whatsoever Adam called every living creature that was the name thereof. And Adam gave names to all cattle, and to the fowl of the air, and to every beast of the field; but for Adam there was not found a help meet for him. Genesis 2:19-20 | The Quran contradicts the Bible, which says Adam named the animals. Koran says God named the animals, told the names to Adam, then made him recite the list before the angels. Then the angels bowed down to Adam. |
| he Shaitan (Satan) made them fall from it, and caused them to ′t from that (state) in which they ä 2:36 | And when the woman saw that the tree was good for food, and that it was pleasant to the eyes, and a tree to be desired to make one wise, she took of the fruit thereof, and did eat, and gave also unto her husband with her; and he did eat. Genesis 3:6 | The Quran teaches that Satan made Adam and Eve fall, but the Bible clearly shows that it was an independent choice of Eve, then Adam. |
| it moved on with them amid ′s like mountains; and Nuh h) called out to his son, and he | And Noah went in, and his sons, and his wife, and his sons' wives with him, into the ark, because of the waters | The Quran says that one of Noah's sons refused to go on the ark, choosing to go to a mountain - and was drowned. |

| | | |
|---|---|---|
| was aloof: O my son! embark with us and be not with the unbelievers. He said: I will betake myself for refuge to a mountain that shall protect me from the water. Nuh said: There is no protector today from Allah's punishment but He Who has mercy; and a wave intervened between them, so he was of the drowned. Surah 11:42-43 | of the flood. Genesis 7:7 | |
| ...then we **made a casting** of them, and thus did the **Samiri (Samaritan)** suggest. So, he brought forth for them a calf, a (mere) body, which **had a mooing sound**, so they said: This is your god and the god of Musa (Moses), but he forgot. Surah 20:87-88 | And he bought the hill Samaria of Shemer for two talents of silver, and built on the hill, and **called the name of the city** which he built, after the name of Shemer, owner of the hill, **Samaria.** 1 Kings 16:24 | The Quran says that a Samaritan created the Golden Calf for Israe the wilderness. *It mooed.* There were no Samaritans until many hundreds of years later. |
| And when Musa prayed for drink for his people, We said: Strike the rock with your staff. So there gushed from it **twelve springs; each tribe knew its drinking place.** Surah 2:60 | Behold, I will stand before thee there upon the rock in Horeb; and thou shalt **smite the rock, and there shall come water out of it that** the people may drink. And Moses did so in the sight of the elders of Israel. Exodus 17:6 | The Quran declared that when Moses struck the rock, twelve springs were created. This is add facts to an event that happened 2,000 years before Mohammed's time. At Elim, the children of Isr did find 12 springs of water. It appears that the Quran has combined two completely separa stories. |
| They said: Call on your Lord for our sake to make it plain to us what her color is. Musa said: He says, Surely, she is a **yellow cow**; her color is intensely yellow, giving delight to the beholders. Surah 2:69 | This is the ordinance of the law which the LORD hath commanded, saying, Speak unto the children of Israel, that they bring thee a **red heifer** without spot, wherein is no blemish, and upon which never came yoke. Numbers 19:2 | The Quran says that God ordere Moses to sacrifice a **yellow** cow Israel's sins, but the Bible says it was a **red** heifer. (Surah 2:73 ad "strike a dead body with a part o the sacrificed cow, thus Allah br the dead to life.") This was neve reported in the Bible. |
| **Pharaoh said: "O Haman!** Build me a lofty palace, that I may attain the ways and means- The ways and means of (reaching) the heavens, and that I may mount up to the god of Moses: But as far as I am concerned, | Then the **king Ahasuerus said** unto Esther the queen and to Mordecai the Jew, Behold, **I have given Esther the house of Haman**, and him they have hanged upon the gallows, **because he laid** | The Quran attempts to move Ha from King Ahasuerus of Shusha Pharaoh of Egypt; placing Hama over 1000 years before his time. Instead of Haman building a gal for Mordechai, the Koran says h was building a tower for Pharao |

| | | |
|---|---|---|
| nk (Moses) is a liar!" Surah 6 | his hand upon the Jews. Esther 8:7 | (similar to Babel) even as Pharaoh declared Moses a liar. |
| ou not know that Allah's is the dom of the heavens and the ., and that besides Allah you no guardian or helper? h 2.107 | But unto the Son he saith, Thy throne, O God, is for ever and ever: a scepter of righteousness is the scepter of thy kingdom. Hebrews 1:8 | The Quran totally denies the kingdom of Jesus Christ, and completely excludes the role of Jesus Christ as Savior of the world, giving all power to Allah. |
| eive) the baptism of Allah, and is better than Allah in baptizing? Him do we serve. Surah 2.138 | One Lord, one faith, one baptism. Ephesians 4:5<br><br>John answered, saying unto them all, I indeed baptize you with water; but one mightier than I cometh, the latchet of whose shoes I am not worthy to unloose: he shall baptize you with the Holy Ghost and with fire: Luke 3:16 | The Quran would totally ignore and replace New Testament baptism. The Bible says there is only one correct baptism. It is a baptism of water and of spirit. "Then Peter said unto them, Repent, and be baptized every one of you in the name of Jesus Christ for the remission of sins, and ye shall receive the gift of the Holy Ghost." Acts 2:38 |
| do **blaspheme** who say God is st, the Son of Mary. h 5:75<br><br>Jesus) was nothing but a servant hom We bestowed favor. h 42:59 | And he (Jesus) said unto them, Ye are from beneath; I am from above: ye are of this world; I am not of this world. I said therefore unto you, that ye shall die in your sins: for **if ye believe not that I am he, ye shall die in your sins.** John 8:23,24 | Islam is completely antichrist. Its denial of the deity of Jesus Christ is a foundational belief. Its hostility toward Christianity cannot be overstated. It is murderous, and has a stated purpose of annihilating all Christians. |
| so seeketh as religion other than Surrender (to Allah) it will not be pted from him, and he will be a in the Hereafter. Surah 3:85<br><br>surely disbelieve who say: Lo! h is the Messiah, son of Mary. ... whoso ascribeth partners unto h, for him Allah hath forbidden dise. His abode is the Fire. For doers there will be no helpers. h 5:72 | Jesus answered and said unto him, Verily, verily, I say unto thee, Except a man be born again, he cannot see the kingdom of God. ...Except a man be born of water and of the Spirit, he cannot enter into the kingdom of God. John 3:3,5 Then said Jesus unto them again, Verily, verily, I say unto you, I am the door of the sheep. ...by me if any man enter in, he shall be saved. John 10:7,9 | Mohammed plainly said that all Christians go to hell. He directly refuted the teachings of Jesus. Jesus Christ asserted that He is the only door to the kingdom of God.<br><br>Speaking of Jesus Christ, Peter said, "Neither is there salvation in any other: for there is none other name under heaven given among men, whereby we must be saved," Acts 4:12.[xxxviii] |

110

After studying the contradiction between the Bible and the Qur'an, one might wonder what he should believe and what he shouldn't? Either he should follow the Bible or the Qur'an?

First of all, one should take into consideration the secular historical facts, which are unbiased toward the Bible and the Qur'an. For example, as the Qur'an claimed that the Samaritan helped Israelites to make a golden calf, and at the time of this event, Samaritans were not in existence on the stage of the World History, then the Qur'an loses its case and the Bible wins. This can also be applied to Haman, who is associated with Pharaoh in Egypt, whereas Haman is associated with King Ahasuerus in Persia. The gap between Pharaoh and Ahasuerus is over 1000 years.

It is very pathetic that Muhammad has mixed up so many Biblical events, and people in the Qur'an, because of him being illiterate and because of his sole dependency on the oral narratives, heretic teaching, and the traditions from here and there.

Secondly, one should take Biblical account more seriously than the Quranic narratives not necessarily that the Bible was in existence before the Qur'an, even though it shouldn't be taken lightly at large, but much more than the fact that the Qur'an itself admonishes to consult with the Bible if someone has doubts and question marks about the Qur'an.

"And if thou (Muhammad) art in doubt concerning that which We reveal unto thee, then question those who read the Scripture (that was) before thee. Verily the Truth from thy Lord hath come unto thee. So be not thou of the waverers" **(Surah 10:94).**

"And We sent not (as Our messengers) before thee other than men whom We inspired - Ask the followers of the Remembrance if ye know not!" **(Surah 16:43).**

The Questioning About The Qur'an is Prohibited:

It is sad to say that Muslims are discouraged from asking questions about their own faith.

*"O ye who believe! Ask not questions about things which if made plain to you, may cause you trouble. Some people before you did ask such questions, and on that account lost their faith."* (Surah 5:101-102)

It appears that questioning or inquiring about Islam is forbidden because it can cause you to lose faith in Islam! This insecurity causes people to keep on believing blindly without enjoying its essence. It is so to speak a RELIGIOUS SLAVERY.

Generally, when someone has something to hide, they do not want it to be questioned.

A famous commentator on the Qur'an, Maududi, warns Muslims against probing too deeply into Islam:

"The Holy Prophet himself forbade people to ask questions--so do not try to probe into such things." (Maududi, The Meaning of the Qur'an, Vol. III, pgs. 76-77)

Bukhari's Hadith tells us how Mohammed responded to those who asked questions:

*"The prophet was asked about things which he did not like, and when the questioner insisted, the Prophet got angry."* (Vol. 1, no. 92)

*"The prophet got angry and his cheeks or his face became read."* (Vol. 1, no. 91)

"We must ask ourselves these questions:

What kind of god is Allah who hates people for asking questions? This is not like the God of the Bible who encourages us to seek, to ask, and to knock!

Why did Muhammad hate the person so viciously who asked him questions?

Why were people warned not to ask any questions?

What is Islam trying to hide?

Is Islam so weak that merely asking questions threaten to destroy it?

Do Muslims assume that blind faith is the way to Islam?"[xxxix]

On the other hand, the people have always been examining the Bible to see if its teachings are true or not.

*Now the Bereans were of more noble character than the Thessalonians, for they received the message with great eagerness and **examined the Scriptures** every day to see if what Paul said was true.* (Acts 17:11)

## SOME QURANIC TEACHING ABOUT:

### 1. Woman:

Muslims often claim that Muhammad promoted women's rights. Islam's most trusted sources, however, tell a different story. According to the Qur'an, the testimony of a woman is only half as reliable as a man's testimony. Muhammad explains why in the hadith, where he declares that women are less intelligent and more immoral than men. When we combine these teachings with other Qur'anic teachings (e.g., Allah allowing men to beat their wives into submission, to rape their female captives, and to have sex with prepubescent girls), Muhammad's view of women becomes perfectly clear.

Here are some sources to consider:
Qur'an 4:34—Men are in charge of women, because Allah hath made the one of them to excel the other, and because they spend of their property (for the support of women). So good women are the obedient, guarding in secret that which Allah hath guarded. As for those from whom ye fear rebellion, admonish them and banish them to beds apart, and scourge them. Then if they obey you, seek not a way against them. Lo! Allah is ever High, Exalted, Great.

112

**Sahih al-Bukhari 2658**—The Prophet said: "Isn't the witness of a woman equal to half of that of a man?" The women said: "Yes." He said: "This is because of the deficiency of her mind."

**Sahih al-Bukhari 1052**—The Prophet said: ".... I saw the Hell-fire and I had never seen such a horrible sight. I saw that most of the inhabitants were women." The people asked: "O Allah's Apostle! Why is it so?" The Prophet said: "Because of their ungratefulness." It was asked whether they are ungrateful to Allah. The Prophet said: "They are ungrateful to their companions of life (husbands) and ungrateful to good deeds."

**Sahih Muslim 142**—[Muhammad said]: O womenfolk, you should give charity and ask much forgiveness for I saw you in bulk amongst the dwellers of Hell. A wise lady among them said: Why is it, Messenger of Allah, that our folk are in bulk in Hell? Upon this the Holy Prophet observed: You curse too much and are ungrateful to your spouses. I have seen none lacking in common sense and failing in religion but (at the same time) robbing the wisdom of the wise, besides you. Upon this the woman remarked: What is wrong with our common sense and with our religion? He (the Holy Prophet) observed: Your lack of common sense (can be well judged from the fact) that the evidence of two women is equal to one man; that is a proof of the lack of common sense.[xl]

Sexual relations with captive female slaves is acceptable (Surah 23:5,6 70:30)

*SAHIH MUSLIM*

*The Messenger of Allah (peace be upon him) said: The (permanent) inhabitants of the Fire are those who are doomed to it, and verily they would neither die nor live in it (Qur'an al-Qur'an, xx.47; liiixii.13). But the people whom the Fire would afflict (temporarily) on account of their sins, or so said (the narrator) "on account of their misdeeds," He would cause them to die till they would be turned into charcoal. Then they would be granted intercession and would be brought in groups and would be spread on the rivers of Paradise and then it would be said: O inhabitants of Paradise, pour water over them; then they would sprout forth like the sprouting of seed in the silt carried by flood. A man among the people said: (It appears) as if the Messenger of Allah lived in the steppe.*

*AL-MUWATTA of Imam Malik (Hadith)*
*Abdullah ibn Abbas*
*Then I saw the Fire - and I have never seen anything more hideous than what I saw today - and I saw that most of its people were women.'*
*They said, 'Why, Messenger of Allah?'*
*He said, 'Because of their ungratefulness (kufr),'*
*Someone said, 'Are they ungrateful to Allah?'*
*He said, 'They are ungrateful to their husbands and they are ungrateful for good behavior (towards them). Even if you were to behave well towards one of them for a whole lifetime and then she were to see you do something (that she did not like) she would say that she had never seen anything good from you.'"*

## 2. Paradise

"The true servants of Allah will be well provided for, feasting on fruit, and honored in gardens of delight. Reclining face to face upon soft couches, they shall be served with a goblet filled at a gushing fountain… delicious to those who drink it. They shall sit with bashful, dark-eyed virgins, chaste as the sheltered eggs of ostriches." -- 37:40-49; 78:32ff.

Qur'an described as place underneath the Earth that flows with rivers of wine and "wide eyed" virgins of beauty. And round about them will (serve) youths of perpetual (freshness): If thou seest them, thou wouldst think them scattered Pearls.

> *20 And when thou lookest, it is there thou wilt see a Bliss and a Realm Magnificent. 21 Upon them will be green Garments of fine silk and heavy brocade, and they will be adorned with bracelets of silver; and their Lord will give to them to drink of a Wine Pure and Holy. 22 Verily this is a Reward for you, and your Endeavour is accepted and recognized.*
> *(Surah 76:19-2; 2 Surah 2:25).*

### 3. Jihad
"Wage war on them until the infidels are no more and Allah's religion reigns supreme."
  8:12 Cut off their fingertips, stab them in the neck.
  48:16,17 Atone for sin by killing in war.
  47:4-6 Martyrdom → Heaven.

### "The verse of the sword"
> *"But when the forbidden months are past, then fight and slay the idolaters wherever ye find them, and take them, and prepare them each ambush. But if they repent and establish worship and pay the poor due, then leave their way free."* (9:5)

### 4. Punishment of enemies
"The punishment of those who wage war against God and his Apostle, and strive with might and main for mischief through the land is: execution, or crucifixion, or cutting off of hands and feet from opposite sides, or exile from the land." (5:36)

### The Yom Kippur or the Idu'l-Azha?:
Islam has copied the Jewish Holy Day-Yom Kippur as Idu'l-Azha. Mohammed observed the Jews of Medina celebrating the Day of Atonement (Leviticus 16) and he saw the role that sacrifice played among the people of the Book, the Jews.
  "We have a greater right in Moses than they" said Mohammed and fasted with the Jews, commanding his followers to do the same.
Mohammed instituted the Idu'l-Azha. He killed two young goats, one for himself and his family and one for the people (Leviticus 16). This feast was instituted to commemorate Abraham's sacrifice of his son Ishmael on Mount Mina near Mecca.

### The Quran on the Bible?:
Say ye: 'We believe in Allah, and the revelation given to us, and to Abraham, Ismail, Jacob, and the Tribes, and that given to Moses, and Jesus, and that given to all prophets from their Lord: WE MAKE NO DIFFERENCE BETWEEN ONE AND ANOTHER OF THEM." (Surah. Baqara 2:136).

**"Allah! There is no God but He, - the Living, the Self subsisting, Eternal ... He sent down Law (of Moses) and the Gospel (of Jesus) ... as a guide to mankind."** (Surah. Al-i-Imran 3:2-3).

114

**"0 ye who believe! Believe in Allah, and His Apostle - and the scripture which He sent before them".** (Surah. Nisaa 4:136).

"People of the Book! ... Stand fast by the Law, the Gospel, and all the revelation that hath come to you from YOUR LORD. It is the revelation that has come to thee from THY LORD." (5: 68).

### The Qur'an on the Jews Killing Christ?:
The Qur'an states that both the Torah and Gospel are revealed. But in contrast, it also claims that Jesus was not crucified:
**"They (the Jews) said (in boast), 'We killed Christ Jesus the son of Mary, the Apostle of Allah', - but they killed him not, nor crucified him, but so it was made to appear to them..."** (Surah 4:157).

# The Contradictory teachings of the Quran

| Meccan Early Revelations | | Medinan Later Revelations | |
|---|---|---|---|
| MODERATE ISLAM | | MILITANT ISLAM | |
| Be patient with what they say, and part from them courteously | 2:191 | kill them wherever you find them, and drive them out from wherever they drove you out | |
| If thou dost stretch thy hand against me, to slay me, it is not for me to stretch my hand against thee to slay thee: for I do fear Allah, the cherisher of the worlds. | 9:123 | Oh, ye who believe! Murder those of the disbelievers and let them find harshness in you. | |
| Speak good to men... | 9:5 | Slay the idolaters wherever you find them | |
| Therefore, be patient with what they say, and celebrate (constantly) the praises of thy Lord, | 8:12 | I will instill terror into the hearts of the unbelievers: smite ye above their necks and smite all their finger-tips off. | |
| We well know what the infidels say: but you are not to compel them | 9:14 | Fight them, and Allah will punish them by your hands, cover them with shame, help you (to victory) over them, heal the breasts of Believers | |
| Those who believe (in the Qur'an), those who follow the Jewish (scriptures), and the Sabaeans and the Christians, any who believe in Allah and the Last Day, and work righteousness, - on them shall be no fear, nor shall they grieve. | 9:29 | Fight those who do not believe in God and the last day... and fight People of the Book, who do not accept the religion of truth (Islam) until they pay tribute by hand, being inferior" | |
| To you be your religion, and to me my religion" | 3:85 | Whoso desires another religion than Islam, it shall not be accepted of him; in the next world, he shall be among the losers." | |
| Those who believe (in the Qur'an), and those who follow the Jewish (scriptures), and the Christians and the Sabaeans, - any who believe in Allah and the Last Day, and work righteousness, shall have their reward with their Lord; on them shall be no fear, nor shall they grieve. | 9:30 | The Jews call 'Uzair a son of Allah, and the Christians call Christ the son of Allah. That is a saying from their mouth; (in this) they but imitate what the unbelievers of old used to say. Allah's curse be on them: how they are deluded away from the Truth! | |
| If it had been thy Lord's Will, they would all have believed, all who are on earth! Wilt thou then compel mankind against their will to believe! | 5:11 | And as for those who disbelieve and reject Our Signs, they are the people of Hell" | |
| Argue with people of the book, other than evil doers, only by means of what are better! and say, we believe in what has been sent down to us and sent down to you. Our God is the same as your God, and we are surrendered to Him. | 9:28 | O you who believe! Verily, the Mushrikûn (unbelievers) are Najasun (impure). So, let them not come near Al-Masjid-al-Harâm (at Makkah) after this year, ..." | |
| There is no compulsion in religion | 2:193 | Fight them on until there is no more tumult and religion becomes that of Allah | |
| Pardon thou, with a gracious pardoning.... | 14:17 | Before him is Hell; and he shall be made to drink boiling water. | |
| But if they strive to make thee join in worship with Me things of which thou hast no knowledge, | 5:33 | The punishment of those who wage war against Allah and His Messenger, and strive | |

| | | | |
|---|---|---|---|
| | obey them not; yet bear them company in this life with justice (and consideration), and follow the way of those who turn to me (in love): in the end the return of you all is to Me, and I will tell you the truth (and meaning) of all that ye did. | | with might and main for mischief throug the land is: execution, or crucifixion, or cutting off of hands and feet from oppos sides, or exile from the land: that is their disgrace in this world, and a heavy punishment is theirs in the Hereafter; |
| 6:108 | and insult not (Revile not) those whom they call upon besides Allah, lest they of out spite revile Allah in their ignorance. Thus, we made alluring to each people its own doings. In the end, they return to their Lord, and we shall then tell them the truth of all that they did | 22:19-22 | But as for those who disbelieve, garmen fire will be cut out for them; boiling flui will be poured down on their heads,<br><br>Whereby that which is in their bellies, a their skins too, will be melted;<br><br>And for them are hooked rods of iron.<br><br>Whenever, in their anguish, they would forth from thence they are driven back therein and (it is said unto them): Taste doom of burning. |
| 5:82 | Thou wilt find the nearest of them in love to the believers (Muslims) are those who say 'We are Christians' | 9:23 | O ye who believe! take not for protecto your fathers and your brothers if they l Infidelity above Faith: if any of you do they do wrong. |
| 60:8 | Allah forbids you not, with regard to those who fight you not for (your) Faith nor drive you out of your homes, from dealing kindly and justly with them: for Allah loveth those who are just. | 25:52 | So, obey not the disbelievers, but strive against them herewith with a great endeavor. |
| 17:53 | Say to My servants that they should (only) say those things that are best: for Satan doth sow dissensions among them: For Satan is to man an avowed enemy. | 66:9 | O Prophet! Strive against the disbeliev and the hypocrites, and be stern with t Hell will be their home, a hapless jour end. |
| 43:88,89 | O Lord, these are people who do not believe,' Bear with them and wish them 'peace.' In the end, they shall know their folly. | 47:4 | When you meet the unbelievers, strike their heads; then when you have made slaughter among them, carefully tie up remaining captives. |
| 50:45 | We know of best what they say; and you (O Muhammad SAW) are not a tyrant over them (to force them to Belief). But warn by the Qur'an, him who fears My Threat. | 8:65, | O Prophet! rouse the Believers to the If there are twenty amongst you, patie and persevering, they will vanquish tw hundred: if a hundred, they will vanqu thousand of the Unbelievers |
| 49.11 | O ye who believe! Let not some men among you laugh at others: It may be that the (latter) are better than the (former): | 3:28 | Let not the believers take for friends o helpers unbelievers rather than believ any do that, in nothing will there be h from Allah. except by way of precaut that ye may guard yourselves from th But Allah cautions you (to fear) Hims for the final goal is to Allah. |

| If Allah had so willed, He would have made you a single people, but (His plan is) to test you in what He hath given you: so, strive as in a race in all virtues | 8:12 | I will instill terror into the hearts of the unbelievers: smite ye above their necks and smite all their finger-tips off them |
|---|---|---|
| Tell those who believe, to forgive those who do not look forward to the Days of Allah: It is for Him to recompense (for good or ill) each People according to what they have earned. | 8:60 | Against them make ready your strength to the utmost of your power, including steeds of war, to strike terror into (the hearts of) the enemies, of Allah and your enemies. |

This dichotomy is explained by some Muslim scholars.

Q 9:5 reads: "*Slay the idolaters wherever you find them*"
So according to Dr. M. Khan in Q. 9:5 Allah ordered Mohammad to cancel all covenants and to fight the pagans, the Jews even the Christians. This contrasts with what Muhammad wrote earlier.
"*Thou wilt find the nearest of them in love to the believers [Muslims} are those who say 'We are Christians'*" (Q. 5:82)

Dr. Khan continues: The "Mujahideen who fight against the enemies of Allah in order that the worship should be all for Allah (alone and not for any other deity) and that the word is Allah's (ie. none has the right to be worshipped but Allah and His religion Islam) should be upper most."

So first it was "*There is no compulsion in religion*" (Q. 2:265) and then "*O who believe! shall I direct you to a commerce that which will save you from a painful torment? That you believe in Allah and His Apostle (Mohammad), and that you strive hard and fight in the cause of Allah with your wealth and your lives. That will be better for you, if you but knew. If you do so He will forgive you your sins, and admit you into gardens of Eternity - that is the great success*" (Q. 61:10-12).

**SUMMARY:**

The Quran is inconsistence in reference to its doctrine and dogma. It lacks historical reliability immensely. The ancient existing Manuscripts of the Quran such as Samarkand, Topkapi MSS, and number of more do not have all the surahs. The present Quran has 114 surahs or chapter, whereas the manuscripts have only 46 surahs. The language is different and it has many internal errors for example 2,270 errors in one manuscripts alone. Sometimes, the words are erases and written on the top. Sometimes, without erasing a word, a word is written on the top. All the manuscripts are flagrant. There are intentional changes done to the manuscripts of the Quran. None of the Manuscripts were written by the companions of Muhammad. All of the Manuscripts have gone through corrections.

# The Process of Standardizing the Quran:

1. **Uthman, third caliph (Political leader) was the first who try to standardize the Quran. Zaid ibn Thabit was given the responsibility to collect the Quran from all different sources.**
2. **Abdul Malik, a political leader (685-705) standardized the Quran after his governor** Hajjaj made some changes.

118

3. Al-Walid son of Abdul Malik, again a political leader standardized the Quran after making some addition and corrections.
4. During Ottoman Empire (Political body) in 1,500 A.D., the Quran was standardized again since there were 14 different readings of Quran in existence. Out of fourteen, one was chosen.
5. In 1924, Quran was finally standardized and canonized. There was a crucial need of doing it, since, there were 80 different Arabic Qurans, people were reading in the Muslim world. The first edition of the Egyptian or Cairo Quran was published on July 10, 1924 in Cairo; subsequent revisions to the text were made in 1924 and 1936 when it was re-published. The text upon release in 1936 became known as the Faruq edition in honor of the Egyptian king Faruq. The religious leaders in Al-Ahzar university other than a political figure or a political body finally embarked upon this task.
6. The present Quran was finally canonized officially by King Fahd of Saudi Arabia in 1985.
7. The (Hafs) Qur'an which is now the most commonly used Qur'an. It is the 1924 Egyptian standard edition based on the transmitted version of Imam Hafs. The (Warsh) Qur'an is according to Imam Warsh's transmitted version and is mainly used in North Africa. When we compare two Qur'ans (Hafs and Warsh), it becomes obvious they are not identical. There are four main types of differences between them.
   a. Graphical/Basic Letter Differences
   b. Diacritical Differences
   c. Vowel Differences
   d. Basmalah Difference

After studies these insurmountable facts, one can come to the conclusion that The Quran is not a Word of God but merely word of man trying to pen so cleverly without proper articulacy and intelligibility. No wonder, Muslims are encouraged to memorize the Quran in Arabic. Whatever the content it contains different or similar as long as, it sound Arabic language can keep its followers under the yoke of religious slavery.

I would like to encourage my Muslim friends to read their so called Holy book with understanding rather than simply memorizing it solely. Your imams (clerics) might prohibit you to read Quran with translation having this strong fear that you might lose faith. Losing your spot in heaven is more tragic than losing your faith. Thinking about eternity is more important than a temporary life on this earth which will be over one day. A religious book is to bring spiritual understanding about a supreme being and about one's purpose on this earth to that Quran fails desperately.

*"Whether Muslim or Christian, no one likes having their holy books criticised. However, if a book is held up as perfect, as having fully preserved the message of God, then its perfection should be demonstrable against all criticism and tests of its contents. The standards and measures chosen should be equally applicable to any book which calls itself inspired."*[xli]

## Differences Between
### The Bible & The Quran

| The Quran | The Bible |
|---|---|
| External sources (the Hadith and Sira) necessary for translating the Quran | Historical context contained within the text of the Bible |
| Must know Arabic in order to "fully understand" the Quran (according to Muslim apologists) | Universal. Can be translated into other languages without excessive commentary. |
| Chronological progression of the Quran is from peace to violence. | Chronological progression of the Bible is from violence to peace. |
| The words 'torture' and 'punishment' appear six times more often in the Quran than in the New Testament. | The word 'love' appears five times more often in the New Testament than in the Quran, |
| Contains not a single original moral value. | The 'Sermon on the Mount' and others. |
| Suffering is an excuse for violent revenge and establishment of Islam by force<br><br>*"And slay them wherever ye find them, and drive them out of the places whence they drove you out, for persecution [of Muslims] is worse than slaughter [of non-believers] ...and fight them until persecution is no more, and religion is for Allah."*<br>(Quran 2:191) | Suffering builds character<br><br>*"We also rejoice in our sufferings, because we know that suffering produces perseverance; perseverance, character; and character, hope"*<br>(Romans 5:4) |
| Emphasis on this World<br><br>*"And Allah has made you heirs to their land and their dwellings and their property"*<br>(Quran 33:27) | Emphasis on the Next<br><br>*"Mine is not a kingdom of this world"*<br>(John 18:36, see also Luke 14:33) |

| | |
|---|---|
| Kill, convert, or subjugate Christians and Jews.<br>(Quran 9:29) | Share one's faith with gentleness and respect.<br>(1 Peter 3:15) |
| **Martyrs as Killers**<br><br>*"Allah hath purchased of the believers their persons and their goods; for theirs (in return) is the garden (of Paradise): they fight in His cause, and slay and are slain"*<br>(Quran 9:111) | **Martyrs as Martyrs**<br><br>*"As it is written, For thy sake we are killed all the day long; we are counted as sheep for the slaughter"*<br>(Romans 8:36) |
| **Killing Apostates**<br><br>*"They but wish that ye should reject Faith, as they do, and thus be on the same footing (as they): But take not friends from their ranks until they flee in the way of Allah (From what is forbidden). But if they turn renegades, seize them, and slay them wherever ye find them"*<br>(Quran 4:89, also Bukhari 52:260, 83:37...)* | **Letting God Judge Apostates**<br><br>*"For we know Him that has said, 'Vengeance belongs unto me, I will recompense,' says the Lord. And again, 'The Lord shall judge his people'"*<br>(Hebrews 10:25-30) |
| **Punishment**<br><br>*"Let not compassion move you from carrying out God's law..."*<br>(Quran 24:2) | **Mercy**<br><br>*"Love is patient. Love is kind... It keeps no record of wrongs"*<br>(1 Corinthians 13:4-5) |
| **Charity and Non-Believers**<br><br>Mercy toward fellow Muslims - ruthlessness toward unbelievers. Muslims are warned not to befriend those outside the faith. They must even ensure that their charity tithe (zakat) stays within their own identity group.<br>(Quran 48:29, 3:28, Sharia) | **Charity and Non-Believers**<br><br>Christians are specifically told that even those who hate them are entitled to kindness and charity. They should be loved and cared for as surely as any fellow believer.<br>(Mark 10:25-37) |
| The Qur'an explicitly instructs men to beat disobedient wives.<br>(Quran 4:34, Sahih Muslim 2127) | *"Husbands, love your wives and do not be harsh with them."* |

| | (No permission to beat women) (Colossians 3:19) |
|---|---|
| Explicitly allows Muslim men to rape their female slaves, even those already married. (Quran 4:24, 70:29-30, 23:5-6...) | Tells masters and slaves to serve each other as if serving God. (Ephesians 6:7-9) |
| *Muhammad is the messenger of Allah. And those who are with him are ruthless to the unbelievers"* (Quran 48:29) | "Do good to them that hate you" (Luke 6:27) |
| Allah wills those that stray and are lost (Quran 16:93) | God wants all people saved (1 Timothy 2:4) |
| Warns Against Questioning Faith. (Quran 5:101-102) | Welcomes Intellectual Challenge. (1 Peter 3:15) |
| Violence as Virtue *"Fighting is prescribed for you, and ye dislike it. But it is possible that ye dislike a thing which is good for you, and that ye love a thing which is bad for you. But Allah knoweth, and ye know not."* (Quran 2:216) | Violence as Sin *"Do not take revenge, my friends, but leave room for God's wrath, for it is written:* *'It is mine to avenge; I will repay,' says the Lord. On the contrary: 'If your enemy is hungry, feed him... '"* (Romans 12:19-20) |
| Hell for unbelief. Good deeds count for naught (Quran 18:102-107) | Hell for bad deeds and the failure to do what is right (Romans 2:6-8, Matthew 16:27, Matthew 25:41-45) |
| Judging *"Strive against the disbelievers and the hypocrites! Be harsh with them..."* (Quran 9:73) | Judge Not *"For when you pass judgment on another person, you condemn yourself..."* (Romans 2:1) |
| Taking wealth from others | Working for and giving wealth to others *"The thief must no longer steal but must work hard and do what is good with his* |

| | |
|---|---|
| *"Allah promiseth you much booty that ye will capture..."* (Quran 48:20) | *own hands, so that he might have something to give to the needy."* (Ephesians 4:28) |
| Calls down Allah's curse on Christians and those of other religions. (Quran 9:30) | Calls down God's blessing on those who curse Christians. (Matthew 5:44) |
| Arrogance & Privilege<br><br>*"Ye are the best of peoples, evolved for mankind"* (Quran 3:110) | Humility & Servitude<br><br>*"If anyone wants to be first, he must make himself last of all and servant of all."* (Mark 9:35) |
| *"O you who believe! do not take My enemy and your enemy for friends: Would you offer them love while they deny what has come to you of the truth?* (Quran 60:1)[xlii] | *"Love your enemies..."* (Luke 6:27) |

# WHAT ABOUT THE HOLY BIBLE?

The Bible is the library of sixty-six books. God inspired more than forty authors to pen the sacred pages of His Word over a span of more than fifteen hundred years. The writers included shepherds, kings, prophets, statesmen, fishermen, tax collector, a doctor, and several anonymous authors. They wrote in three languages: Hebrew, Aramaic, and Greek. They composed their work in three continents: Asia, Africa, and Europe. This divine library includes narratives, legal codes, poetry, wisdom literature, prophecy, parable, sermon, epistles, and apocalypse.

The Bible is a book of great diversity, still convey a unified message of God's love and a universal need of every person on this planet to embrace God's love through Jesus Christ and to receive forgiveness of sins through the finished work of Jesus Christ on the cross. The Bible addresses hundreds of difficult issues without a single contradiction.

The Bible is the most orderly religious book in the world. The simplicity of its sacred message is so easy that even for a child is able to understand, and at the same time, it is so deep even for a scholar to ponder.

The Bible passes tests such as, Historical, archeological, scientific, and prophecy. According to 2 Timothy 3:16 ("All Scripture is given by inspiration of God, and is profitable for **doctrine**, for **reproof**, for **correction**, for **instruction** in righteousness, that the man of God may be complete, thoroughly equipped for every good work."").

The Bible is profitable for:
1. Doctrine-What is right
2. Reproof-What is not right
3. Correction-How to get right
4. Instruction-How to stay right

The Bible is the inspired, uncorrupted, unchanged, Word of God. The evidence of the reliability and authenticity could be demonstrated by the verifiable facts which are internally in corroboration with the Biblical testimonies of itself and at the same time externally in corroboration with the secular history in its immediate setting of the Biblical accounts.
1. Manuscripts
   5,300 Greek, 10,000 Latin vulgates, 24,000 Manuscripts copies or portions. 230 Manuscripts were compiled before Islam in the 7th century.

2. Dating of the Ancient Manuscripts as compared to the Bible

| Author | Date Written | Earliest Copy | Time Span | Copies |
|--------|-------------|---------------|-----------|--------|
| **Secular Manuscripts:** | | | | |
| Herodotus (History) | 480 - 425 BC | 900 AD | 1,300 years | 8 |
| Thucydides (History) | 460 - 400 BC | 900 AD | 1,300 years | ? |
| Aristotle (Philosopher) | 384 - 322 BC | 1,100 AD | 1,400 years | 5 |
| Caesar (History) | 100 - 44 BC | 900 AD | 1,000 years | 10 |
| Pliny (History) | 61 - 113 AD | 850 AD | 750 years | 7 |
| Suetonius (Roman History) | 70 - 140 AD | 950 AD | 800 years | ? |
| Tacitus (Greek History) | 100 AD | 1,100 AD | 1,000 years | 20 |

## Biblical Manuscripts: (note these are individual manuscripts)

| | | | |
|---|---|---|---|
| Magdalene Ms (Matthew 26) | 1st century | 50-60 AD | co-existent (?) |
| John Rylands (John) | 90 AD | 130 AD | 40 years |
| Bodmer Papyrus II (John) | 90 AD | 150-200 AD | 60-110 years |
| Chester Beatty Papyri (N.T.) | 1st century | 200 AD | 150 years |
| Diatessaron by Tatian (Gospels) | 1st century | 200 AD | 150 years Codex |
| Vaticanus (Bible) | 1st century | 325-350 AD | 275-300 years |
| Codex Sinaiticus (Bible) | 1st century | 350 AD | 300 years |
| Codex Alexandrinus (Bible) | 1st century | 400 AD | 350 years |

### 3. Eyewitness accounts

a. Luke whom God inspired to write about the birth, teaching, miracles, crucifixion, and the resurrection of Jesus in an immediate setting of the events that took place. The Gospel according to Luke was written around 63 A.D. whereas Jesus' death and resurrection took place around 30 A.D. In a time span of 30 years while the generation was still alive who had witnessed the crucifixion and resurrection of Jesus Christ. This verses demonstrate the writing of Luke by saying that "**...to compile an account of the things accomplished among us, just as those who from the beginning were eyewitnesses and servants of the Word have handed them down to us, it seemed fitting for me as well, having investigated everything carefully from the beginning, to write it out for you in consecutive order." (Luke 1:1-3).**

b. Peter challenges his Jewish audience on the day of Pentecost that took place fifty days after the crucifixion and resurrection of Jesus and ten days after the ascension of Jesus to heaven by this statement: "**Men of Israel, listen to these words: Jesus the Nazarene, a man attested to you by God with miracles and wonders and signs which God performed through Him in your midst, just as you yourselves know...**" (Acts 2:22). The event is recorded in the Book of Acts that was written in 62 A.D.

c. Paul's testimony before Porcius *Festus* who was procurator (treasury officer) of Judea from about AD 59 to 62 reveals the truth that Jews and as well Roman authorities were well aware of the events that took place in the first half of the first century. "**...Paul said, 'I am not out of my mind, most excellent Festus, but I utter the words of sober truth. For the king knows about these matters, and I speak to him also with confidence, since I am persuaded that none of these things escape his notice; for this has not been done in a corner." (Acts 24:24-26).**

### 4. Hostile accounts

a. Thallus, a Greek historian (52 AD) mentions in his writing about the crucifixion and day suddenly turned dark and earth trembled. This coincide and coheres with the biblical account of the crucifixion of Jesus Christ.

b. Tacitus, a Roman historian (80-84 AD) death of Christ, reign of Tiberius',

c. by governor of Judea, Pontius Pilate

d. **Josephus: a Jewish historian 90-95 AD, death of Jesus, martyrdom of James, John the Baptist, resurrection**

e. **Suetonius: a Greek historian Expulsion from Rome of followers of Crestus, by emperor Claudius, (Acts 18:2)**

f. **Pliny the Younger: A Roman author and administrator 112 AD of the Christian community in Asia Minor, and of their devotion to Christ**

## 5. Translations:

19,284 translations, in 11 languages! (note: 230 examples between 2$^{nd}$ - 6$^{th}$ C.).

| | | |
|---|---|---|
| a. | Latin  150 AD | (over 10,000 examples) |
| b. | Syriac 150-250 AD | (350 examples |
| c. | Coptic early 3rd and 4th centuries | (100 + examples) |
| d. | Armenian    400 AD | (2,587 examples) |
| e. | Gothic 4th century | (6 examples |
| f. | Georgian    5th century | (4,101 examples) |
| g. | Ethiopic    6th century | (2,000 examples) |
| h. | Nubian6th century | |

## 6. Lectionaries

6$^{th}$ Century 2,135 lectionaries

## 7. Early church Father's writings

Dr. Jean Burgon: 86,489 quotes and Sir David Dalrymple: 36,289 quotes before 4$^{th}$ C.

| | |
|---|---|
| Clement of Alexandria | 2,406 quotes |
| Tertullian | 7258 quotes |
| Justin Martyr | 330 quotes |
| Irenaeus | 1,819 quotes |
| Origen | 17,922 quotes |
| Hippolytus | 1,378 quotes |
| Eusebius | 5,176 quotes |
| | **36,289 quotes** |

**More than 36,000 quotes from before 325 AD = all but 11 verses of the New Testament**[xliii]

# THE TESTIMONY OF THE QURAN ABOUT THE BIBLE

Muhammad was asked to consult with the inspired revelations if he has doubts about his own revelation. The Quran says, "So if you are in doubt, [O Muhammad], about that which We have revealed to you, then ask those who have been reading the Scripture before you. The truth has certainly come to you from your Lord, so never be among the doubters" (10:94).

The Quran emphatically ask Muhammad **"And We sent not before you, [O Muhammad], except men to whom We revealed [the message], so ask the people of the message if you do not know" (21:7).**

The Quran even admonishes not to argue with the people of the book (Jews and Christian). **"And do not argue with the People of the Scripture except in a way that is best, except for those who commit injustice among them, and say, "We believe in that which has been revealed to us and revealed to you. And our God and your God is one; and we are Muslims [in submission] to Him" (29:46).**

**"O you who have believed, believe in Allah and His Messenger and the Book that He sent down upon His Messenger and <u>the Scripture which He sent down before.</u> And whoever disbelieves in Allah, His angels, His books, His messengers, and the Last Day has certainly gone far astray" (4:136).**

**"And We sent, following in their footsteps, Jesus, the son of Mary, confirming that which came before him in the Torah; and <u>We gave him the Gospel, in which was guidance and light and confirming that which preceded it of the Torah as guidance and instruction for the righteous.</u> And <u>let the People of the Gospel judge by what Allah has revealed therein. And whoever does not judge by what Allah has revealed - then it is those who are the defiantly disobedient"</u> 5:46-47).**

**Say, "O People of the Scripture, <u>you are [standing] on nothing until you uphold [the law of] the Torah, the Gospel, and what has been revealed to you from your Lord."</u> And that which has been revealed to you from your Lord will surely increase many of them in transgression and disbelief. So, do not grieve over the disbelieving people (5:68).**

These Quranic verses demonstrates the reliability and the authenticity of the Torah and the Gospel. If Muslims have reservation in accepting Quranic testimony about the Bible, then it shows that they defiant, arrogance and disobedient to their own scripture. How could God of Islam encourage Muhammad and his followers to ask from the people of the book if that book is corrupted?

**<u>How could Allah admonish to Muslims to believe the scriptures if they are corrupted.</u>**

# CHAPTER FIVE

## THE TRUTH ABOUT THE DOCTRINE AND RELIGIOUS PRACTICES OF ISLAM

Human behavior flows from three main sources:
desire, emotion, and knowledge.
Plato

# CHAPTER FIVE

## TRUTH ABOUT THE DOCTRINE AND RELIGIOUS PRACTICES OF ISLAM

**The Doctrine of Islam**

The six articles of faith of Islam are:

1. **Belief in Allah:** Muslims believe Allah is one, eternal, creator, and sovereign.

2. **Belief in the angels and jinn (evil spirit).**

3. **Belief in the prophets:** Muslims believe that God sent 124,000 prophets, of which Muhammad is the last and the greatest prophet. They believe men like Lot, Adam, to be a prophet. They lack understanding of the true meaning of prophet-hood.

4. **Belief in the revelations of Allah:** Muslims believe that God gave the Torah to Moses, the Zaboor (Psalms) to David, the Injel (gospel) to Jesus, and the Quran to Muhammad. But to promote the Quran, they do not accept the previous scriptures such as Torah, Zaboor, and Injel to be fully authentic. They have a fallacious and fictitious notion that the early scriptures are corrupted, whereas, the Quran is only pure and a well preserved scripture.

5. **Belief in the last day of judgment and the life hereafter:** Muslims believe that everyone will be resurrected for judgment into either paradise or hell. They also believe that every Muslim will have to go through hell for a short time. For Muslims, paradise is a really a place of sensual and endless sexual activities and pleasure but only for men. Heaven (Paradise) has a Garden (79:41), is a place of bliss and fruit (69:21-24), has rivers (3:198). It is a place where maidens are pure and holy given to men for endless sexual pleasure (4:57). The men will recline on carpets and cushions (88:8-16). One might wonder what about Muslim women. What will happen to them? Sadly, many Muslims even the most sincere and pious Muslims are not certain about heaven.

6. **Belief in predestination:** Muslims believe that Allah has decreed everything that will happen. Muslims testify to Allah's sovereignty with their frequent phrase, *inshallah*, meaning, "if God wills."

### Five pillars of Islam

1. **Confessions of Faith:** *Shahada*- all Muslims must recite this creed "There is no God but God, and Muhammad is the apostle of God".

### The Monotheistic Concept of God is the Basic Tenet of Judeo-Christian Doctrine: The Unity of God
The Judeo-Christian teaching about the oneness of God has been very strict in observance and in its historicity.

*"Hear, O Israel: The LORD our God is one LORD: And thou shalt love the LORD thy God with all thine heart, and with all thy soul, and with all thy might."* (Deuteronomy 6:4-5).

*"For there is **one God** and **one** mediator between **God** and men, the man Christ Jesus,"* (1 Timothy 2:5)

Islam emphasizes the importance of the Character of God. They typically believe in ninety-nine attributes of God, though most acknowledge that He cannot be limited to that many. His Sovereignty, Omnipotence, mercy and compassion are emphasized. One major difference in Character between Islam and Christianity is the justice of God, rather than the grace of God. (The cross being the reconciling factor between the two). For Muslims, God is more a god of judgement than a god who is full of grace and mercy. Out of ninety-nine names or attribute of God, there is not a not a single attribute that would depict Allah as a god of love.

The Confession of Faith, every Muslim pronounces and recites on many important occasions. When a non-Muslims embraces Islam, that person is asked to verbalize the confession of faith (Shahada, Kalima) that has two parts:
**Shahada:** There is no God but Allah, and
**Kalima:** Muhammad is the Prophet of Allah.

The Kalima (Muhammad is the prophet of God), what Muhammad taught to his followers is not something new. Many so called prophets have had been forcing people to accept them whether people like it or not. There is the Manicean influence on Islam, Mani (216-270 A.D.) a Persian painter and "Prophet" made many claims similar to Mohammad 400 years earlier. Mani was a Gnostic, who combined Christian, Buddhist, and Persian Zoroastrian teachings into a belief system

| Mani (216-270 A.D.) | Mohammed (570-632 (A.D.) |
|---|---|
| Called himself Apostle | Called himself Apostle |
| Called himself "the Last Prophet" | Called himself "the Last Prophet" |
| Salvation by obedience to his "System" | Salvation by following Mohammad. |
| Claimed continuous revelation | Claimed continuous revelation |
| Claims Jesus spoke of him in John 14:16 "Paraclete" | Claims Jesus spoke of him in John 14:16 "Paraclete" |
| Angelic messenger revealed the message | Angel Gabriel revealed the message. |
| Followers forbidden to drink wine | Followers forbidden to drink wine.[xliv] |

The confession of faith (Shahada and Kalima) is not mentioned in the Quran, but the Christian Confession of Faith is mentioned in the Bible which is meaningful because eternity hinges on this confession. Christian Confession of Faith not only focuses on a person, but the results that follow after making confessing on that person. The Islamic confession of faith is merely a demand to accept the person (Muhammad) to be an apostle, but what the person receives after making that confession is null and void.

The Bible says, "that if you **confess with your mouth the Lord Jesus** and **believe in your heart that God has raised Him from the dead, you will be saved**" (Romans 10:9).

2. **Ritual Prayer:** *Salat-* ritual prayers are spoken five times a day, along with the correct postures, which all Muslims are expected to perform. (Except women when they are on their menstrual period)

Muhammad borrowed from the Sabaeans-a religious group that existed in Arabia at the time of Muhammad. They prayed seven times every day.

It is also borrowed from Jews who pray three times a day.

*"Now when **Daniel** learned that the decree had been published, he went home to his upstairs room where the windows opened toward Jerusalem. Three times a day he got down on his knees and **prayed**, giving thanks to his God, just as he had done before"* (Daniel 6:10).

It seems that Muhammad choose the middle number between 7 and 3 which is 5, but Muhammad chose the same timings as those of Sabaeans.

Prayers are mere repetition and to some they are measures of religious ostentatious manners of righteousness. The goal of prayer is to accumulate some deeds (religious points) in order to get to heaven. The prayers are more an obligation rather than a manner of deep and awesome relationship with an almighty God. An ordinary Muslim has no knowledge of the Arabic language, so, that person does not have any clue of what he recites in his prayer. It is simply mechanical rather than relational.

It is pity that there are so many sincere and devoted Muslims who observe their religious practices so seriously, but what if at the end of rope, they find out that they did everything for nothing. It was all meaningless. What a disappointment it will bring?

Muslims should be grateful for at least one thing that they do not need to pray for 50 times every day. Initially, Allah commanded Muhammad then to pray 50 times. According to the Islamic sources, Muhammad went to the 7th heaven to meet Allah. Over there, Allah commanded him to go back and pray 50 times. On his way back, Moses asked Muhammad, how many times Allah commanded him to pray? His reply was, 50 times! 50 times is really too much, Moses said to Muhammad. Moses asked Muhammad to go back to Allah and request him to decrease the number of times Muhammad and his Umma (people) could pray. Muhammad went back and forth and made a big bargain with Allah. Eventually, Allah was able to change his mind and Muhammad was able to get a good deal from Allah and that is to pray five time only every day. Allah was really a puppet in the hand of Muhammad.

It is an apt to mention that there is no indication of praying five times a day in the Quran. Praying three times is mentioned in the Quran as the Jews living in Arabia prayed three times every day.

**Allah is discriminatory in crediting prayers from place to place**

Allah grades prayer based on its location. The merit points are exchangeable on the day of resurrection. Here are the merit points for prayers according to the location:

- 1 prayer in Mecca = 100, 000 prayers in an ordinary mosque;

- 1 prayer in the Medina mosque of Muhammad = 10, 000 prayers;

- 1 prayer at Bait al-Muqaddis = 1 000 prayers… (Ghazali, p.1.192)

- Pray in an ordinary mosques = 25 times prayer in house; Jame mosque = 500, Al-Aqsa = 50, 000;  Medina = 50, 000;  Mecca = 100, 000 times…(Mishkat, 2.98)

- One prayer in Muhammad's mosque (in Medina) is better than 1,000 prayers in any other mosque, except the Kaaba mosque… (Sahih Bukhari, 2.21.282)

- A prayer in the mosque of Muhammad is a thousand times better than a prayer in any other mosque except the Masjid al–Haram (Ka'ba)… (Malik's Muwatta, 14.4.9)

**Jesus has taught the pattern of Prayer in (Matthew 6:5-13)**

"And when you pray, you shall not be like the **hypocrites**. For they love to pray standing in the synagogues and on the corners of the streets, that they may be **seen by men**. Assuredly, I say to you, they have their reward. [6] But you, when you pray, go into your room, and when you have shut your door, pray to your Father who *is* in the secret *place;* and your Father who sees in secret will reward you openly.[7] And when you pray, do not use **vain repetitions** as the heathen *do.* For they think that they will be heard for their many words.
[8] "Therefore do not be like them. For your Father knows the things you have need of before you ask Him. [9] In this manner, therefore, pray:
Our Father in heaven, **(PRAISE)**
Hallowed be Your name.
[10] Your kingdom come. **(PRIORITY)**
Your will be done
On earth as *it is* in heaven.
[11] Give us this day our daily bread. **(PETITION)**
[12] And forgive us our debts, **(PURITY)**
As we forgive our debtors.
[13] And do not lead us into temptation, **(PROTECTION)**
But deliver us from the evil one.
For Yours is the kingdom and the power and the glory forever. Amen **(OWNER)**.

The Biblical model of prayer starts with our Father that shows a close and deep relationship with a mighty God who is in heaven. Let His name be hollowed and his kingdom come (lordship), and His will be done. There is praise, petition for daily needs, prayer for purity and protection. It ends with exalting the majestic God of this universe.

## SOME MUSLIMS HAVE NO RESPECT FOR THE HOLY-DAY

Friday is the day of prayer for Muslims. It is the day when Muslims go to the mosques, offer special Friday (Jumma) prayers and hear the sermons from the clerics. It is wonderful, if someone does that with such devotion and dedication but, it is sad to say that sometimes, the Day of Prayer and Meditation turn into a Day of Protests, Violence, terrorist attacks, and many other lawless activities. The Holy day becomes the time of planning, instigating, and propagating evil, rather than a time of prayer, meditation, and the day to something good.

*The Bible says, He hath showed thee, O man, what is good; and what doth the LORD require of thee, but to do justly, and to love mercy, and to walk humbly with thy God?* (Micah 6:8)

### PRAYING TOWARD MECCA

An idol was set at the Kaaba along with all the other idols. The pagans prayed toward Mecca and the Kaaba, because, it is where their gods were. It was like facing their god at the time of prayer. Since Allah was the moon god, at Mecca, they prayed toward Mecca. The worship of the moon god extended far beyond the Allah-worship in Arabia. The entire fertile-crescent was involved in the worship of the moon. This, in part, explains the early success of Islam among Arab groups that traditionally had worshiped the moon god. The use of the crescent moon as the symbol for Islam, is placed on the flags of Islamic nations and on the top of mosques and minarets is a throwback to the days when Allah was worshiped as the moon god in Mecca.[xlv]

### THE CHANGE OF DIRECTION FOR PRAYER FROM MECCA TO JERUSALEM AND BACK TO MECCA

Muhammad had also commanded Muslims to pray towards Jerusalem, the prayer direction of the Jews, but when the Jewish community did not accept Muhammad as a prophet, he was disappointed. With deep frustration, he changed the direction from Jerusalem to Mecca. The choosing of Jerusalem as a direction for prayer was an attempt to win favor from the Jews and to convert them to Islam. The Qur'an records the reaction of the people when Muhammad decided to change the direction of prayer:

*"The fools among the people will say: "**What hath turned them from the Qibla to which they were used?**" Say: To God belong both east and West: He guideth whom He will to a Way that is straight. Thus, have We made of you an Ummat justly balanced, that ye might be witnesses over the nations, and the Apostle a witness over yourselves; and We appointed the Qibla to which thou wast used, only to test those who followed the Apostle from those who would turn on their heels (From the Faith). Indeed, it was (A change) momentous, except to those guided by God. And never would God Make your faith of no effect. For God is to all people Most surely full of kindness, Most Merciful. We see the turning of thy face (for guidance) to the heavens: **now Shall We turn thee to a Qibla that shall please thee. Turn then Thy face in the direction of the sacred Mosque**: Wherever ye are, turn your faces in that direction. The people of the Book know well that that is the truth from their Lord. Nor is God unmindful of what they do. Even if thou wert to bring to the people of the Book all the Signs (together), they would not follow Thy Qibla; nor art thou going to follow their Qibla; nor indeed*

134

*will they follow each other's Qibla. If thou after the knowledge hath reached thee, Wert to follow their (vain) desires, - then wert thou Indeed (clearly) in the wrong" S. 2:142-145 Y. Ali*

Thank God, Christians are not bound to pray in any particular direction, because they believe that God of this immense universe is everywhere who hears prayers, prayed in any language, when someone diligently, whole heartedly, and righteously prays to him.

3. **Obligatory Alms:** *Zakat*-alms that are a percentage of their possessions, or earnings given once a year. This reminds them that there are others in need. The offering goes to help those in need.

It is a charitable deed for a Muslim which is legal and compulsory. The slaves are exempt from paying Zakat. Generally, it is 1/10th of the fruits and produce of the soil, but 1/40th of money and merchandise. This is done before the beginning of the month of Muharram, the first of the new year. Giving Zakat is considered an act of worship.

Once again Zakat, a charitable deed is not something new. Giving tithe (10%) has been considered as an act of worship by the community of Judeo-Christian faith.

**Recipients of Zakat Funds (Quran 9:60)**

1. Those (Muslims) who are in power.
2. Those who cannot meet their basic needs
3. Those who collect the Zakat
4. Those who propagate and persuade non-Muslims to convert to Islam
5. To bring people out of slavery
6. Those who have incurred an overwhelming debt
7. Those who fight for the Jihad
8. Those who travel on an Islamic goal

4. **The Fast of Ramadan:** *Saum*- fasting during the ninth month of the lunar calendar, the month of Ramadan. It moves year to year. The fast lasts for 30 days from sunrise to sunset. They should not eat or drink, smoke, have sexual relations, swear or become angry. It is a time when the believers seek to draw closer to God, and renew their spiritual strength. If a Muslim is unable to fast due to some sickness or some other reasons, he might help the poor and needy with food at the time of breaking the fast. In return, Allah adds all the rewards (religious points) to the account of that person. Islamic faith focuses on debit and credit. Allah gives credit for good deeds and debit or deduct for every bad deed.

According to Muslim sources, Muhammad at first adopted the Jewish day of fasting, which happened to take place on the Day of Atonement, when he arrived at Medina:
Narrated Ibn 'Abbas:
**The Prophet came to Medina and saw the Jews fasting on the Day of Ashura**. He asked them about that. They replied, **"This is a good day, the day on which Allah rescued Bani Israel from their enemy. So, Moses fasted this day."** The Prophet said, "We have more claim over Moses than you." So, the Prophet fasted on that day and

ordered (the Muslims) to fast (on that day). (*Sahih al-Bukhari*, Volume 3, Book 31, Number 222)

Narrated Ibn Abbas:
When the Prophet arrived at Medina, the Jews were observing the fast on 'Ashura' (10th of Muharram) and they said, "This is the day when Moses became victorious over Pharaoh," On that, the Prophet said to his companions, "You (Muslims) have more right to celebrate Moses' victory than they have, so observe the fast on this day." (*Sahih al-Bukhari*, Volume 6, Book 60, Number 202)

Narrated 'Aisha:
The people used to fast on 'Ashura (the tenth day of the month of Muharram) before the fasting of Ramadan was made obligatory. And on that day the Ka'ba used to be covered with a cover. When Allah made the fasting of the month of Ramadan compulsory, Allah's Apostle said, "Whoever wishes to fast (on the day of 'Ashura') may do so; and whoever wishes to leave it can do so." (*Sahih al-Bukhari*, Volume 2, Book 26, Number 662)

Narrated Ibn 'Umar:
The Prophet observed the fast on the 10th of Muharram ('Ashura), and ordered (Muslims) to fast on that day, but when the fasting of the month of Ramadan was prescribed, **the fasting of the 'Ashura' was abandoned**. 'Abdullah did not use to fast on that day unless it coincided with his routine fasting by chance. (*Sahih al-Bukhari*, Volume 3, Book 31, Number 116)[xlvi]

It is an undeniable reality that Muhammad borrowed his religious practices from the Jews. When it comes to the number of days of fasting, it is precisely taken from the Sabaeans. Even though, the religious practice like fasting is borrowed, but the fasting itself has great meaning and benefits in regards to the spiritual relationship with God, physical health in many aspects. But it is pathetic that many Muslims fast in order to show how religious they are and for the sake of adding some points to their account that would help them go to heaven. It is very tragic that even the moderate Muslims become so aggressive and militant during Ramadan. It should be a time of deeper spiritual relationship with God, more tolerant, loving, caring, and aiming to fulfill the purpose of God for mankind which is: LOVING GOD AND LOVING OTHER HUMAN BEINGS. Fasting is a time of feasting in the Islamic world. During the month of Ramadan, more food is sold as compared to rest of the year.

5. **The pilgrimage to Mecca:** *Hajj-* Every Muslim that has the ability, physically and financially must go to Mecca for the Hajj. It is part of the purification process and a point when all despite their social standing, are considered equal. It is the duty of every Muslim to perform a Hajj (Pilgrimage) to Mecca at least once in his lifetime. The pilgrim runs around the Ka'ba seven times, drinks from the well, Zamzam, and performs other running exercises and acts of devotion.

Every religious group and community of faith feels attached to the places where their faith started. The Jews have deep sense of attachment with Jerusalem, whereas the Christians feel some sort of connection with the Biblical places such as Jerusalem, Bethlehem, the river Jordan and so on. Muslims have a same sentimental attachment to the birth place of Islam.

## HAJJ-THE PILGRIMAGE TO MECCA IS THE CONINUATION OF ACIENT IDOLATRY AND THE BUSINESS OF MULTI-BILLION DOLLARS

Muslims believe that they only worship one god called Allah and all their religious activities are aimed at and associated with the worship the only true God. It might sound good, and even look in accordance with their sayings, but the reality speaks differently. In connection to the Hajj, there are several features that were characteristic already to the Arabs' faith and idolatry before Islam and Muhammad. These features are:

> Mecca, the Destination of pilgrimage
> Circumambulation of the Ka'ba
> Kissing or touching the black stone
> Standing at Arafat
> Throwing stones ("stoning the Devil")
> Sacrifice at Minah

**MECCA-THE DESTINATION OF THE PILGRIMAGE:** It has its roots in the idolatry of the Arabs during the time of Muhammad. Arabs and the ancient worshippers of pagan gods also had a custom to make pilgrimages to Mecca and to take part in the cultic ceremonies in the temple of Kaaba, which housed 360 heathen gods there. The Quraysh tribe, the tribe of Muhammad was the guardian of the Kaaba. Muhammad's grandfather was a man responsible and a distinguished figure in the tribe.

At the time of Muhammad, every year, during the time of the pilgrimage to Mecca, the tribal disputes were halted, no bloodshed was expected, and the people were encouraged to have a time of peace, celebration, and of different festivals.

The same development continued until Muhammad, who himself had been a guard in the Kaaba Temple when there were still the 360 heathen gods. In 630 A.D., Muhammad decided to close the town from all except the followers of Islam. He destroyed all the gods, and declared that there is only one god-Allah. The reality of one god might be there, but all the rituals of the old religion and idolatry have not disappeared. Without the idolatrous rituals of the past, the Hajj is incomplete.

**CIRCUMAMBULATION OF THE KA'ABA:** Muslims walk around the Kaaba seven times. This was also a part of the ancient idolatry during the pilgrimage. The people did so in showing respect for the temple, and also kissed the black stone in the temple.

People of Quraysh had Hubal one of their revered deities in the Kaaba. The same deity stood near the well, Zamzam, where the sacrifices were offered. They also worshipped Isaf and Na'il next to Zamzam. Aabe-Zamzam is considered to be a holy water that cleanses sins and brings healing.

**KISSING THE BLACK STONE:** One of the rituals of the Hajj, is kissing or touching of the black stone. The Arabs in the old days used to kiss this stone and worship it as a god. The black stone was the most honored object in the ancient temple and the focus of worship. The Bedouins also worshipped many other stones before and during the time of Muhammad. In addition to holy stones, springs, and trees were worshipped as well.

The Arabs in the past believed that the black stone was dropped from heaven by the moon god-Hubal. However, Muhammad and Muslims now believe that the stone was sent by

137

the angel Gabriel from Paradise. It was originally white but has turned black because it sucks the sins of the people, when they kiss or touch it.

There is such ignorance at its climax that even the intelligent and well educated Muslims refuse to believe that this Black Stone is nothing but probably a meteorite that has fallen to the Earth.

Muhammad could have been successful in fooling the Bedouins of his time, but even so many Muslims in the twenty first century living in the age of science and technology have been so deceived by this dire deception.

Muhammad's companions had a question mark in venerating the Black Stone. They did it because Muhammad asked them to do it. The reference to this reality justifies it. For example:

Narrated 'Abis bin Rabia: **'Umar came near the Black Stone and kissed it and said "No doubt, I know that you are a stone and can neither benefit anyone nor harm anyone. Had I not seen Allah's Apostle kissing you I would not have kissed you."** (Bukhari Hadith 1494)

Similar has been narrated about the First Caliph, Abu Bakr (RA). See Suyuti's *Tarikh Al-Khulafa* 1/35 cf. *Ilal al-Darqutni*

**STANDING AT ARAFAT:** The pilgrims go to Arafat and they pretend to hear the final sermon of Muhammad which he delivered on this mountain. I don't know how many people can hear Muhammad's voice since he is dead a long time ago. Yes, with modern technology, if the association and organizers of the Hajj put some hidden speakers at different places and play Muhammad's final sermon over and over again, then it might work, but of course, there is no recording of Muhammad's original voice, since the technology didn't exist at that time. Anyhow, these are just mystical things with which the Muslims are linked.

**THROWING STONES ("STONING THE DEVIL"):** Pilgrims throw pebbles, usually about 70 at three spots where Satan is believed to have tempted the Prophet Ismail. Muslims really need to think twice that how many pebbles they need to throw at so many places where Muhammad had been tempted. Throwing stones were also a ritual of pilgrimage among the ancient idolatrous community.

In 2016, the Saudi authorities had to shorten the ritual of Hajj that is stoning Satan after a deadly stampede that led to the death of about 2,300 people in 2015. Satan must be rejoicing since he has to get less hits. Satan must be very grateful to the Hajj committee.

**SACRIFICE AT MINAH:** Pilgrims sacrifice an animal (usually a sheep or goat). This, according to their belief is to commemorate the incident related in the Old Testament when the Prophet Ibrahim/Abraham was about to sacrifice his son and God accepted a sheep instead. Nowadays many pilgrims pay someone to slaughter the animal on their behalf and obtain a certificate to say that the sacrifice has been carried out. The meat is not wasted: much of it is frozen and distributed to poor countries.

The animal sacrifice was also part of the pilgrimage and religious ceremonies during the time of Muhammad. He just changed it into the commemoration of the sacrifice of Abraham's son.

If Muslims have had been visiting merely their holy site (pilgrimage), then it would have been really acceptable, but the Hajj with all its rituals which are directly linked to the idolatrous practices of the pre-Islamic times is nothing short of idolatry and a business of multi-billion dollars for Saudis. To justify my statement, it is apt to document a report about the Hajj-as a big business.

## The Hajj is A Big Business

Saudi Arabia is not too happy about the news that Arab health ministers want to restrict Hajj travel by young and elderly pilgrims. Saudi officials have insisted the ban, which is pending the approval of the Saudi authorities, will not result in a reduction in any country's quota of pilgrims. Every country is allotted a number of Hajj visas amounting to 0.1 per cent of the total population, or 1,000 pilgrims per million people.

Lest you think Saudi Arabia is just concerned about the Ummah's spiritual well-being, remember that the Hajj is a $7 billion-a-year industry for the kingdom. Interestingly, according to *The National*, the Saudi government is accusing Arab health ministers of imposing the young-and-old ban for their *own* economic reasons -- since people will spend their money at home, instead of in Saudi Arabia. (Gregg Carlstrom | July 27, 2009).

## The Ka'ba the Cube-Baitu'llah, "The House of God"

According to Islamic tradition, <u>Allah</u> ordained a place of worship on Earth to reflect the house in heaven.

According to the Qur'an, the Kaaba was built by the prophet Abraham and his son <u>Ishmael</u>.

Muslim writers are excellent in fabrication. They even go one step ahead of the Qur'an by saying that Adam, the first man, built the Ka'ba on earth, exactly below the spot its perfect model occupies in heaven. The Ka'ba refers to the building in which the black stone is housed. Recently, I was watching a program about the Kaaba. A Muslim scholar was not shy at all by saying that Allah himself built the Kaaba. Supposedly, one thousand angels have been appointed to guard the structure. Apparently, they were careless in their duties because Abraham and his son Ishmael are said to have rebuilt it after a flood destroyed it!

Several centuries later, the Meccans had to reconstruct it again after another flood. The stone within the Ka'ba structure is shaped somewhat like an egg and is about seven inches long. Muslims believe that at first it was whiter than milk, but it has become black from the sin of those who touched it.

### What is inside the Kaaba?

Dr. Muzammil Siddiqi is the president of the Islamic Society of North America (ISNA). He had the opportunity to go inside the Kaaba in October 1998. In an interview with Sound Vision, he described the following features:
- There are two pillars inside (others report 3 pillars)
- There is a table on the side to put items like perfume
- There are two lantern-type lamps hanging from the ceiling
- The space can accommodate about 50 people
- There are no electric lights inside - the walls and the floors are of marble
- There are no windows inside
- There is only one door

- The upper inside walls of the Kaaba were covered with some kind of curtain with the Kalima written on it.[xlvii]

The "far distant place of worship" mentioned in (Surah Bani Isra'il 17:1) refers to the Aqsa Mosque, which was built as a church in Jerusalem by the Crusaders during the twelfth century. In 1187 Saladin made it a mosque after he conquered the Holy Land. In other words, no such place existed at the time of the so-called heavenly journey. Even the Dome of the Rock mosque was not built until AD 691.

As to the description of what Muhammad saw in the various levels of heaven, one can find an earlier record of the very same details in The Testament of Abraham.

Although Muhammad claimed he went to Jerusalem and worshipped at the temple in his spirit, whereas, the temple had been destroyed by Titus 570 years before the vision!

There is nothing new in regards to the religious tenets that the religion and the prophet of Islam has originated or initiated which must be esteemed so highly. Even The Qur'an testifies this fact with these words, "*Nothing is said to thee (Muhammad) that was not said to the Apostles before thee,* that thy Lord has at His command (all) forgiveness as well as a most grievous penalty" (Surat-u Fussilat 41:43).

The religion of Islam has adopted many practices that were already common, particularly among the Jews hundreds of years prior to the advent of Muhammad.

The following is a brief list of some Muslim practices that have their counterparts in the Bible. Contrary to what some Muslims would have Christians to believe, these were not a new set of customs for a new religion.

| BIBLICAL PRACTICES | MUSLIMS PRACTICES |
|---|---|
| eeting of peace (Luke 10:5) | 1. As-salamu alai kum (peace be unto you) |
| ashing before prayer (Exodus 40:31-32) | 2. Ablutions, "wudu" |
| moval of shoes in God's presence (Exodus | 3. No shoes inside the mosque |
| ostrate during prayer (Psalm 95:6) | 4. Prostrate during prayer, "sajda" |
| iimal sacrifices (Deuteronomy 16:1-6) | 5. Eid-ul Adha / Eid-ul Qurban, Feast of animal sacrifice |
| lgrimage (Acts 8:26-28) | 6. Pilgrimage to Mecca, "hajj" |
| ad covering for women (1 Corinthians 11:5- | 7. Women wear head-covering |
| rcumcision (Luke 2:21) | 8. Circumcision, "khilan" |
| fering of sacrifice at birth of a child (Luke | 9. Offering of sacrifice at birth of a child, "akika" |
| rolonged fasting (Exodus 34:28, 1 Kings Matt. 4:2) | 10. Thirty-day fast during Ramadhan, "saum" |
| bstinence from pork (Leviticus 11:7)[xlviii] | 11. Muslims abstain from eating pork |

Muslims claim that Muhammad came to establish a new religion that supersedes all other religions prior to him in regards to doctrine and practices. It seems that there is nothing but ignorance at its climax.

The basic tenets of Islam were already in existence even with greater importance and impetus. For example, the Sabaeans-a religious group in Arabia during the time of Muhammad observed the following customs:

- 7 daily prayers, 5 of them at the same times as those chosen by Muhammad
- prayers for the dead
- fasted 30 days from night to sunrise
- observed Eed from the setting of 5 starts
- venerated the Ka'ba

Someone might say, *"Don't judge the Muslims that you know by Islam and don't judge Islam by the Muslims that you know. "*

Islam is an ideology. No ideology is above critique, particularly one that explicitly seeks political and social dominance. Muslims are individuals who should have all the rights to live side by side with other human beings. No Muslim should be harmed, harassed, stereotyped or treated differently anywhere in the world solely on account of their status as a Muslim. Likewise, Muslims should respect non-Muslims, and exhibit a great desire of living with peace and harmony with others.

Not all them Muslims are terrorists. Many have condemned terrorism openly that has even cost them their lives. But it is extremely difficult for the moderate Muslims to condemn the Quranic teachings on killing of the non-Muslims. It has gone to such extreme that the terrorists are determined to kill anybody, and even the people of their own faith. They do not shy away in doing so even in their holy months and sacred festivals since they firmly believe that during a holy month a martyr will goes to heaven.

Unfortunately, there is bad news for all those who have erroneous beliefs about heaven. The Bible says, "you shall not kill" (Exodus 20:13). On the basis on this command, God will not allow any killer to enter into his holy and beautiful paradise. Heaven is not a bar or brothel. The Bible tells that heaven is a holy place. "Nothing impure will ever enter it, nor will anyone who does what is shameful or deceitful, but only those whose names are written in the Lamb's book of life" (Revelation 21:27). "But the cowardly, the unbelieving, the vile, the murderers, the sexually immoral, those who practice magic arts, the idolaters and all liars—they will be consigned to the fiery lake of burning sulfur. This is the second death." (Revelation 21:7).

There is a loving God who forgives sins not on the merit of one's righteousness, but because of His grace and mercy. He has provided a way and that is to accept the righteousness of God on the basis of the demonstration of God's love through the sacrificial death of Jesus on the cross. The Bible say, "In fact, **the** law requires that nearly everything be cleansed with **blood, and without the shedding of blood the**re is no forgiveness" (Hebrews 9:22). People do not need to shed their own blood for their forgiven. They need to put their trust in Jesus who shed His blood on the cross for the forgiveness of all humanity. "But if anybody does sin, we have an advocate with the Father—Jesus Christ, the Righteous One. He is the atoning sacrifice for our sins, and not only for ours but also for the sins of the whole world" (1 John 2:1-2).

141

When a person puts his faith in the sacrificial death of Jesus, asks forgiven of his/her sins, God in return offers that person His righteousness that is found is Jesus Christ and his redemptive work on the cross. Then that person has an assurance for salvation and certainty for eternity. That person will spend eternity with God in the place called heaven where there is peace, love, joy. "And God will wipe away every tear from their eyes; there shall be no more death, nor sorrow, nor crying. There shall be no more pain, for the former things have passed away." (Revelation 21:4).

# CHAPTER SIX

---

# THE TRUTH ABOUT
# SHARIAH LAW

Sharia is the most oppressive system on earth.
It encourages people to lie, if it's for the benefits of Islam.
It doesn't allow Muslims to leave Islam,
and there's a death penalty in all the schools of Sharia
against those that leave Islam. Sharia defines what jihad is.
(Mark Durie)

# CHAPTER SIX
## THE TRUTH ABOUT SHARIAH LAW

### WHY DO WE NEED LAWS?

Laws are important to protect the rights of every individual in a society. The law and regulations give a proper guideline and order for the behavior for all men and to sustain an equity. Without law there would be chaos and conflicts between individuals and social groups. Laws are made not to punish, but to protect people or a society.

In the Old Testament, God also gave laws for the establishment of a healthy and safe community.

The Hebrew word for "Law" is Torah. It means "to teach or to instruct". It refers to either human instruction or divine instruction. Through the Law, God shows His interest in all aspects of man's life. God instructs His people in the way of wisdom and knowledge. It was for the protection and prosperity of people. The Laws of the Old Testament addresses almost every aspect of life. It deals with theology (who God is and how one should worship Him), politics, international and domestic relationships, family life, business, and social life. The Ten Commandments in Exodus 20 deals with one's relationship to God and, also, with fellow human beings. The first four commandments are related to God, while the last six are related to human relationships. There are 613 Laws in the Old Testament that teach about God; how to treat the poor and unfortunate, how to treat strangers and foreigners, how to have healthy marital and family relationships, how to have a healthy life physically, how to deal fairly in business with each other, how to deal with employees, servants and slaves and how to show justice to different groups of people.
Jesus sums up these Laws with two simple, yet profound and powerful commandments. Jesus said...., "*'You shall love the LORD your God with all your heart, with all your soul, and with all your mind.* [38] This is *the* first and great commandment. [39] And *the* second *is* like it: *'You shall love your neighbor as yourself.'* [40] On these two commandments hang all the Law and the Prophets" (Matthew 22:37-40).

### WHAT IS SHARIAH LAW?

The term Sharia means "way" or "path" to be followed. It is the Islamic law, both for civil and criminal justice as well as regulating individual conduct, both in the personal and moral arena.
*These laws are based upon the Quran, which Muslims consider to be the literal word of God; "Sunnah" the divinely guided traditions of Islam's Prophet Muhammad, the Hadith (the collection of Mohammed's sayings,) and the Sira (Mohammed's biography). The commandments of the Sharia law are derived from the Quran (14%) and the example of sayings of Muhammad (86%). Only 200 verses of Quran deal with the legal matters out of 6236 total verses. The Quran is quite limited in creating laws that would be beneficial for the humanity and that would bring safety and security for a community. The Quran at large, is a repetitious as well as a tedious document. The collection of sayings and examples of Muhammad are the compilation of Hadith. Muslim scholars have even admitted very regretfully as well as remorsefully, that many collections of Hadith are unreliable and fallacious. In essence, the formation and foundation of Sharia law is quite shaky. It lacks immense sustainability and substantiality in its claim to be the sole divine law as Muslims have believed for years. It is*

145

based on very little amount of the Quranic teachings which Muslims believe to the first, supreme and final authority, and then the example of Muhammad from Hadith which most of them are not even reliable. So, conclusively, the starting point of Sharia law does not seem good at all even for Muslims who have no choice but the follow those laws that are imposed upon them. It seems that religious leaders complied the laws in such a way that would give them authority over people to control their lives in whatever way they could in the name of Allah. It is very evident that in some Muslims countries, religion and sharia law has been used forcefully by the dictators who are afraid even to hear the name of democracy. They impose the sharia law with such intensity and demonize its citizen so that no one has the right to question or challenge either the laws or a group of people responsible for presenting and imposing laws in the name of Theocracy (ruled by God). If anyone dares to challenge any Islamic law, that person is silenced with threats, intimidation, and eventually wiped out from the scene. This is what is happening in Saudi Arabia, Iran, Pakistan, Bangladesh and in many parts of the world.

Sharia law has a very little amount of derivation of its commandments from the Quran. It is instituted by four main schools of Sharia law:

- **Hanbali:** This is the most conservative school of Sharia. It is used in Saudi Arabia and by some states in Northern Nigeria.
- **Hanifi:** This is the most liberal school, and is relatively open to modern ideas.
- **Maliki:** This is based on the practices of the people of Medina during Muhammad's lifetime.
- **Shafi'i:** This is a conservative school that emphasizes on the opinions of the companions of the Prophet Muhammad.

The principal sources for Islamic law are: The Quran, Tradition, Consensus (*ijma'*), and Reason (*qiyas*). The Shi'ites reject the 'consensus' and substitute what is for them the divinely appointed, infallible spiritual guide (*Imam*)".[xlix]

Sharia law was formatted between the 8th and 10th centuries, some 200 to 300 years after Muhammad received his first revelation. The core components of Sharia had been exhaustively debated. That said, changes in Islamic society force scholars to look at Sharia anew, with new interpretations expressed in fatwas (religious edicts) and opinion. Interpreting Sharia is done by jurists known as "fuqahaa" who look at the practicality of both time and place regarding how a ruling can be applied. In places where Sharia has official status, it is interpreted by judges known as "qadis." It covers personal and collective sphere of daily life.[l]

**Sharia law is divided into two main sections:**
  **I. The acts of worship, or al-ibadat, these include:**
    1. Ritual Purification
    2. Prayers
    3. Fasts (marxva)
    4. Charities
    5. Pilgrimage to Mecca
  **II. Human interaction, or al-mu'amalat, which includes:**
    1. Financial transactions
    2. Endowments (shecirva)
    3. Laws of inheritance (memkvidreoba)
    4. Marriage, divorce, and child care
    5. Foods and drinks (including ritual slaughtering and hunting)

6. Penal punishments
7. Warfare and peace
8. Judicial matters (including witnesses and forms of evidence)[li]

"Traditionally, the Islamic *umma* [community or nation] is divided into three regions: the territory of Islam (*dar al-Islam*) the territory of peace (*dar al-sulh*), and the territory of war (*dar al-harb*). In regions such as Pakistan, Iran, and Libya, Islamic law is assumed to form the basis of government. The second territory represents regions such as India and Africa where Muslims are in the minority but are permitted for the most part to live in peace and to practice their religion freely. The rest of the world comprises the third territory, which is viewed more as an ideological battleground contested by groups with conflicting values than as a literal theatre of war. Within this territory holy war (*jihad*) is waged against all non-Muslims or infidels (*kafir*) in perpetuity until they too are absorbed into the world of Islam.[lii]

In a Theocratic state that is governed by Sharia law, this consists of a hierarchal system with Allah, Muhammad, Ulema (religious teachers), Umma (Muslims), and then non-Muslims. The Sharia law has been used by Islamic states as a mean of dictatorship to snatch away the rights of individuals with regards to freedom of speech and expression and freedom of worship. The Sharia law is a discriminatory and barbaric in its core.

**Under Sharia law:**
- There is no freedom of speech
- There is no freedom of religion
- There is no freedom of expression
- There is no equality of people. There is clear distinction between Muslims and non-Muslims who can never get equal rights.
- There are no equal rights for women.

**According to the Sharia law:**

1. A Caliph who is the head of an Islamic state is exempt from being charged with serious crimes such as murder, adultery, robbery, drinking and in some cases, rape.
2. It is obligatory to obey the commands of the Caliph, even if he is unjust.
3. Criticizing or denying any part of the Quran is punishable by death.
4. Criticizing Muhammad and Islam is a blasphemy that is punishable by death (Qur'an 33:57).
5. To apostate is punished by death.

**MUSLIMS AND NON-MUSLIMS UNDER SHARIA LAW:**

1. A Muslim will be forgiven for murdering: 1) an apostate; 2) an adulterer; 3) a highway robber. Honor killing is acceptable.
   Narrated by 'Abdullah: Allah's Apostle said, "The blood of a Muslim who confesses that none has the right to be worshipped but Allah and that I am His Apostle, cannot be shed except in three cases: In Qisas for murder, a married person who commits illegal sexual intercourse and the one who reverts from Islam (apostate) and leaves the Muslims." (Bukhari 9, 83, 17)
2. A Muslim is exempt from the death penalty if he kills a non-Muslims, but a non-Muslim will get it for killing a Muslim.
3. A non-Muslim who leads a Muslim away from Islam is a crime punishable by death.

4. A non-Muslim man who marries a Muslim woman and converts her to his religion is a crime punishable by death. But if a non-Muslim converts to Islam and marries a Muslim, it is permitted.

Here Sura 109:1-6 is completely ignored and absolutely disregarded.

Say: "O disbelievers!

I worship not that which ye worship;

Nor worship ye that which I worship.

And I shall not worship that which ye worship.

Nor will ye worship that which I worship.

**Unto you your religion, and unto me my religion."**

5. Non-Muslims are not equal to Muslims under the law. They must comply with Islamic law if they are to remain safe. They are forbidden to publicly partake of wine or pork, recite their scriptures or openly celebrate their religious holidays or funerals. They are forbidden from building new churches or building them higher than mosques.

6. It is a crime for a non-Muslim to sell weapons to someone who will use them against Muslims.

7. A percentage of Zakat (charity) must go toward Jihad

8. Muslims may engage in (Taqiyya) deceiving and lying to non-Muslims to advance Islam.

9. A Muslim may marry a non-Muslim woman but first force her to convert to Islam.

## WOMEN UNDER SHARIA LAW:

1. A woman can have 1 husband, but a man can have up to 4 wives if he can afford them and slave women captured in war. An enslave woman who is married, her marriage is then annulled. None of them have a right to divorce him, even he is polygamous. In theory, Islamic law allows spouses to divorce at will, by saying, **"I divorce you"** three times in public. In practice, divorce is more involved than state proceedings which vary. In 2003, for example, a Malaysian court ruled that, under *Sharia law*, a man may divorce his wife via text message as long as the message was clear. Such a divorce, known as the "triple talaq" is not allowed in most Muslim states.

2. A man can unilaterally divorce his wife, but a woman needs her husband's consent to divorce. If in the future, if either the man or woman desire to remarry the divorced partner, the woman must first marry another man, consummate her marriage with this husband, then divorce him. Eventually, she is allowed to remarry her former husband.

3. A woman loses custody if she remarries.

4. Testimonies of four male witnesses are required to prove rape against a woman (Quran 4:15).

5. A woman who has been raped cannot testify in court against her rapist(s).

6. A rapist may only be required to pay the bride-money (dowry) without marrying the rape victim.

7. A Muslim woman must cover every inch of her body, which is considered "Awrah," a sexual organ. Not all Sharia schools allow the face of a woman to be exposed.

8. A man can beat his wife for insubordination.

Men are in charge of women by [right of] what Allah has given one over the other and what they spend [for maintenance] from their wealth. So righteous women are devoutly obedient, guarding in [the husband's] absence what Allah would have them guard. But those [wives] from whom you fear arrogance - [first] advise them; [then if they persist], forsake them in bed; and [finally], strike them. But if they obey you [once more], seek no means against them. Indeed, Allah is ever Exalted and Grand. (Surah 4:34).

9. A Muslim man is forgiven if he kills his wife at the time he caught her in the act of adultery. However, the opposite is not true for women, since the man "could be married to the woman he was caught with."
10. There is no age limit for marriage of girls. The marriage contract can take place any time after birth and can be consummated at the age 8 or 9.
11. A female heir inherits half of what a male heir inherits (Surah 4:11).
12. A woman cannot drive a car, as it leads to *fitnah* (upheaval).
13. A woman cannot speak alone to a man who is not her husband or relative.
14. A woman's testimony in court, allowed only in property cases, carries half the weight of a man's.

*"O you who have believed, when you contract a debt for a specified term, write it down. And let a scribe write [it] between you in justice. Let no scribe refuse to write as Allah has taught him. So let him write and let the one who has the obligation dictate. And let him fear Allah, his Lord, and not leave anything out of it. But if the one who has the obligation is of limited understanding or weak or unable to dictate himself, then let his guardian dictate in justice. And bring to witness two witnesses from among your men. **And if there are not two men [available], then a man and two women from those whom you accept as witnesses** - so that if one of the women errs, then the other can remind her. And let not the witnesses refuse when they are called upon. And do not be [too] weary to write it, whether it is small or large, for its [specified] term. That is more just in the sight of Allah and stronger as evidence and more likely to prevent doubt between you, except when it is an immediate transaction which you conduct among yourselves. For [then] there is no blame upon you if you do not write it. And take witnesses when you conclude a contract. Let no scribe be harmed or any witness. For if you do so, indeed, it is [grave] disobedience in you. And fear Allah. And Allah teaches you. And Allah is Knowing of all things" (Surah 2:282).*

Narrated by Abu Said Al-Khudri
The Prophet said, "Isn't the witness of a woman equal to half of that of a man?" The women said, "Yes." He said, "This is because of the deficiency of a woman's mind." (Bukhari 3,48,826; Abu Dawaud 11, 2155; Bukhari 1,6,301).

15. An adulteress is stone to death
Narrated by Zaid bin Khalid and Abu Huraira:
The Prophet said, "O Unais! Go to the wife of this (man) and if she confesses (that she has committed illegal sexual intercourse), then stone her to death." (Bukhari 3,38,508; 8,82,803).

## LIVING UNDER SHARIA LAW
1. In court, a testimony is unacceptable from people of low-level jobs, such as street sweepers or bathhouse attendants.
2. Meat to be eaten must come from animals that have been sacrificed to Allah - i.e., Halal.
3. Sharia Law also includes a set of crimes that invoke hudud penalties, which are the penalties specified in the Quran and therefore cannot be mitigated or reduced. They

include amputating the right hand of a thief, amputating the right hand and left foot of an armed highway robber, stoning an adulterer, flogging a fornicator or sodomizer 100 lashes and banishing the person 50 miles for one year, flogging a false accuser of adultery 80 lashes, and flogging a person 40 lashes for drinking even a glass of wine. Except for the latter crime, all of these penalties apply to Muslims and non-Muslims alike in an Islamic State.

## SHARIA LAW IN COMPARISION

| LAWS BASED ON JUDEO-CHRISTIAN SCRIPTURES | SHARIA LAW BASED ON THE QURAN AND HADITH |
|---|---|
| **Love your Neighbor:**<br>"You have heard that it was said, 'You shall love your neighbor and hate your enemy.' [44] But I say to you, love your enemies, bless those who curse you, do good to those who hate you, and pray for those who spitefully use you and persecute you, [45] that you may be sons of your Father in heaven; for He makes His sun rise on the evil and on the good, and sends rain on the just and on the unjust. [46] For if you love those who love you, what reward have you? Do not even the tax collectors do the same? [47] And if you greet your brethren only, what do you do more *than others?* Do not even the tax collectors do so? [48] Therefore you shall be perfect, just as your Father in heaven is perfect. (Matthew 5:43-48).<br>Therefore "If your enemy is hungry, feed him;<br>If he is thirsty, give him a drink; For in so doing you will heap coals of fire on his head." [21] Do not be overcome by evil, but overcome evil with good. (Romans 12:20-21) | Muhammad is the Messenger of Allah; **and those with him are forceful against the disbelievers, merciful among themselves.** You see them bowing and prostrating [in prayer], seeking bounty from Allah and [His] pleasure. Their mark is on their faces from the trace of prostration. That is their description in the Torah. And their description in the Gospel is as a plant which produces its offshoots and strengthens them so they grow firm and stand upon their stalks, delighting the sowers - so that Allah may enrage by them the disbelievers. Allah has promised those who believe and do righteous deeds among them forgiveness and a great reward. (surah 48:29).<br>**Islam always distinguish between Muslims and Non-Muslims and make laws accordingly.** |
| **Do not Murder:**<br>"You shall not murder" (Exodus 20:13). | **Murdering an apostate is permitted.**<br>A parent might kill his/her children or grandchildren which is called honor killing. |
| **Do not commit Adultery:**<br>"You shall not commit adultery" (Exodus 20:14) | Sex with multiple wives (m6.10), sex with slaves and captives (Quran 33:50), and sex with temporary wives (Quran 4:24). |
| **Do not bear false witness:** | Muslims may engage in (Taqiyya) deceiving and lying to non-Muslims to |

| | |
|---|---|
| "You shall not bear false witness against your neighbor" (Exodus 20:16) | advance Islam, protecting Muslims and Islam. |
| **Freedom of Religion:**<br>In a country like Saudi Arabia, Christian cannot build churches. They are not allowed to visit Mecca and Medina, the holy cities of Islam. In the western world, Muslims build Mosques and enjoy all the freedom of worship.<br>In some staunch Muslim countries, Muslims are not allowed to change their religion whereas Non-Muslims are forced to do it. | They wish you would disbelieve as they disbelieved so you would be alike. So do not take from among them allies until they emigrate for the cause of Allah. But if they turn away, then seize them and kill them wherever you find them and take not from among them any ally or helper. (Surah 4:89)<br><br>**Narrated by 'Ikrima**<br>Some Zanadiqa (atheists) were brought to 'Ali and he burnt them. The news of this event, reached Ibn 'Abbas who said, "If I had been in his place, I would not have burnt them, as Allah's Apostle forbade it, saying, 'Do not punish anybody with Allah's punishment (fire).' I would have killed them according to the statement of **Allah's Apostle, 'Whoever changed his Islamic religion, then kill him.'"** (Bukhari 9:84:57) |
| **Freedom of Speech:**<br>The books and literature that shed light on Islam, Muhammad and Quran are banned. The authors of such literature are threatened and even killed. | Speech of insulting Islam or Muhammad is considered "blasphemy" and is punished by death. |
| **Right to self-defense:** | Non-Muslims cannot possess sword, firearms or weapons of any kind under Sharia law. |
| **Right to have a fair trial:** | Hadith Sahih Bukhari, Muhammad said, Muhammad said, "No Muslim should be killed for killing a kafir (infidel)" (Sahih Bukhari 9:83:50). Non-Muslims are forbidden from testifying against Muslims. A woman's testimony is equal to half of a man's (Surah 2:282).<br>*Men are superior to women (Qur'an 2:228).* |

**SUMMARY:**
Saima Baig, a Muslim woman from Pakistan has argued that Muslims have this tendency of explaining to others that Islam provided rights to women in an era where they did not have those rights. I tend to disagree with that but that is a whole other debate. Let's assume that they were provided with these rights. And these rights were perfect. The thing to understand is that

they were perfect for 7th century Arabia. They are not perfect today. In fact, they are not even rights but just methods to subjugate women.

As a 21st century woman, I do not want the perverted, bearded gents that comprise the CII (Council of Islamic Ideology) to tell me what my rights are. I am very well aware of my rights and I do not need a bunch of men to give them to me. My rights are to live my life as an individual and are not based on my gender. I am not my gender; I am a human being.

No, the Sharia does not provide women with the rights they should demand in this day and age. It is very clear to anyone with half a brain cell.

Sharia law is discriminatory and highly biased towards a certain groups of people. It brings slavery and snatches personal freedom to its climax. Sharia law must be forbidden in any civilized society and people must work hard to eradicate such cruel and discriminatory laws that enslave and treat people ruthlessly.

In the Old Testament, God commanded his people to have the same law for everybody in a community.

*'Whoever kills any man shall surely be put to death. [18] Whoever kills an animal shall make it good, animal for animal. [19] 'If a man causes disfigurement of his neighbor, as he has done, so shall it be done to him— [20] fracture for fracture, eye for eye, tooth for tooth; as he has caused disfigurement of a man, so shall it be done to him. [21] And whoever kills an animal shall restore it; but whoever kills a man shall be put to death. [22] **You shall have the same law for the stranger and for one from your own country;** for I am the LORD your God'"* (Leviticus 24:17-22).

The world should wake up. The leaders of the nations and the law makers around the world ought to stand together against the laws that are against human rights and endeavor to defend them against any set of law whether it is religious or political basis.

# CHAPTER SEVEN

## THE TRUTH ABOUT JIHAD

The Quran contains at least 109 verses that call Muslims to war with nonbelievers for the sake of Islamic rule. Some are quite graphic, with commands to chop off heads and fingers and kill infidels wherever they may be hiding. Muslims who do not join the fight are called 'hypocrites' and warned that Allah will send them to Hell if they do not join the slaughter.

# CHAPTER SEVEN
## THE TRUTH ABOUT JIHAD

Tashfeen Malik pledged her support for Islamic jihad in her private messages which she sent before entering the United States. Malik hoped to eventually become a jihadist. And that is what she did. On December 2, 2015, Tashfeen Malik together with her husband, Syed Rizwan Farook killed 14 people and seriously injured 22 in a terrorist attack at the Inland Regional Center in San Bernardino, California, which consisted of a mass shooting and an attempted bombing.

There are thousands of Islamic jihadists, religious extremist and fanatics who have pledged their support to the terrorist organizations like ISIS, Al Qaeda, Boko-Haram, Al Shabab, Hamas, Lashkar-e-Tayyiba, Lashkar Jhangvi, Sipah-I-Sahaba and the Muslim brotherhood. The Jihadists have waged war against the West, particularly and against other religious groups at large.

The word Jihad has turned into a very familiar word because it is in the news almost daily. It is immensely related to the religion of Islam. Islam means submission. It does not mean peace as sometimes people have been made to believe. Linguistically, "SALAM", means peace. It is the letter "I" that changes the meaning. Whenever and wherever the letter "I" exists emphatically and forcefully, it always changes the meaning. For example, the middle letter in SIN and PRIDE is "I". Whenever, the focus is on "I" self, it brings the absence of peace which is found very vividly in Islam.

Muslims are forced to submit to Allah and Muhammed even though they might have many questions about their faith. It is also the religious duty of good Muslims to force others to submit to Islam. That is why, terrorists condemn moderate and peaceful Muslims who do not take part in Jihad, either financially or being active in Jihad through pen, imposing laws, or taking sword in the hand.

### WHAT IS JIHAD?

The Arabic word "jihad" is often translated as "holy war. " But the literal meaning of Jihad is to struggle or strive. It is described as internal as well as external efforts to be a good Muslims or believer, as well as working to inform people about the faith of Islam. It is referred to as a religious duty or obligation. Some Muslim scholars view it as the sixth pillar of Islam.
The five basic pillars of Islam which are:
1. **Shahada: Faith**
2. **Salat: Prayer**
3. **Zakāt: Charity**
4. **Sawm: Fasting**
5. **Hajj: Pilgrimage to Mecca**
6. **Jihad (optional)**

**Islamic scholars agree about the military form of jihad. It is required to defend and protect the faith by using legal, diplomatic, and political means. Islam also allows for the use of force. The moderate Muslims might use legal or political means of protecting the faith, whereas religious fanatics esteem taking the "sword verses" in the Quran which are**

155

**as many as one hundred and forty-nine, very seriously and take Muhammad as their role model with regards to him as a militant leader.**

Muhammad's life is divided into two parts: the life in Mecca, where he labored for fourteen years to convert people to Islam; and then, his life in Medina (Yathrib) where he became a powerful political and military leader more than merely a religious leader. The Quran is also divided into two parts: Meccan Quran that presents Islam as a peaceful religion whereas Medinan Quran, which is a militant faith in its notion. In Mecca, Muhammad preached about repentance and charity; whereas in Medina, he wages war against all those who opposed him and killed or asked his followers to kill all those who did not accept him or insulted him. When Muhammad was weak and needed favor and support from others, he preached and advocated peace, but when he was strong, and had an army who would fight for him, he planned and fought at least sixty-seven wars against unbelievers (Christians, Jews, and others). This is the same strategy Muslims use even to this day.

### JIHAD AS DEFINED PLAINLY BY THE MULISM BROTHERHOOD:

Lt. General William G. Boykin has highlighted that Jihad is to create caliphate, and Islamic world-wide super state which will usher in the reign of Islamic Messiah (Mahdi). There have been multiple caliphates established for example during the reign of Ottoman empire and so on. The Ottoman empire was the last hope for Muslims to see the establishment of the Islamic caliphate whereas that hope was shattered as Ottoman empire was defeated after the Word War I. In 1924, Kamal Ataturk of Turkey abolished the caliphate, and sharia law, and declared the country to be a secular country with Muslim population.

Hasan Al-Banna was disappointed over the demise of Ottoman empire and disappearance of that great hope of caliphate   founded the Muslim Brotherhood in 1928, which today is the most powerful organization in Egypt second to the government, itself. In this treatise, Al-Banna cogently argues that Muslims must take up arms against unbelievers. He states, "The verses of the Qur'an and the Sunnah (saying and action of Muhammed) summon people in general (with the most eloquent expression and the clearest exposition) to jihad, to warfare, to the armed forces, and all means of land and sea fighting."

Muslim Brotherhood motto:
  "All is our way;
  The Qur'an is our constitution;
  Muhammad is our leader;
  Jihad is our way;
  Dying for the same of Allah is our highest aspiration."

This is what members of the Muslims Brotherhood chant everyday as they meet in mosques or jihadi camps.

Hasan Al-Banna had the support of Sayyid Qutb who gained support of 800 members in ten years. Hasan Al-Banna moved to Germany where he was living as a guest of Adolf Hitler. Hitler asked an advice from Hanan Al-Banna, how he could help him to deal with the Jews living in Europe. Hasan Al-Banna introduced Hitler to Amin Al-Husseini, the grand mufti of Jerusalem. In that meeting of two hours, Hitler asked Husseini to stop Jews coming to Palestine. In return, Hitler promised to grant him and the Muslim Brotherhood with millions of dollars. Hitler promised him to kill Jews systematically with great brutality to get rid of Jews in Europe and to give favor to the Muslim Brother. The grand mufti of Jerusalem helped in formation of Muslim armies in the Balkan to fight for Hitler.

All Muslims are required Jihad. Jihad is an obligation from Allah on every Muslim and cannot be ignored nor evaded. Allah has ascribed great importance to jihad and has made the reward of the martyrs and the fighters in His way a splendid one. Only those who have acted similarly and who have modeled themselves upon the martyrs in their performance of jihad can join them in this reward. Furthermore, Allah has specifically honored the Mujahideen {those who wage jihad} with certain exceptional qualities, both spiritual and practical, to benefit them in this world and the next. Their pure blood is a symbol of victory in this world and the mark of success and felicity in the world to come.

For those who only find excuses, however, have been warned of extremely dreadful punishments and that Allah has described them with the most unfortunate of names. He has reprimanded them for their cowardice and lack of spirit, and castigated them for their weakness and truancy. In this world, they will be surrounded by dishonor and in the next they will be surrounded by the fire from which they shall not escape though they may possess much wealth. The weaknesses of abstention and evasion of jihad are regarded by Allah as one of the major sins, and one of the seven sins that guarantee failure. Islam is concerned with the question of jihad and the drafting and the mobilization of the entire Umma {the global Muslim community} into one body to defend the right cause with all its strength than any other ancient or modern system of living, whether religious or civil. The verses of the Qur'an and the Sunnah of Muhammad (PBUH {Peace Be Unto Him}) are overflowing with all these noble ideals and they summon people in general (with the most eloquent expression and the clearest exposition) to jihad, to warfare, to the armed forces, and all means of land and sea fighting.[liii]

The Muslim brotherhood has given birth to the terrorist organizations such as Hamas, Hizballah, Al Quaeda, and many more around the world.

One might argue that there are extremist and fanatics in every religion, of which Islamic faith is not exempt from. Certainly, it is important to be honest and fair about judging, but in regards to fanaticism, one must take heed to the basic teaching of any faith in this matter.

## QURANIC TEACHINGS ON JIHAD DEFINES IT AS HOLY WAR:

*In Mecca, Muhammed had the message of religious tolerance which is quite evident in Surah 50:45; 109:6; 2:256). But in Medina, Muhammed's message had a completely different tone.*

*For example:* "And fight them until there is no more Fitnah (disbelief and polytheism: i.e. worshipping others besides Allah) and the religion (worship) will all be for Allah Alone [in the whole of the world]. But if they cease (worshipping others besides Allah), then certainly, Allah is All-Seer of what they do" (Surah 8:39).

"It is not for a Prophet that he should have prisoners of war (and free them with ransom) until he had made a great slaughter (among his enemies) in the land. You desire the good of this world (i.e. the money of ransom for freeing the captives), but Allah desires (for you) the Hereafter. And Allah is All-Mighty, All-Wise" (Surah 8:67).

*"Therefore, when ye meet the Unbelievers (in fight), smite at their necks; at length, when ye have thoroughly subdued them, bind a bond firmly (on them): thereafter (is the time for) either*

157

*generosity or ransom: Until the war lays down its burdens. Thus (are ye commanded): but if it had been God's Will, He could certainly have exacted retribution from them (Himself); but (He lets you fight) in order to test you, some with others. But those who are slain in the way of God, He will never let their deeds be lost. Soon will He guide them and improve their condition. And admit them to the Garden which He has announced for them. O ye who believe! if ye will aid (the cause of) God, He will aid you, and plant your feet firmly. But those who reject (God), for them is destruction, and (God) will render their deeds astray (from their mark)" (47:4-8).*

"Then when the Sacred Months (the 1st, 7th, 11th, and 12th months of the Islamic calendar) have passed, then kill the Mushrikun {unbelievers} wherever you find them, and capture them and besiege them, and prepare for them each and every ambush. But if they repent and perform As-Salat (Iqamat-as-Salat {the Islamic ritual prayers}), and give Zakat {alms}, then leave their way free. Verily, Allah is Oft- Forgiving, Most Merciful" (9:5).

*"Fight those who believe not in God nor the Last Day, nor hold that forbidden which hath been forbidden by God and His apostle, nor acknowledge the religion of truth, (even if they are) of the People of the Book, until they pay the Jizya with willing submission, and feel themselves subdued" (9:29).*

*surah 9 is considered to be the final revelation Muhammed received at the end of his life. The sword verses in the Quran themselves speak for itself that Islam is not a religion of peace since Muslims consider the Quran as the divine revelation from Allah take it as their final authority.*

## SUNNAH AUTHENTICATES JIHAD AS HOLY WAR

Narrated Anas: "The Prophet cut off the hands and feet of the men belonging to the tribe of Uraina and did not cauterize (their bleeding limbs) till they died" (Sahih Bukhari Volume 8, Book 82, Number 795).

**Narrated by Abu Huraira:** Allah's Apostle was asked, "What is the best deed?" He replied, "To believe in Allah and His Apostle (Muhammad). The questioner then asked, "What is the next (in goodness)? He replied, "To participate in Jihad (religious fighting) in Allah's Cause." The questioner again asked, "What is the next (in goodness)?" He replied, "To perform Hajj (Pilgrim age to Mecca) 'Mubrur, (which is accepted by Allah and is performed with the intention of seeking Allah's pleasure only and not to show off and without committing a sin and in accordance with the traditions of the Prophet)" (Sahih Bukhari Volume 1, Book 2, Number 25).

## THE HISTORY VALIDATES JIHAD AS HOLY WAR

The Sira (Biography of Muhammed) and Hadith (saying and doing of Muhammad) shed a bright light on Jihad as a Holy War, especially during the last ten years of Muhammed's life (622-632 A.D). After Muhammed's life, the four prominent caliphs, and numerous other caliphs, carried out the mission of the Islamic submission and domination even to the present day. Muhammad had twenty-five people killed who criticized him. He was involved in twenty-nine battle campaigns.

Islam is not only a religion. It is also a political ideology. Muslims have typically divided the world into two domains, known as the *Dar al-Islam*—the "house of Islam" or "house of submission" to God—and the *Dar al-Harb*, or "house of war"—those who are at war with God.

The *Dar al-Harb* must be brought under the control of the Muslim government and made part of the *Dar al-Islam*. The *Dar al-Harb* by its nature is at war with God, it is unlikely that it will submit to God without a fight. Individual groups might be convinced to lay down their arms and join the Muslim community by various forms of pressure—economic or military—that fall short of war. In history, some groups have become Muslim in this way, either fearing Muslim conquest, desiring Muslim military aid against their own enemies, or aspiring to good trade relations with the Muslim world. But many peoples would rather fight than switch. This has been particularly true of Christians, who have put up more resistance to the Muslim advance than have pagan and animistic tribes. Because of the need to expand God's dominion by wars of conquest, Islam's ideology imposes on Muslims the duty to fight for God's community. As eminent French sociologist Jacques Ellul notes, "*Jihad* is a religious obligation. It forms part of the duties that the believer must fulfill; it is Islam's *normal* path to expansion."[liv]

A fourth and final consequence of Islam's view of itself as a theocracy is that in theory all Muslims should not only form one religious community but should be subject to one government as well—God's government, a kind of Muslim super state. Yet this has not happened. Muslims have been ruled by different governments since the early days of Islam.

According to Dr. Bill Warner, "Data bases of ancient documents" reveals that Islam has fought 548 battles from the dawn of Islam and throughout the history of 1400. The Battle of Badr; The Battle of Uhud; The Battle of Medina (Trench); and The battle of Khybair are the examples where Muhammed and his followers attached, fought, and killed the Meccan caravans and anyone who did not submit to Muhammad and his followers. During this time of brutality, 800 Jews were butchered, the women were raped, taken as sex slaves and the innocent children were enslaved.

The Muslims apologists call it the battles as a form of self-defense against the persecution Muhammad and his followers were facing. But history and even the very own history of Islam, speaks very differently. These battles and Jihad were an attempt to purge the land from anyone who was not in alignment with Islam and refused to submit to Muhammad. Islam is not merely a religion telling people about the way to worship God and teaching people a way of life to live that would build communities where people live with peace and harmony. Islam has a political agenda and that is to wipe out the existing culture, and belief system that people had or have and to impose its Islamic tenets by any and every means possible civilization faith and belief people have and to impose its culture and belief system by any and every means.

Muhammed said, "No infidel [unbeliever] should be left on his land. He added, 'I was commanded to fight the people ...'"[lv] (Bukhari Vol. I, p. 13)

"Muhammad sent Khalid Ibn al-Walid to the tribe of the children of Haritha and told him: 'Call them to accept Islam before you fight with them. If they respond, accept that from them, but if they refuse, fight them.' Khalid told them: 'Accept Islam and spare your life.' They entered Islam by force. He brought them to Muhammad. Muhammad said to them: 'Had you not accepted Islam I would have cast your heads under your feet'" (ibn Hisham, "The Biography of the Apostle", part 4, p. 134; also, Al Road Al Anf, part 4, pp. 217, 218)

"The apostle of God started to send military detachments from among his followers to the various Arab tribes which were scattered in the Arab Peninsula to carry out the task of calling (these tribes) to accept Islam If they did not respond; they would kill them. That was during the 7th Higira year. The number of the detachments amounted to ten." (*Dr. Muhammad Sa'id Ramadan al-Buti, "Jurisprudence in Muhammad's Biography", 7th ed., p. 263*)

"Ali Ibn Abi Talib encountered a man called 'Umru and told him, `I indeed invite you to Islam.' 'Umru said, `I do not need that.' 'Ali said, 'Then I call you to fight.' (This was the same policy Muhammad used with those who rejected his invitation.) 'Umru answered him, `What for my nephew? By God, I do not like to kill you.' `Ali said, `But, by God, I love to kill you'" (*ibn Hisham, "The Biography of the Prophet", part 3, p. 113; see also Al Road Al Anf part 3, p. 263*).[lvi]

* Narrated Jubair bin Haiya:
'Umar sent the Muslims to the great countries to fight the pagans. When Al-Hurmuzan embraced Islam, 'Umar said to him. "I would like to consult you regarding these countries which I intend to invade." Al-Hurmuzan said, "Yes, the example of these countries and their inhabitants who are the enemies of the Muslims, is like a bird with a head, two wings and two legs; If one of its wings got broken, it would get up over its two legs, with one wing and the head; and if the other wing got broken, it would get up with two legs and a head, but if its head got destroyed, then the two legs, two wings and the head would become useless. The head stands for Khosrau, and one wing stands for Caesar and the other wing stands for Faris. So, order the Muslims to go towards Khosrau." So, 'Umar sent us (to Khosrau) appointing An-Numan bin Muqrin as our commander. When we reached the land of the enemy, the representative of Khosrau came out with forty-thousand warriors, and an interpreter got up saying, "Let one of you talk to me!" Al-Mughira replied, "Ask whatever you wish." The other asked, "Who are you?" Al-Mughira replied, "We are some people from the Arabs; we led a hard, miserable, disastrous life: we used to suck the hides and the date stones from hunger; we used to wear clothes made up of fur of camels and hair of goats, and to worship trees and stones. While we were in this state, the Lord of the Heavens and the Earths, Elevated is His Remembrance and Majestic is His Highness, sent to us from among ourselves a Prophet whose father and mother are known to us. Our Prophet, the Messenger of our Lord, has ordered us to fight you till you worship Allah Alone or give *Jizya* (i.e. tribute); and our Prophet has informed us that our Lord says: -- "Whoever amongst us is killed (i.e. martyred), shall go to Paradise to lead such a luxurious life as he has never seen, and whoever amongst us remain alive, shall become your master." (Al-Mughira, then blamed An-Numan for delaying the attack and) An-Nu'man said to Al-Mughira, "If you had participated in a similar battle, in the company of Allah's Apostle he would not have blamed you for waiting, nor would he have disgraced you. But I accompanied Allah's Apostle in many battles and it was his custom that if he did not fight early by daytime, he would wait till the wind had started blowing and the time for the prayer was due (i.e. after midday)." (*Sahih Bukhari 4.386*)

Gregory David, call it "The First Major Wave of Jihad," Arabs started in 622 that would continue until 750 AD. Muslims fought and subdued the people of the Middle East, Africa, Asia, and Europe in the name of Allah. In Hindustan (India) 26,000 Hindus were attacked and killed, the nobles in Armenia were burned, and in Ephesus 7000 Greeks were enslaved. Caliph Umar conquered Jerusalem and made Christians and Jews dhimmis (second class citizen in an Islamic state).

The Muslim offensive was finally stopped in the West at the Battle of Poitiers/Tours, not far from Paris, on the 10th of October in 732 AD. The battle pitted Frankish and Burgundian forces under Austrian Mayor of the Palace Charles Martel against an army of the Umayyad Caliphate led by 'Abdul Rahman Al Ghafiqi (died 732), Governor-General of al-Andalus. The Franks were victorious. 'Abdul Rahman Al Ghafiqi was killed, and Charles subsequently extended his authority in the south. Ninth-century chroniclers, who interpreted the outcome of the battle as divine judgment in his favor, gave Charles the nickname *Martellus* ("The Hammer"). Notably, the Frankish troops won the battle without a cavalry. Later Christian chroniclers and pre-20th century historians praised Charles Martel as the champion of Christianity, characterizing the battle as the decisive turning point in the struggle against Islam, a struggle which preserved Christianity as the religion of Europe.[lvii] However, In the east, the jihad penetrated deep into Central Asia.

This first wave of jihad engulfed much of the Byzantine, Visigothic, Frankish, and Persian Empires and left the newborn Islamic Empire controlling territory from Southern France, south through Spain, east across North Africa to India, and north to Russia. Early in the second millennium AD, the Mongol invasion from the east greatly weakened the Islamic Empire and ended Arab predominance therein.[lviii] During this era, all new churches were destroyed, with the massive enslavement. Egyptian Christians revolted over the Jizyah (a tax required for non-Muslims in an Islamic state).

Dr. Bill Warner has highlighted Jihad throughout the centuries in his lecture on "Why we are so afraid" that bring authenticated and factual teaching on the subject of Islamic Jihad from the very beginning of the Islamic faith to the present day. For example:

In the 10[TH] century, the Muslim Jihad enslaved 22,000 Thessalonians, Christians were massacre in Seville, and 30,000 Churches destroyed in Egypt and Syria.

In the 11[TH] century, 6000 Jews of Morocco, hundreds of Jews in Cordoba and 4000 Jews of Granada were killed. Georgia and Armenia were invaded and in Hindustan (India) 15,000 were killed and 500,000 were enslaved

In the 12[TH] century, Jews in Yemen were asked either to convert or die. Christians of Granada were deported to Morocco, and in India, many cities were destroyed. People were asked either to convert or die. 20,000 were enslaved just in one town.

In the 13[TH] century, in India, 50,000 Hindu slaves were freed after their conversion to Islam. A 20-year campaign created 400,000 new Muslims out of Hindus. Buddhist monks were butchered, nuns were raped. In Damascus and Safed - Christians were mass murdered. Jews of Marrakesh were massacred and there was a forced conversions of Jews in Tabri.

In the 14[TH] century, during the Cairo riots churches were burned. Tamerlane (Timur) in India killed as many as 90,000 in a day. Tughlaq took 180,000 slaves.

The Turkish wave of jihad reached its farthest extent at the failed sieges of Vienna in 1529 and 1683, where, in the latter instance, the Muslim army under Kara Mustapha was thrown back by the Roman Catholics under the command of Polish King, John Sobieski. In the decades that followed, the Ottomans were driven back down through the Balkans, though they were never ejected from the European continent entirely. Still, even while the imperial jihad faltered, Muslim land- and sea-borne razzias into Christian territory continued and Christians were being abducted into slavery from as far away as Ireland into the 19th century.

In the 15[TH] century, Tamerlane (Timur) in India devastated 700 villages. Tamerlane annihilated Nestorian and Jacobite Christians.

Zahir ud din Babur (1483-1530), the founder of the Mughal Empire is presented as an example of Muslim tolerance. However, the history speaks differently as narrated in his own words in his autobiography "Baburnama" about the infidel prisoners of Jihad campaigns: "Those who were brought in alive [having surrendered] were ordered beheaded, after which, a tower of skulls was erected in the camp."[lix]

After 700 years of attacks, Islam captured and destroyed Constantinople.
Paul Fregosi in his book Jihad describes the scene following the final assault on Constantinople:
Several thousand of the survivors had taken refuge in the cathedral: nobles, servants, ordinary citizens, their wives and children, priests, and nuns. They locked the huge doors, prayed, and waited. {Caliph} Mahomet {II} had given the troops free quarter. They raped, of course, the nuns being the first victims, and slaughtered. At least four thousand were killed before Mahomet stopped the massacre at noon. He ordered a muezzin {one who issues the call to prayer} to climb into the pulpit of St. Sophia and dedicate the building to Allah. It has remained a mosque ever since. Fifty thousand of the inhabitants, more than half the population, were rounded up and taken away as slaves. For months, afterward, slaves were the cheapest commodity in the markets of Turkey.
Mahomet asked that the body of the dead emperor be brought to him. Some Turkish soldiers found it in a pile of corpses and recognized Constantine {XI} by the golden eagles embroidered on his boots. The sultan ordered his head to be cut off and placed between the horse's legs under the equestrian bronze statue of the emperor Justinian. The head was later embalmed and sent around the chief cities of the Ottoman empire for the delectation of the citizens. Next, Mahomet ordered the Grand Duke Notaras, who had survived, be brought before him, asked him for the names and addresses of all the leading nobles, officials, and citizens, which Notaras gave him. He had them all arrested and decapitated. He sadistically bought from their owners {i.e., Muslim commanders} high-ranking prisoners who had been enslaved, for the pleasure of having them beheaded in front of him. (Fregosi, Jihad, 256-7.)

In the 16TH century, the son of Tamerlane destroyed temples and there was forced conversions in India. Generals built two towers of human heads after victories. At this time of bloody and brutal time of atrocities, noble women commit mass suicide to avoid sexual slavery and rape.

In the 17TH century, Jews of Yemen and Persia were forced to convert. There was forced conversions of Greek Christians to Islam in Persia (Iran). The persecution against Zoroastrian increased. In India 600,000 Hindus were killed by Aurangzeb.

In the 18TH century, the persecution against Zoroastrian intensifies. Jews of Jedda, Arabia were expelled. Jews of Morocco were massacred and the persecution against Hindus continues.

In the 19TH century, there was a forced conversion of Jews in Iran. The Jews of Baghdad were massacred. About 250,000 Armenian Christians were slaughtered in Turkey.

In the 20TH century, over 1,000,000 Turkish Armenians were killed in jihad.

The anti-Christian jihad culminated in 1922 at Smyrna, on the Mediterranean coast, where 150,000 Greek Christians were massacred by the Turkish army under the indifferent eye of Allied warships. All in, from 1896-1923, some 2.5 million Christians were killed, the first modern genocide, which to this day the Turkish government has denied.[lx]

As Gregory M. Davis, has highlighted that the first wave of Jihad was started by the Arabs (622-750) while the Second Major Wave of Jihad was led by the Turks (1071-1683 AD). The Ottoman army was defeated outside Vienna on September 11, 1683 by Polish forces. Islam went into a period of strategic decline in which it was overwhelmingly dominated by the European powers. Much of dar al-Islam was colonized by the European powers who employed their superior technology and exploited the rivalries within the Muslim world to establish colonial rule.[lxi]

It seems that September 11, 2001 was a well-planned attack on the western world in an attempt to defeat the west because the Jihadist were defeated on September 11, 1683 in Vienna by the west and the Islamic invasion was stopped at the gates of Vienna. The majestic twin towers of the World Trade Center in New York city were the icon of New York financial center and the symbol of the Greatness of American economy and her leading role in the free world was targeted to be brought down. The Jihadist are always after controlling the financial systems and sectors of the world while destroying the commercial citadel of non-Muslims.

Four reasons why September 11 might be significant to Islam which are:
1. Battle of Vienna when Ottoman army was defeated took place on September 11-12, 1683.
2. The Great Siege of Malta was closed on September 11, 1565. Malta saved Europe and Christianity
3. Muslims expulsion from Spain announced was announced on September 11, 1609). The "little Moors" fled from Spain.
4. The Battle of Zenta took place September 11, 1697. Zenta was the last decisive step to force the Ottoman Empire into the Treaty of Karlowitz (1699), ending the Ottoman control of large parts of Central Europe.

Not known for sure how Jihadists put great significance of historical dates but fits in their right the wrongs of past failures of defeat by Christians.

There are different ways of Jihad which are:
Jihad of Womb is done by having many children into order to outnumber a country.
Political Jihad is done by subjugating the culture and its freedom.
Banking Jihad is done by subjugating the financial institutions.
Judicial Jihad is done by subjugating the legal and court systems.
Jihad is done in controlling media, education, and freedom of speech.

The Muslim fanatics have strategically planned three forms of Jihad which are called Jihad through pen, laws and then, sword.

Jihad through pen means to write against other religions, bring doubt about their belief systems deceptively and try to silence others with threats and attempt to kill if possible. The religious thugs and hooligans think that they have all the rights to criticize other religions, while they are intolerant of hearing the truth, even when it is documented by their own authenticated sources of writing. Without a shadow of doubt, I have every reason to believe that if a sincere, open-minded person who loves the truth would read Quran, biography of Muhammad, history and hadiths would certainly have earnest desire to leave the Islamic faith and look for the truth from elsewhere. They do not need to go further than the Bible. Muhammad himself was admonished to go back to the people of the book to clarify his doubts. "And *if thou*

163

*(Muhammad) art in doubt concerning that which We reveal unto thee*, then question those who read the Scripture (that was) before thee. Verily the Truth from thy Lord hath come unto thee. So be not thou of the waverers. *And be not thou of those who deny the revelations of Allah, for then wert thou of the losers.*" Surah 10:94-95 Pickthall.

I want to encourage our Muslim friends who are really the seeker of truth to come back to the Bible. The Word of God (Bible) that leads to the truth, the person Jesus Christ who is God's Word in flesh. Jesus said, "I am the way, the truth, and life." (John 14:6). Jesus also said, "you shall know the truth and the truth shall set you free." (John 8:32). Muslims do not need to be antagonistic toward Jews and Christians, neither do they need to question aimlessly the authenticity and reliability of their scripture. Muhammad himself was admonished to consult from "the people of the book" if he had doubts about his own revelation (surah 10:94-95).

The Jihad through scale or law means to impose Sharia laws, first in their own communities and then continue to do so on non-Muslims. There are over 100 sharia courts in The Great Britain and sharia law zones. There is an implementation of sharia law in many part of Europe and Canada which is always gaining its momentum.

Once the Muslims are in majority, the third phase or form of Jihad is sword. It is through violence trying to impose sharia law on non-Muslims and to convert them by force.

Dr. Martin Luther King Jr. has said so wisely that:
Darkness cannot drive out darkness;
only light can do that.
Hate cannot drive out hate;
only love can do that.
Hate multiplies hate,
**violence multiplies violence,**
and toughness multiplies toughness
in a descending spiral of destruction....
The chain reaction of evil --
hate begetting hate,
wars producing more wars --
must be broken,
or we shall be plunged
into the dark abyss of annihilation.

Dr. Martin Luther King was a true follower of Jesus Christ. Jesus taught his followers the message of tolerance and even to love the enemies in his Sermon on the Mount (Matthew 5:38-48). Jesus said to his disciple called Peter, "Put your sword back where it belongs. All who use swords are destroyed by swords" (Matthew 26:52). Tolerance could be misled which means to accept anything and everything even when it is against someone's beliefs and values. Tolerance does not mean politically correctness. It means to love those who do evil and firmly stand against evil in order to bring what is good and right for the society.

One might ask what about the teaching of Jesus in Matthew 10:
32 "Whoever acknowledges me before men, I will also acknowledge him before my Father in heaven. 33 But whoever disowns me before men, I will disown him before my Father in heaven. **34 Do not suppose that I have come to bring peace to the earth, but a sword.** 35 For I have come to turn

a man against his father,
a daughter against her mother,
a daughter-in-law against her mother-in-law—
36 a man's enemies will be the members of his own household [Micah 7:6]
37 Anyone who loves his father or mother more than me is not worthy of me; anyone
who loves his son or daughter more than me is not worthy of me; and anyone who
does not take up his cross and follow me is not worthy of me. 39 Whoever finds his
life will lose it, and whoever loses his life for my sake will find it."

## I came, not to send peace, but a sword.

Jesus is called the prince of peace (Isaiah 9:6). He came to bring peace between God and man
and between fellow human being. During Jesus' life and ministry on this earth, he preached
about a life peace and harmony with others. He also practiced what he preached. However, this
Bible verse is puzzling to many and especially Muslim apologists frequently quote Matthew
10:34, which mentions a sword. To justify Jihad that was originated and initiated by
Muhammad and has been carried out over the centuries by his followers who take Muhammad
as a role model draw a parallel between Christianity and Islam that Jesus and Muhammad both
endorse jihad.

The Bible teacher and theologian John Gill has commented on this Bible verse that convey
very different meaning of sword as violence but separation between those who accept the
message of Jesus and who reject it.

By the "sword" may be meant the Gospel, which is the means of dividing and separating the
people of Christ from the men of the world, and from their principles and practices, and one
relation from another; as also of divisions, discords, and persecutions arising from it: not that
it was the intention and design of Christ, in coming into the world, to foment and encourage
such things; but this, through the malice and wickedness of men, was eventually the effect and
consequence of his coming; see ( Luke 12:51 ) where, instead of a "sword", it is "division";
because the sword divides asunder, as does the sword of the Spirit, the word of God.[lxii]

The historical context is this verse in Matthew 10 is that Jesus called his disciples and He gave
them power *over* unclean spirits, to cast them out, and to heal all kinds of sickness and all kinds
of disease (v. 1). They were sent out to with a mission (vv. 7-8) which was:

1. To preach, that 'The kingdom of heaven is at hand.'
2. To Heal the sick, cleanse the lepers, raise the dead, cast out demons.
3. To do it Freely without charging anything.

Jesus predicts that some towns may not receive the disciples and that the authorities may put
them on trial and flog them. In that eventuality, they should shake the dust off their feet, pray
for them, and flee to another city (not attack the people or the authorities, which Muhammad
did to his Meccan persecutors).

The one key element in this passage is the word "sword," and its meaning is now clear. It
indicates that following Jesus in his original Jewish society may not bring peace to a family,
but may "split" it up, the precise function of a metaphorical sword. This kind of spiritual sword
invisibly severs a man from his father, and daughter from her mother, and so on (Micah 7:6).
It is only natural that Matthew, the traditional author of the most Jewish of the Gospels, would
include a periscope (a unit or section) like 10:32-39. Given Jesus' own family resistance early
on (they later came around), it is only natural he would say that no matter what the cost, one

165

must follow him to the end, even if it means giving up one's family. But this applies only if the family rejects the new convert, not if the family accepts him in his new faith; he must not reject them because the whole point of Jesus' advent is to win as many people to his side as possible, even if this divides the world in two, but never violently.[lxiii]

William Barclay also explain this verse in his commentary on the Gospel According to Matthew very vividly. He does it by telling that It so happens that Jesus was using language which was perfectly familiar to the Jew. The Jews believed that one of the features of the Day of the Lord, the day when God would break into history, would be the division of families. The Rabbis said: "In the period when the Son of David shall come, a daughter will rise up against her mother, a daughter-in-law against her mother-in-law." "The son despises his father, the daughter rebels against the mother, the daughter-in-law against her mother-in-law, and the man's enemies are they of his own household." It is as if Jesus said, "The end you have always been waiting for has come; and the intervention of God in history is splitting homes and groups and families into two." When some great cause emerges, it is bound to divide people; there are bound to be those who answer, and those who refuse, the challenge. To be confronted with Jesus is necessarily to be confronted with the choice whether to accept him or to reject him; and the world is always divided into those who have accepted Christ and those who have not.[lxiv]

Conclusively, as the bible verse goes through the scrutiny of cultural and historical background, it is every evident that Jesus never exhibited and encouraged violence, use of sword and neither his disciples did. This verse, Jesus referring to Christians becoming victims of the sword of godless men. When a disciple used a sword to attack Jesus' enemies. Jesus actually healed the injured ear of the man and never appreciated but rebuked his disciple (Luke 22:49-51). The disciples and the early church were persecuted vehemently. But they in return preached the message of love to those who were filled with hatred and hostility.

Someone might this question, "what about the crusaders". Fair enough, it is good you ask this question and I hope that you would find the truth about crusades (holy wars).

## THE TRUTH ABOUT CRUSADES:

When I was in 8th grade studying in a school where all the teachers and students were Muslims, I was the only one Christian in my class. One day, the principal of that school humiliated me in front of the entire class by talking about crusades and how Christians attacked the innocent Muslims for many years. God gave me courage me to stand up to defend my faith without any fear and intimidation. I spoke with confidence and told the principal that what he was speaking was not truthful by telling him that Christians are not violent people. They are peace loving and peaceful people who believe in the beautiful teachings of Jesus of non-violence and tolerance.

As I confronted the principal, he could not handle it. He thought I was rude to him, whereas I was not. I was afraid that I might be kicked out of the school. The principal asked me not to come to school unless I bring my father with me. I had no choice but to ask my father to come to school with me. In the office of the Principal, in the presence of my father, I defended my position by telling him that his image about Christianity and Christians as a whole is absolutely wrong and he must check his facts. My father asked me to apologize if I was too forceful in my opinion and lost respect for a man of authority in a school. Sure enough, I did, but I hang on to my position which I firmly believe that Christianity is the most non-violent and tolerant faith in the world. The disciples of Jesus Christ have had been facing persecution over the years around the world. Right now, severe persecution against Christians is going on, especially, in the Islamic countries like Saudi Arabia, Iran, Iraq, Syria, Afghanistan, and the list continues.

In both the Western as well as in the Islamic world, the Crusades are considered as wars of aggression European Christian fought against peaceful Muslims. A War is a terrible thing no matter in what form or feature it takes place. It is very important to understand what caused the crusades at the first place? Why European Christians traveled to a far land knowing that they were embarking upon a terrible journey.

## What caused crusades?

With the rise of Islam, Christendom faced with two options which were: fight or be destroyed. It started with Muhammad and his followers. After conquering Mecca, Muhammad and his followers waged war against every Arab tribe very systematically and strategically. As they were dominated one by one and brought under the submission of Islam into a united force, it transformed the Arabs into world conquerors. Muhammad excited his followers to fight and to kill the non-Muslims in order to secure a place in paradise where they will have beautiful virgins to pleasure them unceasingly.

Muhamad preached aggression towards others as he told his followers that "I will cast terror into the hearts of those who disbelieved, so strike [them] upon the necks and strike from them every fingertip." (Quran 8:12). "When the sacred months are over, slay the idolaters wherever you find them. Arrest them, besiege them and lie in ambush everywhere for them" (Quran 9:5).

As Mohammed was gaining ground, he was soon in a position to declare himself the supreme religious and military leader over Arabia. He sent delegates to every Arabian city offering two options: submit to Mohammed's rule or face war. A few cities tried to defend themselves against Muhammad's aggression (Jihad), but tragically, the entire Arabian Peninsula surrendered in 632.

After the death of Muhammad, his close friend and father-in-law Abu Bakr was designated to be his successor. He led the Muslims to suppress thousands of people under his military commander Khalid ibn al-Walid. The Muslim swept through the lands winning several battles and crushing all who showed any sort of resistance to Islam.

In 633 the Muslim forces under the leadership of Mohammed's cousin marched around South Arabia making sure to remind all the Arabs that any further resistance would result in death. Abu Bakr ordered his Muslim forces to begin attacking the Persians in Mesopotamia who were mainly Zoroastrians initiating a series of invasions that would ultimately result in the total conquest in the Persian Empire by Islam. During this time the Muslims also attacked Byzantine empire which was heavily Christian populated. The Jihadist attacked Christians ruthlessly and massacred mercilessly.

Bat Ye'or summarize the wanton destruction and massacres that accompanied these jihad conquests, as follows:
Abu Bakr organized the invasion of Syria [Syro-Palestine] which Muhammad had already envisaged. He gathered tribes from the Hijaz, Najd, and Yemen and advised Abu Ubayda, in charge of operations in the Golan, to plunder the countryside, but due

to a lack of adequate weaponry, to refrain from attacking towns. Consequently, the whole Gaza region up to Caesarea was sacked and devastated in the campaign of 634. Four thousand Jewish, Christian, and Samaritan peasants who defended their land were massacred. The villages of the Negev were pillaged by Amr b. al-As, while the Arabs overran the countryside, cut communications, and made roads perilous. Towns such as Jerusalem, Gaza, Jaffa, Caesarea, Nablus, and Beth Shean were isolated and closed their gates. In his sermon on Christmas day 634, the patriarch of Jerusalem, Sophronius, lamented over the impossibility of going on pilgrimage to Bethlehem, as was the custom because the Christians were being forcibly kept in Jerusalem: 'not detained by tangible bonds, but chained and nailed by fear of the Saracens,' whose 'savage, barbarous and bloody sword' kept them locked up in the town...Sophronius, in his sermon on the Day of the Epiphany 636, bewailed the destruction of the churches and monasteries, the sacked towns, the fields laid waste, the villages burned down by the nomads who were overrunning the country.[lxv]

In 634 Abu Bakr was succeeded by Umar ibn-al-Khattab who continued to wage wars against the Byzantines at the Battle of Fihl in 635 and the Battle of Yarmouk in 636. Most of the Fertile crescent, virtually all of Palestine was under Muslim's rule except Jerusalem. In the name of Allah, Muslims plundered everything, men were killed while women and children were enslaved and even turned them into sex slaves. Caliph Umar considered this a blessing from Allah and thanked him for blessing him with all the sex slaves.

In 638 Caliph Umar arrived in Jerusalem on what seemed to a be a friendly visit. With the Patriarch of Jerusalem as his guide, he toured one of the most splendid ancient Christian cities. A month later, the Muslims attacked Jerusalem and the Christians became dhimmis (second class citizen). The law of Dhimmitude was imposed upon Christians.

**The following are the terms imposed upon the Jews and Christians in the Charter of Caliph Umar II-**

1. All Dhimmis had to pay a very onerous Jizzya/Poll tax which was a very important source of income to the imperialist Arabs. Sometime Jizzya was 20% of the income with addition to some other taxes…
2. They were required to wear distinctive, unflattering, and humiliating dress to distinguish them from the pious 'Muslims' and hence have them subjected to ridicule and insults.
3. Dhimmis were denied access to public baths and other public spaces because they are inferior and unclean beings.
4. They were not greeted with the civility that Muslims did for each other.
5. They had to keep to the opposite side of the street where Muslims were walking.
6. They were invariably assigned distasteful duties such as removing dead animals or cleaning public toilets.
7. They were not allowed to practice their faith openly
8. They were forbidden from displaying their joy and grief in public.
9. They were forbidden to build any dwelling equal to or higher than that of a Muslims.
10. No churches were to ring bells or display crosses.
11. Churches and Synagogues were rarely respected and were burned or demolished at will. New churches or synagogues were not allowed to be built.
12. They were invariably subjected to massacres for whatever political or theological reason deemed useful to the leaders at the time.

13. They were not accepted as witnesses or able to defend themselves under Sharia 'law'
14. Their word against Muslims carried no value and weight whatsoever.
15. In many recorded historical instances, they were subjected to mass murder or mass conversion, both contrary to the Quranic injunction not to do so: **2:256 *Let there be no compulsion in religion.*** *Truth stands out clear from error; whoever rejects evil and believes in Allah hath grasped the most trustworthy hand-hold that never breaks. And Allah hears and knows all things*
16. Male children of the dhimmis were taken from their parents to convert them as well as to use them as mercenary troops for the service of the Caliph as in the (Janissaries)
17. A murderer of any unbeliever would never carry a death penalty but only a small monetary compensation, whereas, a murderer of a Muslims should get death penalty.
18. Big churches must be turned into Mosques. Only small churches could be left where Christian could worship God quietly.
19. An unbeliever had to bow down before the Muslim tax collector and then be beaten across the head and verbally abused of any violations of terms that could result in death.
20. Anyone who wish to leave Islam and become a Christian must be executed.

No wonder, this is the same that ISIS is carrying out in Iraq and Syria and the Taliban in Afghanistan upon Christians even today. For example:

"ISIS Issues Dhimma Contract for Christians to Sign, Orders Them to Pay Jizyah": ISIS has forced Christians living in Al-Qaryaten to sign a Dhimma contract, requiring each of them to pay the jizya poll tax with 11 clauses:

1. Christians may not build churches, monasteries, or hermitages in the city or in the surrounding areas.
2. They may not show the cross or any of their books in the Muslims' streets or markets, and may not use amplifiers when worshiping or during prayer.
3. They may not make Muslims hear the reciting of their books or the sounds of church bells, which must be rung only inside their churches.
4. They may not carry out any act of aggression against ISIS, such as giving refuge to spies and wanted men. If they come to know of any plot against Muslims, they must report it.
5. They must not perform religious rituals in public.
6. They must respect Muslims and not criticize their religion.
7. Wealthy Christians must pay an annual jizya of four gold dinars; middle-class Christians must pay two gold dinars, and the poor must pay one. Christians must disclose their income, and may split the jizya into two payments.
8. They may not own guns.
9. They may not engage in commercial activity involving pigs or alcohol with Muslims or in Muslim markets, and may not drink alcohol in public.
10. They may maintain their own cemeteries.
11. They must abide by ISIS dress code and commerce guidelines.

The contract states that a Christian violating any of the articles will be treated as an enemy combatant. (September 3, 2015)

**Document of submission**: On conquering the northern city of Raqqa, Syria, the Islamic State in Iraq, and Syria gave 20 Christian leaders there the classic three Islamic options: to convert to Islam; to remain Christian as *dhimmi*s; or to "face the sword." They opted for the second choice and promised, in return for assurances of physical safety to agree to a long list of conditions. These include to:

- Abstain from renovating churches or monasteries in Raqqa;
- Respect Islam and Muslims and say nothing offensive about them;
- Pay the jizya tax worth four golden dinars for the rich, two for the average, and one for the poor, twice annually, for each adult Christian;
- Refrain from drinking alcohol in public;
- Dress modestly.

And not to:

- Display crosses or religious symbols in public;
- Use loudspeakers in prayer;
- Read scripture indoors loud enough for Muslims standing outside to hear;
- Undertake subversive actions against Muslims;
- Carry out any religious ceremonies outside the church;
- Prevent any Christian wishing to convert to Islam from doing so;

The document ends with: "If they adhere to these conditions, they will be close to God and receive the protection of Mohammed his prophet ... none of their religious rights will be detracted nor will a priest or monk be wronged. But if they disobey any of the conditions, they are no longer protected and ISIS can treat them in a hostile and warlike fashion." (February 27, 2014)

**Jizya Tax on Christians in Egypt and Syria**: As Islamists control portions of these two countries, they impose the additional taxes due from non-Muslims.

In Egypt, the Muslim Brotherhood has imposed jizya on all of the 15,000 Copts of Dalga, "without exception," according to Fr. Yunis Shawqi. "[The] value of the tribute and method of payment differ from one place to another in the village, so that, some are being expected to pay 200 Egyptian pounds per day, others 500 Egyptian pounds per day." Some families not able to pay have been attacked and as many as 40 Christian families have fled Dalga.

In Syria, jihadi rebels went into a Christian man's shop and "gave him three options: become Muslim; pay $70,000 as a tax levied on non-Muslims, known as jizya; or be killed along with his family." (September 10, 2013)

**"Non-Muslims want equal funeral rights in Turkey"**: Municipalities in Turkey pick up most funeral expenses for Muslims but the tiny number of non-Muslims must shoulder these costs all on their own. The authorities use the excuse that they are unfamiliar with non-Muslim funeral practices. It also turns out that mosque utility bills are picked up by the national government but not so for non-Muslim sanctuaries. (January 17, 2013).

Muslim rule in the Holy Land began after Muslims Jihadist subjugated Damascus and Jerusalem under the leadership of Caliph Umar. After the initial bloody jihad, Christian and Jewish life over there was tolerated within the strictures of the Law of dhimmitude and

170

collecting jizya from non-Muslims which proved to be a lucrative business for the Muslim state.

Before Islam, the Middle East was populated by millions of Christians and Jews. Zoroastrians and Arab polytheists were also in great number. Muhammad himself comes from polytheistic background whose ancestors worshipped 360 deities of whom Allah was one of them.

The Christian Church had by five major religious centers whose capitals were: Alexandria in modern-day Egypt, Antioch located in modern-day Turkey was known as the cradle of Christianity, Constantinople located in modern-day Istanbul, Turkey, Jerusalem of course the holy ground of Christianity and Judaism and Rome.

In 613 Zoroastrian Persians captured modern-day Turkey. Several decades later the Persian Empire was conquered by the Muslims and Antioch came under Muslim rule.

In 637-38 Muslim captured Jerusalem.

In 641 Alexandra fell in Muslim hands.

In 674 Muslims forces first besieged Constantinople the capitol of the Christian Byzantine Empire, but after four years of fighting the Muslims were finally repelled. However, the Muslims returned to Constantinople with a vengeance in 717 and laid siege to the city once again. The Byzantine Empire was aware of the Muslim threat and had signed a treaty with the Bulgarian Empire. Under terms of the Treaty Tervel, Bulgarian Empire was bound to help propel the Muslims at Constantinople. So, the Bulgarian army attacked the invading Arabs and forced them to fight a war on two fronts. The Muslims were gradually worn down and eventually lost the battle to Bulgarian onslaught that ended with the successful defense of Constantinople. The defeat for Muslims not only protected the fall of Constantinople, but prevented Muslims from entering Europe from the east and to do to Europe what they had done to the Middle East and North Africa.

The Muslims first invaded southern Italy which was then a part of the Byzantine Empire in 667 and relentless raids continued until the island of Sicily was eventually fully conquered in 902. An Islamic state the Emirate of Sicily was established on the island. The Muslims would remain in control of it for two hundred and sixty-four years. The Muslims took millions of Europeans into absolutely brutal slavery. Using Sicily as their base of operations, Muslim began to raid the southern part of the Italian peninsula for hundreds of years. The island of Corsica and Sardinia were also repeatedly ravaged by Muslim raids.

In 846 the Muslims launched an attack on Rome but was stopped by Emperor Louis II in 872. However, the invading Muslims sacked the outskirts of the city killing men and women regardless of their age. Most importantly with regard to Christianity, at least, they desecrated St. Peter's and St. Paul's Basilica (church). They also desecrated the burial place of the St. Peter and St. Paul.

There was a second attack on Rome that was thwarted in 849 after a coalition of maritime cities joined the papal forces to defeat in invading Muslims. The Muslim occupation of Italy posed a serious threat to Rome for centuries. The last Arab strongholds in southern Italy fell in 1091. It was that for years before a pope preached about the First Crusade.

In the early 10th century a Christian Alliance, an early precursor to the Crusades was formed between the Franks, the Byzantines, and the Lombards who were a Germanic tribe and the Italian city of Naples. The goal of the alliance was to repel the Muslim invaders of Italy. The threat of Muslim invasions and aggression was real since by the end of the seventh century three of the five Christian capitals were under Muslim control. Constantinople was besieged twice by Muslims. Rome was attacked and had its holy shrines pillaged and desecrated. So, one could imagine why the Christians might be rather upset by this continual Muslim onslaught.

In 711 Muslims invaded Spain which was inhabited by Christians. They established first Islamic state on European territory. The Emirate of Córdoba, the Reconquista of the period in which the Christians tried and tried to retake Spain and Portugal in an endless series of bloody battles, lasted for approximately seven hundred and seventy years. The Muslim rulers were fully expelled from Spain in 1492, the year Christopher Columbus sailed for India but came to the West Indies.

Once the Muslims secured control over the Iberian Peninsula, they tried to conquer the rest of Europe, however, French people (Franks) again stood in their way. In 732 one of the most important battles in the history of the world took place near the city of Tours France, Frankish forces led by Charles Martel, who defeated an invading Muslim army and put an end to Muslim expansions into Europe from the southwest.[lxvi]

The things get from bad to worse when in the 11th century, the Arab administration of the Holy Land was replaced with that of Seljuk Turks, due to civil war in the Islamic Empire. Throughout the latter half of the 11th century, the Turks waged war against the Christian Byzantine Empire and pushed it back from its strongholds in Antioch and Anatolia (now Turkey). In 1071, Byzantine forces suffered a crushing defeat at the Battle of Manzikert in what is now Eastern Turkey. The Turks resumed the jihad in the Holy Land, abusing, robbing, enslaving, and killing Christians there and throughout Asia Minor. They threatened to cut off Christendom from its holiest site, the Church of the Holy Sepulcher in Jerusalem, which was rebuilt under Byzantine stewardship after it was destroyed by Caliph Al-Hakim Bi-Amr Allah in 1009. The persecution and forced conversion of many Christians was rapidly growing.

**In 1095 Pope Urban II proclaimed that:**
> The Muslims had invaded the lands of those Christians and has depopulated them by the sword, pillage, and fire; it has led away a part of the captives into its own country, and a part it has destroyed by cruel tortures; it has either entirely destroyed the churches of God or appropriated them for the rites of its own religion. They destroy the altars, after having defiled them with their uncleanness. They circumcise the Christians, and the blood of the circumcision they either spread upon the altars or pour into the vases of the baptismal font. When they wish to torture people by a base death, they perforate their navels, and dragging forth the extremity of the intestines, bind it to a stake; then with flogging they lead the victim around until the viscera having gushed forth the victim falls prostrate upon the ground. Others they bind to a post and pierce with arrows. Others they compel to extend their necks and then, attacking them with naked swords, attempt to cut through the neck with a single blow. What shall I say of the abominable rape of the women? To speak of it is worse than to be silent. The kingdom of the Greeks is now dismembered by them and deprived of territory so vast in extent that it cannot be traversed in a march of two months. On whom therefore is the labor of avenging these wrongs and of recovering this territory incumbent, if not upon you? You, upon

whom above other nations God has conferred remarkable glory in arms, great courage, bodily activity, and strength to humble the hairy scalp of those who resist you.[lxvii]

In this scenario of suffering and religious persecution in the Middle East, the Roman Pope, Urban II, issued a call in 1095 to Western Christians to help the Christians in the Holy hand. The Franks who took part in crusades were exactly those who had faced jihad and razzias for centuries along the Franco-Spanish border and knew better than most the horrors to which Muslims subjected Christians.

Conquering territory for God in the mode of jihad was an alien idea to Christianity and it should not be surprising that it eventually died out in the West and never gained ascendancy in the East.

The Crusades was an answering the cry for help against aggression of the Muslims who had destroyed 30,000 churches under one Caliph alone. The Christians and Jews under Islamic rule were dhimmis (second class citizen): There were numerous incidents of brutality against Christians for four hundred years. The Christians were fleeing their ancient homes. The Byzantine Emperor plead for help.

The crusades protected Europe and its values that are based on the Judeo-Christians principles such as: human rights, freedom of speech and freedom of religion. These precious values give a sense of dignity to every human being. No wonder, people from all over the world who face religious persecution, social discrimination, and financial hardship endeavor to come and want to settle in the Western world where they can breathe freely and feel the value and worthiness of their being. Muslims as a whole do not enjoy freedom in other Muslim countries where they are treated worse than animal. They can never get the equal rights their own citizens have and status of the citizenship in an Islamic state. They are always considered as slaves and servant no matter how long they live in the country.

The crusades also united Europeans who were fighting each other for political dominance for years. The warriors from England, France, Spain, Germany, and Italy suddenly were bond together to crush the evil of aggression. The crusades brought a new religious zeal. The Christianity became important part of European culture and a way of life. New churches were built, chronicles were written, new songs were composed, statues of remembrance were erected, and glass stain windows were dedicated.

Significantly, while the West has for some time now lamented the Crusades as mistaken, there has never been any mention from any serious Islamic authority of regret for the centuries and centuries of jihad and dhimmitude perpetrated against other societies. But this is hardly surprising: while religious violence contradicts the fundamentals of Christianity, religious violence is written into Islam's DNA. The four Sunni Madhhabs (schools of fiqh [Islamic religious jurisprudence]) — Hanafi, Maliki, Shafi'i, and Hanbali — all agree that there is a collective obligation on Muslims to make war on the rest of the world. Furthermore, even the schools of thought outside Sunni orthodoxy, including Sufism and the Jafari (Shia) school, agree on the necessity of jihad. This war is not merely a war to defend Islam and Muslims (Dar-ul-Islam) but to wage war on non-Muslims (Dar-ul-Harb: house of war). The Jihad extends to the moderate peaceful Muslims a well as to the Muslims who have different interpretation of Quran and have different opinion on Islamic teaching.[lxviii]

At the time of this writing, the "Religion of Peace data" base shows 28444 Islamic terrorist attacks since September 11, 2001 on the World Trade Center in New York city. These attacks have been perpetrated in the name of Allah (Allahu Akbar=Allah is Great is a shout after and during every attack) on Muslims and Non-Muslims alike.

A war is still a war no matter how it is interpreted or justified. In a war, no one wins. It brings pain and sufferings and swallow lives of many even the lives of innocent people in its sea of death and destruction. We wish people live with peace and harmony regardless of their creed and color, religious beliefs and practices, social status, and diversified set of opinion.

It can happen when there is a change of heart. Jesus said, *"For out of the heart proceed evil thoughts, murders, adulteries, fornications, thefts, false witness, blasphemies"* (Matthew 15:19). The piousness ideology of world domination is an evil thought of an evil heart. Those who believe and practice this ideology, they feel like giving service to their god. Jesus said, *"…. yes, the time is coming that whoever kills you will think that he offers God service"* (John 16:2).

Jesus also said, *"For **what** will it profit **a man** if he gains the whole world, and **loses his own soul?**"* (Mark 8:36).

Alexander the Great did conquered most of the world at age of 32. Many Great Empires like Egyptian, Babylonian, Persians, and many more have come and gone. They are nothing but just part of the pages of world history. The zeal of Muslims for world domination in the name of Allah has also happened to some extent. Let's assume, somehow, Muslims gain the whole world, but what about, at the end they lose their own soul. This is not a good bargain at all. Every great Empire has fallen. The history is quite honest about it. Every great empire has fallen from inside and from outside as well. **The word of Jesus must be taken seriously who said, "those kill with the sword will be killed by the sword". What we sow, we will have to reap it one day.**

There is great deception of Jihad in terms of killing others, dying as a martyr, and securing a place in paradise for the sake of enjoying never-ending sexual pleasure with 72 virgins and boys with cup full of wine. It is nothing but a lie from the pit of hell to encourage and excite young men for Jihad. An unmarried suicide bomber was arrested before he was about to blew himself said, "my 72 virgins are waiting for me in heaven, so why I should prefer only one here? He was determined to kill as many as he could even his family members, innocent children and all the Muslims who are not involved in Jihad directly or indirectly after his release from prison.

The moderate, peaceful Muslims have come to the conclusion that there is no promise of 72 virgins or even 1 virgin for martyrs, terrorists, or suicide bombers anywhere in the Quran. The section many people claim promises this is in (surah 78:29-24).

"But all things We have enumerated in writing.
So, taste [the penalty], and never will We increase you except in torment.
Indeed, for the righteous is attainment Gardens and grapevines
And full-breasted [companions] of equal age
And a full cup."

Tragically, because of the ignorance of many fanatics and because of some power-hungry monsters who brainwash such ignorant and innocent people by inventing lies using religion are taking the lives of many. That's why The Bible says, "The thief cometh not, but for to steal, and to kill, and to destroy: I am come that they might have life, and that they might have it more abundantly" (John 10:10). In The Bible Satan is a symbol of thief who steal the childhood and youth of these children and young men and women, kill them and destroy them. But there is a Good News that Jesus came to give life and life to its fullness here on this earth and eternal life in heaven.

Muhammad, the great Jihadist who is a role model for all the Jihadists had no assurance about his own place secured in paradise. He was quite honest at least, on this matter. Muhammad, himself said: "I am no bringer of new-fangled doctrine among the messengers, **nor do I know what will be done with me or with you**. I follow but that which is revealed to me by inspiration; I am but a Warner open and clear." (surah. 46:9). Narrated 'Um al-'Ala: An Ansari woman who gave the pledge of allegiance to the Prophet that the Ansar drew lots concerning the dwelling of the Emigrants. 'Uthman bin Maz'un was decided to dwell with them (i.e. Um al-'Ala's family), 'Uthman fell ill and I nursed him till he died, and we covered him with his clothes. Then the Prophet came to us and I (addressing the dead body) said, "O Abu As-Sa'ib, may Allah's Mercy be on you! I bear witness that Allah has honored you." On that the Prophet said, "How do you know that Allah has honored him?" I replied, "I do not know. May my father and my mother be sacrificed for you, O Allah's Apostle! But who else is worthy of it (if not 'Uthman)?" He said, "As to him, by Allah, death has overtaken him, and I hope the best for him. **By Allah, though I am the Apostle of Allah, yet I do not know what Allah will do to me.**" By Allah, I will never assert the piety of anyone after him. That made me sad, and when I slept I saw in a dream a flowing stream for 'Uthman bin Maz'un. I went to Allah's Apostle and told him of it. He remarked, "That symbolizes his (good) deeds." (**Sahih Bukhari** Volume 5, Book 58, Number 266).

The Bible says, "If the Son (Jesus) therefore shall make you free, ye shall be free indeed" (John 10:36). Religion brings bondage while Jesus Christ brings freedom. Jesus gives a person freedom to worship God almighty and a privilege to call him Abba father. He is the one who gives assurance for eternity. Jesus said, *"Let not your heart be troubled; you believe in God, believe also in Me. ² In My Father's house are many mansions; if it were not so, I would have told you. I go to prepare a place for you. ³ And if I go and prepare a place for you, I will come again and receive you to Myself; that where I am, there you may be also"* (John 14:1-3).

*Jesus said, "Because I live, you will live also"* (John 14:16).

*Jesus said…., "I am the resurrection and the life. He who believes in Me, though he may die, he shall live."* (John 11:25).

Muslims believe that a prophet does not lie and especially Jesus who is a supreme prophet and is highly venerated.

And when Allah said: O Isa, I am going to terminate the period of your stay (on earth) and cause you to ascend unto Me and purify you of those who disbelieve and make those who follow you above those who disbelieve to the day of resurrection; then to Me shall be your return, so I will decide between you concerning that in which you differed (surah 3:54 Shakir translation).

[Mention] when Allah said, "O Jesus, indeed I will take you and raise you to Myself and purify you from those who disbelieve and make those who follow you [in submission to Allah alone] superior to those who disbelieve until the Day of Resurrection. Then to Me is your return, and I will judge between you concerning that in which you used to differ" (surah 3:54 *Sahih International translation).*

As Allah said, "O Isa, (Jesus) surely, I am taking you up to Me, and I am raising you up to Me, and I am purifying you of the ones who have disbelieved. And I am making the ones who have closely followed you above the ones who have disbelieved until the Day of the Resurrection. Thereafter to Me will be your return; so, I will judge between you as to whatever you used to differ in (surah 3:54 Dr. Ghali translation*).*

Behold! Allah said: "O Jesus! I will take thee and raise thee to Myself and clear thee (of the falsehoods) of those who blaspheme; I will make those who follow thee superior to those who reject faith, to the Day of Resurrection: Then shall ye all return unto me, and I will judge between you of the matters wherein ye dispute (surah 3:54 Yusuf Ali translation*).*

**The Quran even testifies very vividly that God will make followers of Jesus superior to all who reject him.**

# CHAPTER EIGHT

---

# THE TRUTH ABOUT
# SALVATION IN ISLAM

## THE DIFFERENCE BETWEEN THE TWO RELIGIONS

People say, "Now hold on a minute, there are many religions in the world. There's Buddhism, Hinduism, Islam, Christianity, Judaism, and so on, ... aren't we all praying to the same God? Aren't there more than just two belief systems in the world?" **No, when it comes right down to it, there are only two belief systems in the world today.** Yes, the one religion may come in a different package, a different wrapping paper, or in a different box, but the content is the same, it doesn't change, ... it's either this belief system or the other belief system.

Now, **one belief system is self-centered and teaches what man can do to please God and how mankind can find acceptance before God. But it's all self-centered, the effort, the performance of a human being to please whatever god their belief system worships.** And sadly, we see this type of belief system throughout all the so-called religions in the world. There's always a ritual, a set of rules, a rigid creed and so on, prescribed to followers of such a religion, what they can and should do to impress their god. The emphasis is always on self-effort and performance, ... what man can do for God.

**On the other hand we have this other religion or belief system. And this one is centered in God and what He has done for mankind. It eliminates any self-effort or performance, but instead it lets God do the work and only glorifies God and not men for any work accomplished.** Although God is concerned about an individual, a person needs to make a personal decision to accept the gift from God. This religion or belief system is solely based and centered in God Himself, instead of the performance or the efforts by an individual.

You can find the first belief system, the one that is self-centered virtually everywhere. Even in Christianity this system of self-effort and therefore self-centeredness can be found in many places. Every thought, every attitude, every philosophy, every sentence is either based in God's value system or it's based apart from God in a self-effort/performance system.

As human beings, God invites us constantly to learn of Him and to freely receive His value system and to become part of His "religion" so to speak, ... although this is not really a religion, but rather a personal relationship with God freely offered through His Son Jesus Christ. Now let's take a look what the work of God really is. And let's have Jesus Christ Himself answer that question.

> " 'What can we do to perform the works of God?' they asked." (John 6:28)

> "Jesus replied, **'This is the work of God: that you believe in the One He has sent.'** "(John 6:29)

(Dietmar Scherf)

# CHAPTER EIGHT
# THE TRUTH ABOUT SALVATION IN ISLAM

The main purpose of the creation of Man is to worship his creator and glorify Him in every aspect of his life on this earth. Sin deteriorates and destroys this purpose in Man. Upon the forgiveness of sin, this purpose is restored and Man starts to fulfill this purpose on the earth. But there are millions of people who live with guilt, and condemnation. There is no assurance of forgiveness in their hearts. But the Bible says,

> *"There is therefore now no condemnation to them which are in Christ Jesus, who walk not after the flesh, but after the Spirit" (Romans 8:1).*

Once a person relies on his own efforts in attaining the forgiveness of sins, he will always find himself falling short of what since he feels that his good deeds are not sufficient in attaining forgiveness. As someone has said in this way that the ladder of good deeds is never long enough in reaching to the heaven where one could find forgiveness of sins from God. There must be someone reaching from heaven down to earth to a person in need of mercy and forgiveness. When a person relies on the mercies of God, and lives with this realization that God imparts his grace in abundance, and reaches out with His mighty hand of abundant and amazing grace, then the assurance of forgiveness of sin is possible. The Bible says,

> *"For by grace are ye saved through faith; and that not of yourselves: it is the gift of God: Not of works, lest any man should boast" (Ephesians 2:8-9)*

This concept of the forgiveness of sin is extremely difficult for Muslims to understand. They struggle and strive by means of their good deeds in conjunction with the instrumentality of their self-efforts, yet at the end of the day, they live with uncertainty about forgiveness of their sins on this earth, and without an assurance of salvation for eternity.

Even Muhammad was not certain of heaven when he died; whereas Jesus said very confidently that:

> *"Let not your heart be troubled: ye believe in God, believe also in me. In my Father's house are many mansions: if it were not so, I would have told you. I go to prepare a place for you. And if I go and prepare a place for you, I will come again, and receive you unto myself; that where I am, there ye may be also" (John 14:1-3)*

When a dying criminal on the cross confessed his sins, Jesus said to him,

> *".... Verily I say unto thee, to day you will be with me in paradise" (Luke 23:43).*

The Apostle Paul under the inspiration of the Holy Spirit said,

> *"We are confident, I say, and would prefer to be away from the **body** and at home with the Lord" (2 Corinthians 5:8).*

Since Muslims have no certainty of the forgiveness of sins and of the assurance of salvation, they believe that everybody will pass through Hell and even some Muslim will spend time in Hell until their sins are burned away and Mohammad intercedes for them.

The Quran says,

*"Every soul shall have a taste of death: And only on the Day of Judgment shall you be paid your full recompense. Only he who is saved far from the Fire and admitted to the Garden will have attained the object (of Life): For the life of this world is but goods and chattels of deception." (Surah 3:185)*

But, tragically speaking, Muhammad himself was not sure of his own fate whether he will go to hell or heaven.

## Mohammad was not sure about his Final Destination:

Mohammad wasn't sure about his destination while all the Bible prophets were sure and confident that they were going to heaven after death.

*Jabir reported that the Prophet of Islam said: "No good works of yours can ever secure heaven for you, nor can they save you from hell -- not even me, without the grace of God."*

*Abu Huraira related that when the verse, "Cause thy near relatives to fear," was revealed to the Prophet of Islam, the Prophet arose and began to proclaim: "Oh people of the Quraysh, and you sons of Abdul Manaf, and you Abbas, son of Abdul Muttalib, and you, Safiyyah my aunt, I cannot save you from the punishment of the Day of Resurrection. Take care of yourself, O my daughter Fatimah; you may use my property, but I cannot save you from God. Take care of yourself" (Bukhari).*

*Abu Huraira reported that the Prophet of Islam said: "No one of you will enter Paradise through his good works." They said: "Not even you, O Apostle of God?" "Not even I," he replied, "unless God cover me with His grace and mercy. Therefore, be strong, and morning and evening, nay every moment, try to do good."*

## Muhammad's prayer for asking forgiveness:

*Narrated Abu Huraira:*
*Allah's Apostle used to keep silent between the Takbir and the recitation of Qur'an and that interval of silence used to be a short one. I said to the Prophet "May my parents be sacrificed for you! What do you say in the pause between Takbir and recitation?" The Prophet said, "I say, 'Allahumma, ba'id baini wa baina khatayaya kama ba'adta baina-l-mashriqi wa-l-maghrib. Allahumma, naqqim min khatayaya kama yunaqqa-ththawbu-l-abyadu mina-ddanas. Allahumma, ighsil khatayaya bil-ma'i wa-th-thalji wal-barad (O Allah! Set me apart from my sins (faults) as the East and West are set apart from each other and clean me from sins as a white garment is cleaned of dirt (after thorough washing). O Allah! Wash off my sins with water, snow and hail.)" (Volume 1, Book 12, Number 711)*

Here a simple conclusion that is so easily to understand once a person is free from religious pride and prejudices that Jesus Christ forgives sins, while Muhammad asks forgiveness of his sins. Jesus was sure where he was going, while Muhammad was not sure whether he will go to hell or heaven.

## PLEASE DON'T TAKE THE RISK!

I would like to request Muslims not to take any risk. It is the biggest risk in life a person can take.

When people take some risks on this earth, it might not affect them a lot. They might have a chance to rectify it. But when someone takes the risk in regards to eternity they will never have a chance to rectify it. IT WILL BE TOO LATE!

As Muslims believe that everybody will go to hell, and then upon the intercession of Muhammad, Muslims will make a transit from hell to heaven. Here are **some important questions that must be pondered keenly and considered seriously:**
What about if Muhammad himself would be looking for someone to intercede for him, since he asked forgiveness of his sins over and over and again he was not even sure of going to heaven?

What about if Muhammad never intercedes for his followers, and then all that is left is the fire of hell for eternity and no way to come out of it?

**PLEASE DON'T TAKE THE RISK OF FOLLOWING THE ONE WHO WAS UNCERTAIN ABOUT HEAVEN AND ABOUT WHERE HE WILL SPEND HIS ETERNITY!!!**

**I would like to request my Muslims friends that "Why don't you make decision of following the one who is perfectly righteous, who has authority to forgive sins, and who is sure about heaven and even has given that assurance of salvation to his followers. His name is Jesus. The Quran itself has mentioned this great prophet (Jesus Christ) more than prophet Mohammed. Even though, Jesus is more than a prophet. He has been given a name that is above every name.**

**The Bible says,**

> "Let this mind be in you which was also in Christ Jesus, [6] who, being in the form of God, did not consider it robbery to be equal with God, [7] but made Himself of no reputation, taking the form of a bondservant, *and* coming in the likeness of men. [8] And being found in appearance as a man, He humbled Himself and became obedient to *the point of* death, even the death of the cross. [9] Therefore God also has highly exalted Him and given Him the name which is above every name, [10] that at the name of Jesus every knee should bow, of those in heaven, and of those on earth, and of those under the earth, [11] and *that* every tongue should confess that Jesus Christ *is* Lord, to the glory of God the Father" (Philippians 2:5.

**Jesus is the only Savior who save people from their sins.**

**The Bible says,**

> Nor is there salvation in any other, for there is no other name under heaven given among men by which we must be saved." (Acts 4:12).

Jesus who is the personification of truth, said about himself and gave assurance of salvation and eternity to his followers by these winsome words,

"Let not your heart be troubled; you believe in God, believe also in Me. ² In My Father's house are many mansions; if *it were* not *so,* I would have told you. I go to prepare a place for you. ³ And if I go and prepare a place for you, I will come again and receive you to Myself; that where I am, *there* you may be also. ⁴ And where I go you know, and the way you know."

⁵ Thomas said to Him, "Lord, we do not know where You are going, and how can we know the way?"

⁶ Jesus said to him, **"I am the way, the truth, and the life. No one comes to the Father except through Me.** (John 16:1-6)

**The Bible says,**

He who believes in the Son has everlasting life; and he who does not believe the Son shall not see life, but the wrath of God abides on him." (John 3:36)

## DIVERSE WAYS TO COLLECT DEEDS (RELIGIOUS POINTS) IN ISLAM:

Muslims believe that there are Diverse Ways, that might help Muslims to attain forgiveness of sins and might facilitate Muslims to enter heaven. Muslim theologians disagree about the number of ways in which a Muslim can receive forgiveness for both greater and lesser sins. The most common ways are based on verses in the Quran and Hadith (sayings and teachings of Mohammed and the caliphs Mohammed's followers). Those ways are:

1. **Doing good:** Muslims believe that God will judge them by using a balance to weigh the good deeds against the bad deeds. In trying to increase the weight of good deeds, Muslims believe that there are some deeds of which God multiplies the weight by ten. The Friday prayer in the mosque is one example. Every step a man takes to get closer to the mosque, the better deeds he gains. Some verses in the Quran say, *"Those who avert evil with good—theirs shall be the Ultimate Abode, gardens of Eden which they shall enter; and those who were good to their parents and wives and their seed" (Surah 13:22,23). "For those things that are good remove those that are evil" (Surah 11:1 14).*

2. **Fasting:** Man can also atone for sins through fasting. In Surah 33:35, it says, "Men who fast and women who fast for them God has prepared forgiveness and a mighty wage." If a Muslim is unable to fast due to some sickness or some other reasons, he might help the poor and needy with food at the time of breaking of the fast. In return, Allah adds all the rewards (religious points) to the account of that person. Islamic faith focuses on debit and credit. Allah gives credit for good deeds and debit or deduct for every bad deed.

3. **Children who die before their parents secure their parents' entry into paradise:** The Hadith says that the deceased child stands at the door full of anger saying, "I will not enter paradise without my parents," whereupon it is said, "Let his parents in with him" (quoted by Nisaai and Ibn Hayan, after Abi Huraira).

4.  **Approval of a wife by her husband secures her entry to paradise:** The Hadith says that Mohammed stated, "Every woman who dies while her husband approves of her enters paradise" (quoted by Tarmazi).

5.  **Reciting the Quran:** In the Hadith, according to Ibn Masoud (one of Mohammed's friends, also known as an al Sahaba), Mohammed said, "He who reads the Quran and commits it to memory, Allah ushers him into paradise and grants him for his intercession ten relatives deserving the fire."

6.  **Confessing the two creeds:** The two creeds are that there is no god but Allah and Mohammed is the prophet of Allah. It is related that Abi Thur (one of the al Sahaba) said: "I came upon God's prophet [Mohammed] sleeping in a white robe. He awoke saying, 'Anyone who says there is no God but Allah is assured of entering Paradise.' I said, 'Even if he commits adultery and steals?' He said, `Even if he commits adultery and steals.' I said, 'Even if he commits adultery and steals?' He said again, 'Even if he commits adultery and steals!"'

7.  **A wife's obedience to her husband wins forgiveness for her father:** Ibn Malik (an al Sahaba and one of the Quran's rectors) shared a story about a man who went on a journey and asked his wife not to leave her room upstairs. Her father lived downstairs and became ill. The woman sent to ask the prophet's permission to visit her father on the lower level of the house. He replied, "Obey your husband." Her father died and was buried without her. Later the prophet informed her that Allah had forgiven her father as a result of her obedience to her husband.

8.  **Prayer:** In the Hadith, according to Abu Baker (Mohammed's best friend and the father-in-law), that Mohammed said, "There is no man who if he sins, if he cleanses himself then goes up to pray [a formal printed prayer] but that God will forgive him."

9.  **The Pilgrimage (the Hajj):** One receives forgiveness by going on a pilgrimage to Mecca in Saudi Arabia (Mohammed's birthplace). The Qur'an says that *"whoever makes the Pilgrimage to the House, or the Visitation is not to be faulted." (Surah 2:158)*

This list reveals that Muslims have a couple of choices of obtaining forgiveness and accumulating points of good deeds that might be sufficient, but still the assurance of salvation is far from reaching the standard that God Almighty has set. There is no need for Muslims to live in an uncertainty in regards to eternity. Muslims as Christians can rejoice the forgiveness that is not based on doing good works or on the opinions or judgments of others, but on the **grace of God and redemption through the blood of Jesus Christ** (Ephesians 2:8,9; Galatians 2:21).

The Bible says,

"But God, who is rich in mercy, because of His great love with which He loved us, [5] even when we were dead in trespasses, made us alive together with Christ (by grace you have been saved), [6] and raised *us* up together, and made *us* sit together in the heavenly *places* in Christ Jesus, [7] that in the ages to come He might show the exceeding riches of His grace in *His* kindness toward us in Christ Jesus. [8] **For by grace you have been saved through faith, and that not of yourselves; *it is* the gift of God, [9] not of works, lest anyone should boast."** (Ephesians 2:4-9)

In all the religions of the world including Islam, people try to go heaven with their own efforts. In Christianity, God reaches down to man in the person of Jesus Christ, and taken them to heaven once they put their faith in him.

In all the religions of the world, people try to pay for their sins in exchange for their good deeds. In Christianity alone, Jesus paid for the sins of the world. He gives His righteousness once a person asks the forgiveness. God who is a righteous judge does not look at the personal righteousness of a person, which the Bible says is like dirty rags ["But we are all like an unclean *thing,* And all our righteous nesses *are* like filthy rags; We all fade as a leaf, And our iniquities, like the wind, Have taken us away" (Isaiah 64:4).].

In all the religions of the world, there is no Savior. In every religion, people want to save themselves, but Christianity alone offers a Savior (Jesus Christ).

The Bible says,

"For the wages of sin is death, but the free gift of God is eternal life in Christ Jesus our Lord" (Romans 6:23).

"[11] For the grace of God has appeared, bringing salvation for all people, [12] training us to renounce ungodliness and worldly passions, and to live self-controlled, upright, and godly lives in the present age, [13] waiting for our blessed hope, the appearing of the glory of our great God and Savior Jesus Christ, [14] who gave himself for us to redeem us from all lawlessness and to purify for himself a people for his own possession who are zealous for good works" Titus 2:11-14).

# CHAPTER NINE

## TESTIMOINES OF
## THE MUSLIM CONVERTS

"And they have conquered him by the blood of the Lamb
and by the word of their testimony,
for they loved not their lives even unto death."
(Revelation 12:11-The Holy Bible)

# CHAPTER NINE

## TESTIMOINES OF
## THE MUSLIM CONVERTS

### "The Holy Quran" converted me to Christianity
### said Mario Joseph, a former Imam (Muslim Cleric)

Mario Joseph (Imam Suleiman) grew up in India. His family were devout Muslims. His mother dedicated him to Allah to be a Muslim Cleric before he was born. She had rejected the Doctor's advice to abort him when she had an infected womb during the pregnancy.

Mario was sent to a Muslim Arabic school in the southern Indian state of Kerala at the age of eight. He studied philosophy and theology for ten years. By the time, he was eighteen, He became an Imam (Muslim cleric) in a local mosque.

One day, someone in his mosque asked him about **who Jesus was**? Because Mario couldn't give him a solid answer, he began to investigate from the Quran where upon, he discovered that the name of Jesus was mentioned more often than the name of Mohammed, the prophet of Islam. According to Mario, the Quran mentions Muhammad four times, while Jesus Christ is mentioned twenty-five times. It struck him to consider why the Quran would "give more preference to Jesus", and less to Mohammad. Secondly, Jesus' mother Mary is the only woman mentioned by name in the Quran. Not even Muhammad's mother received that kind of honor. The Quran describes Jesus as the **"Word of God"** and the **"Spirit of God."** Additionally, it states **that Jesus healed the sick**, and **raised the dead to life,** and **went to heaven alive.** It does not depict the Prophet Mohammed as doing any of these things, Mario explained as is found about Jesus in Surah 3:45-55.

According to Mario, this is in stark contrast to Muhammad, who performed no miracles, had a normal death, was buried in Medina, and has no promise of returning. Neither is he called the word of God or the spirit of God.

So as a Muslim cleric, Mario realized that Jesus had a more prominent role in the Quran than Muhammad. When he talked about his findings with the lead Imam in the mosque, Mario started getting into trouble because he was questioning Muhammad's supremacy over Jesus.

One day, Mario went to his religious mentor with this question. Sir, how did God create this universe? His mentor replied that God created the universe through the word. Then Mario asked another question which was: Sir, is the word a creator or creation? He also reminded his mentor that The Quran teaches Jesus as the word of God. Mario's mentor was really in a great dilemma. If he says that the word is a creator, then by that acknowledging, he had no choice but accept Jesus as a creator and to become a Christian. He was nervous to say that the word is the creation, since he already acknowledged that everything was created through the word.

Out of deep desperation and frustration, the mentor pushed Mario out of the room.

After being rebuffed by his mentor. Mario put the Qur'an on his chest and asked Allah what he should do and who should he accept? He was confused. Because Allah's Quran tells that Jesus is still alive and Muhammad is dead.

Shortly after that prayer, Mario opened the Qur'an to an interesting verse which says: *"So if you are in doubt, [O Muhammad], about that which We have revealed to you, then ask those who have been reading the Scripture before you. The truth has certainly come to you from your Lord, so never be among the doubters"* (Surah 10:94).

This verse admonished Muhammad to enquire from the people of the Book (Jews and Christians) who had scriptures long before Muhammad supposedly got them. To clear up his doubts and dilemma, Muhammad was asked to clarify and confirm from the people of the book. Mario realized that if Muhammad was asked to enquire from the people of the book, then he was to do even the same even more. With this, he started reading the Bible to clear up his doubts.

Mario found out that according to John 1:1, Jesus is called the Word in the Bible. *"In the beginning was the Word, and the Word was with God, and the Word was God. ² He was in the beginning with God. ³ All things were made through Him, and without Him nothing was made that was made"* (John 1:1).

He had every reason to believe that Jesus was the Word of God as it is mentioned both in The Bible and The Quran. In addition, the Bible says that: *"And the Word became flesh and dwelt among us, and we beheld His glory, the glory as of the only begotten of the Father, full of grace and truth"* (John 1:14).

Mario was overwhelmed with joy to find out that a person could become a child of God if he/she believes in Jesus as he read John 1:12 that says: *"But as many as received Him, to them He gave the right to become children of God, to those who believe in His name:"*

According to Mario, The Qur'an teaches Allah is the master and his worshippers are his slaves. There is no love relationship between a slave and a master.

**"Whenever Mario thinks that the creator of the universe is his dad, he has a kind of joy which he cannot express," he said in an interview. He wanted God as a loving heavenly father. With this motivation, he decided to accept Jesus.**

However, his conversion to Christianity triggered a violent reaction from family members. When Mario's father found him in a Catholic retreat center, he beat him badly, to the point that he lost consciousness. When he awoke, he found himself naked in a small room at his family's home. His arms and legs were chained and chili had been put in his mouth and on his wounds to torment him as much as they could. For the next three weeks, the family provided him no food and drink hoping that he would starve to death. His brother came in one day and urinated in Mario's mouth as he asked for a drink to quench his thirst of so many days.

One day, his father came with a knife and asked Mario to renounce Christianity and to come back to Islam. He warned: "If you want to be a Christian, I have to kill you."

Mario Joseph said that his father was obeying the law of the Quran, which teaches to punish those who leave Islam. Even though Islam also teaches that there is no compulsion in religion (surah 2:256). Pathetically, **The Quran is full of contradictions.**

"When I knew that it was my last moment… I thought, '**Jesus died, but He came back to life. If I believe in Jesus and die, I, too may get my life back to life'."** He said at this point he felt energized, pulled his father's hand down, and cried out the name of Jesus.

His father then fell down with a severe cut by his own knife, which caused him to foam at the mouth, Mario Joseph said. When family members took his father to the hospital, they forgot to lock the room. Mario then ran out and caught a taxi. The driver, a Christian, helped him to get food and drink. **"That day, really I understood that my Jesus is alive even now. When I called Him for my need, he saved me."**

Mario Joseph said, he did not expect that he would still be alive eighteen years from following his conversion. He said that people are still trying to kill him. His parents held a mock funeral ceremony for him to signify that he was an outcast. On the mock grave, they marked the date of his death as the date of his baptism.

Mario still loves his family so dearly. He wishes that God would save them and take them to heaven.

Over the years, the extremists have tried to kill Mario. Though his life is in constant danger, but he believes that God has kept him alive with a purpose and to finish a task he has installed for him. He believes that it is foolishness to fear death because every person living on this earth will eventually die one day. Death is certain for every person. **But the question is: what happens after death?** If a person believes in Mohamed and dies, what will happen to him and is the question to ask, Mario said. Evidently, Muhammad died, people buried him and afterward no one knows where he went since he was not sure about heaven either. if someone believe in him, he will never know where he will go? It applies to believing all other gods and goddesses. But when someone believes in Jesus, who died, but he came back to life. So, this gives a believer a bright hope. If a person dies believing Jesus, then he/she will come back to life. Jesus also said, *"Let not your heart be troubled; you believe in God, believe also in Me. ² In My Father's house are many mansions; if it were not so, I would have told you. I go to prepare a place for you. ³ And if I go and prepare a place for you, I will come again and receive you to Myself; that where I am, there you may be also. ⁴ And where I go you know, and the way you know"* (John 14:3). It is imperative to be sure about eternity, said Mario Joseph.

Mario explains the plan of salvation in a very simple way by stating that:
Every religion says that there is a separation between God and man because of sin. In Islam, people believe in offering animal sacrifices to restore this relationship. In Hinduism, there is an endless cycle of reincarnations. But only in Christianity, Jesus took upon himself our sins and punishment. He removes sins once a person believes in him. He presents that person righteous before God who is a Holy God. Jesus tells his father, I have removed his sins, made him righteous, and present him purified to you. Now you can take him to heaven. So, Jesus become the Savior. Jesus is a perfect man who never sinned. Since we are in need of a savior, Jesus offered himself to be the perfect savior. Since, we need eternal life which only God has, and can give. The consequence of sin is death. To remove death there must be life. It is like removing darkness one has to bring light. In the Old Testament, people offered animal sacrifices, because they believe the life is in blood. But to remove death, we need eternal life.

But the question is, where can we get that from? Since, Jesus was God in flesh, he gave that life by dying on the cross. He is the one who gives eternal life. That is why The Bible says, *"For God so loved the world that He gave His only begotten Son, that whoever believes in Him should not perish but have everlasting life. [17] For God did not send His Son into the world to condemn the world, but that the world through Him might be saved"* (John 3:16-17).

# Why did God create me less intelligent?

I was ashamed to be a woman. I thought, God made a mistake by creating me a woman. I wanted to be a man, said Amy Ghazal in an interview broadcast on the Christian Broadcasting Network.

Amy Ghazal grew up in Syria born to a Muslim family. Her parents and religious leaders taught her that women had little value. Many times, she was beaten up for asking questions. Questions like, why I am created an unclean woman? Why did God create me less intelligent? (**Sahih al-Bukhari 2658**—The Prophet said: "Isn't the witness of a woman equal to half of that of a man?" The women said: "Yes." He said: "<u>This is because of the deficiency of her mind</u>."). Why do I have men having dominion over me? According to her family's beliefs, a woman had no guarantee where she'd spend eternity even if she had lived a good life.

There is no grace and mercy in Islam for women. Many women in that culture do their best to be a good person. But, despite all this, they're desperate for God to accept them, and allow them an entry to heaven.

Amy was never at peace with Islam. She read the Quran, but she felt that an evil spirit or someone was choking her.

At the age of eighteen, Amy and her family moved from Syria to Egypt. Over there, she openly renounced Islam. She stopped praying, fasting, and taking part in any religious ceremony.

Amy learned English in college and took a job with a travel agency. While on a business tour to the United States, she met and married an American Muslim doctor. But her husband began abusing her. Six months into their marriage, the abuse started. "Even though, he was a religious man, but he had the mentality of Muhammad in controlling and dominating women," she said. She was abused verbally many times. After almost three years of marriage, Amy and her husband divorced. She felt like a failure because she thought, she failed in everything. She lost herself totally. She didn't know why she was alive? Why should she continue with her life? At the same time, she was plagued with the Islamic idea of hell. She felt like when she dies, God will send his angel to torment her in the grave. She could not sleep. She thought, nobody wants to be her friend, because her face looked so miserable. There was bitterness or resentment in her heart against everybody. She had the feeling of being a victim of everybody. At that time of desperation, she thought, if she had courage to kill herself, she would do it without thinking twice.

One day, one of Amy's co-workers invited her to the church. She agreed to go there but she couldn't believe that Jesus was God. It was so confusing for her that Jesus is God, he is the son of God, and he is man also at the same time. She said God, "I'm not going to be deceived again. If Jesus is truly your son, and he is God, and He is the one who died on the cross for me to provide forgiveness of sins for me, then you must prove it to me.

A few months, later, Amy became very ill with gallstones. As she lay in the hospital waiting for the surgery she called out to Jesus. Jesus, I know, you have healed many people in the past. Would you please come and heal me, if you are true? I am broken financially, I am alone, I don't have family to care of me, and I cannot just survive during this surgery, she said.

After she finished praying, she realized that the room was full of light and out of that light Jesus came to her in a real human body. He stretched his hands as he was standing closely by Amy's bed. He said to her, *"Come to Me, all you who labor and are heavy laden, and I will give you rest."* The word Amy heard in that hospital room were the same words Jesus had spoken in Matthew 11:28. But Amy had never read this verse. She saw nails in his hands. That's the way, her friends had described it to her about Jesus' death on the cross. It was so real, said Amy. When Jesus appeared to her, she felt like she was full of sin and he is so holy, and righteous.

Her doctors ran a scan to check in her gallstones again before surgery. They couldn't find any. She was completely healed as all the test came back negative. There were no stones, and no infection at all. Amy was discharged from the hospital. She started reading the Bible and went back to the church with her friend.

She decided to follow Jesus whole heartedly. After a while, she felt like something has changed her life dramatically. Her relationship with Jesus started to deliver her from the lies she learned in her childhood.

She feels that Jesus has given her a guarantee of eternal life, and she is a new creation in Christ now, not that woman who was created less intelligent, and for men to have dominion over her. She thanks God for having the power of God Almighty to live a life with joy and purpose. She rejoices that she is not going to go to hell. She believes that hell is not for her anymore. She knows that she is going to have eternal life with Jesus.

The Bible says, **"He who believes in the Son has everlasting life; and he who does not believe the Son shall not see life, but the wrath of God abides on him"** (John 3:36).

# ENDNOTES:

[i] Steve Keohane, Mohammed (Bible Probe.com) 20.

[ii] Al-Rassooli, I.Q. History of the Arabs: Pre-Islamic Age of Jahiliyah, May 16, 2009.

[iii] The material is adapted from Truth net.com

[iv] Al-Rassooli, I.Q. History of the Arabs: Pre-Islamic Age of Jahiliyah, May 16, 2009.

[v] What is Islam: The History of Islam. http://www.truthnet.org/islam/whatisislam.html

[vi] The Arabian Peninsula, http://inthenameofallah.org/history.html.

[vii] Michael Siemer, It's too Late for Muhammad, He is Burning in Hell, But it's not too late for you. Cult & False Teachings List, http://solascriptura-tt.org/ Seitas/

[viii] Perveen Singh, Islam, copyright © 1995-2009 Leadership U. All rights reserved. Updated: 1 August 2007, Accessed http://www.leaderu.com/wri/articles/islam-singh.html, July 8, 2009

## [ix] The Quotes from the Hadith:

"Ali reported that the Apostle of Allah said, 'There is in Paradise a market wherein there will be no buying or selling, but will consist of men and women. When a man desires a beauty, he will have intercourse with them.'" (Al Hadis, Vol. 4, p. 172, No. 34).

"The virgins will not urinate, relieve nature, spit, or have any nasal secretions" - Sahih Bukhari 4:55:544

'Everyone that God admits into paradise will be married to 72 wives; two of them are houris and seventy of his inheritance of the [female] dwellers of hell. All of them will have libidinous sex organs and he will have an ever-erect penis.' " - Sunan Ibn Majah, Zuhd (Book of Abstinence) 39

"The Holy Prophet said: 'The believer will be given such and such strength in Paradise for sexual intercourse. It was questioned: O prophet of Allah! can he do that? He said: "He will be given the strength of one hundred persons." - Mishkat al-Masabih Book IV, Chapter XLII, Paradise and Hell, Hadith Number 24

The prophet Muhammad described his view with the following words, "The smallest reward for the people of paradise is an abode where there are 80,000 servants and 72 wives, over which stands a dome decorated with pearls, aquamarine, and ruby, as wide as the distance from Al-Jabiyyah [a Damascus suburb] to Sana'a." (Surah Al-Rahman 55, 72, as interpreted by Ibn Kathir, who died in 1373 CE)

Apart from sex, Allah promises all the other things 7th century Arabians lusted after: abundant water (Surah 13:35), wine (56:7-40), fruit (55: 68, 69), jewels, fancy cutlery, and fabrics (43:68-73, 55:70-77, 56:7-40)ix.

**Note: Allah has forbidden Muslim to touch wine on this earth, but he will offer them wine in his paradise. It is ironic that no Islamic scholar with some sanity and rationality has challenges this contradictory phenomenon, but willing and determine to follow it recklessly as well as uncritically.**

[x] Keohane, 23.

[xi] James F. Gauss, Islam and Christianity: A Revealing Contrast (Excerpt from Islam and Christianity: A Revealing Contrast), http://www.CBN.com. Accessed, July 2, 2009.

[xii] Guass.

[xiii] Guass.

xiv Guass

xv Dr. Labib Mikhail, Islam, Muhammad, and The Qur'an, 4.

xvi **Satyameva Jayate,** Prophet Of Terror and "Religion Of Peace"-Part I.

http://www.flex.com/~jai/satyamevajayate/index.html

xvii Information taken from the article "MUHAMMAD, MOHAMMAD, MOHAMET" posted on http://www.bible.ca/islam/dictionary/index.html

xviii Islam & World Events: What is Qur'an. http://www.truthnet.org/Islam

xix Dr. Labib Mikhail, ISLAM MUHAMMAD AND THE Qur'an. P.29.

xx Islam & World Events: What is Qur'an. http://www.truthnet.org/Islam

xxi Steve Koehane, True History of Islam, Mohammed, and the Koran: Muhammad Terrorist or Prophet, p. 64-65

xxii Islam & World Events: What is Qur'an. http://www.truthnet.org/Islam, p.3

xxiii The Qur'an in Islam by Goldsack.

xxiv The Bible and The Qur'an, July 17, 2009 (Emmanuel Evangelical Church 2009) ·

xxv John Gilchrist, The Qur'an: The Scripture of Islam, p.60.

xxvi "Is the Qur'an Pure?" by Harvard House, 17 Feb, 2008

xxvii The Origins of the Koran: Classic Essays on Islam's Holy Book, Edited by Ibn Warraq; Prometheus Books, 1998, Arthur Jeffrey, Abu 'Ubaid on the Verses Missing from the Koran (pp. 150-153)

xxviii Christ, Muhammad, and I, (38-45).

xxix The Origins of the Koran: Classic Essays on Islam's Holy Book, Edited by Ibn Warraq; Prometheus Books, 1998, Alphonse Mingana, (pp. 76-96).

xxx Father Zakaria Boutros, Sources of Islam, Episode 53, p.4.

xxxi The Origins of the Koran: Classic Essays on Islam's Holy Book, Edited by Ibn Warraq; Prometheus Books, 1998, W. St. Clair-Tisdall. (pp. 227-292)

xxxii The Origins of the Koran: Classic Essays on Islam's Holy Book, Edited by Ibn Warraq; Prometheus Books, 1998, W. St. Clair-Tisdall. (pp. 275-286)

xxxiii Reality with Bite: Erroneous Science and Contradictions in the Qur'an (Prepared by: Syed Kamran Mirza).

xxxiv Reality with Bite: Erroneous Science and Contradictions in the Qur'an (Prepared by: Syed Kamran Mirza).

xxxv Koehane, p.10.

xxxvi Reality with Bite: Erroneous Science and Contradictions in the Qur'an (Prepared by: Syed Kamran Mirza).

xxxvii Reality with Bite: Erroneous Science and Contradictions in the Qur'an (Prepared by: Syed Kamran Mirza).

xxxviii Facts About Islam, with Comparisons to the Bible, Ken Raggio.

xxxix Islam-A Study by Parveen Singh.

xl http://www.answeringmuslims.com/2014/03/muhammads-view-of-women.html

xli p. xvii, S. Masood, Bible, and Qur'an.

xlii http://www.thereligionofpeace.com/pages/articles/jesus-muhammad.aspx

xliii The Bible vs. The Qur'an (A critical assessment): Jay Smith, Roxbury 2011.

xliv Challenging the Cults: Answering Muslims. http://www.truthnet.org/Christianity/Cults/answeringislam4/

xlv The Cult of the Moon God (Excerpts from "The Islamic Invasion" by Dr. Robert Morey; Harvest Home Publishers, 1992).

xlv Sam Shamoun, Muhammad's Changing of the Qiblah, Answering Islam.

xlvii Adapted from The Muslim Observer, Vol II, Issue Eleven, March 17-23, 2000.

xlviii Information from answering Islam.

xlix http://www.gotquestions.org/Sharia-Law.html

l http://www.huffingtonpost.com/2013/07/29/sharia-law-usa-states-ban_n_3660813.html

li Islamic Law-Sharia and Fiqa.

lii http://www.gotquestions.org/Sharia-Law.html

liii Islam 101 by Gregory M. Davis (p. 17-18)

liv http://www.catholic.com/documents/endless-jihad-the-truth-about-islam-and-violence

lv Dr. Muhammad al-Amin, "The Method of Islamic Law"

lvi http://www.answering-islam.org/Index/F/fighting.html

lvii https://en.wikipedia.org/wiki/Battle_of_Tours

lviii Islam 101 by Gregory M. Davis (p. 27)

lix Scot, Daniel & Abdulhaq, Michael (Share the Gospel with Muslims): Queensland, Australia, 2009.

lx ibid

[lxi] Islam 101 by Gregory M. Davis (p. 38)
[lxii] http://www.biblestudytools.com/commentaries/gills-exposition-of-the-bible/matthew-10-34.html
[lxiii] http://www.answering-islam.org/Authors/Arlandson/sword.htm
[lxiv] http://www.studylight.org/commentaries/dsb/matthew-10.html
[lxv] http://www.americanthinker.com/blog/2010/09/jihad_islamization_and_the_ara.html
[lxvi] Notes taken from "The Truth about the Crusades" by Stefan Molyneux
[lxvii] "The Truth About the Crusades" by Clay Jones
[lxviii] Islam 101 by Gregory M. Davis.

Made in the USA
San Bernardino, CA
03 February 2017